Contents at a Glance

Table of Contents

About the Author

Chuck Easttom has been in the IT industry for many years working in all aspects including network administration, software engineering, and IT management. For the past 10 years he has been part-time teaching at colleges and doing corporate training. For the past 7 years, he has also been an independent consultant working with a variety of companies and serving as an expert consultant/witness in various computer cases. Chuck holds more than 28 different IT industry certifications, including the CISSP, ISSAP, Certified Ethical Hacker, Certified Hacking Forensics Investigator, EC Council Certified Security Administrator, and EC Council Certified Instructor. He has served as a subject matter expert for the Computer Technology Industry Association (CompTIA) in the development or revision of four of their certification tests, including the initial creation of their Security+ certification. Most recently he worked with the EC Council to develop their new advanced cryptography course, which he is teaching around the world.

In addition to this book, Chuck has authored 12 other titles on topics such as computer security, web development, programming, Linux, and computer crime. Chuck also is a frequent guest speaker for computer groups, discussing computer security. You can reach Chuck at his website www.chuckeasttom.com or by email at chuck@chuckeasttom.com

About the Technical Reviewer

Dr. Louay Karadsheh has a Doctorate of Management in information technology from Lawrence Technological University, Southfield, MI. He teaches information assurance, operating system, and networking classes. His research interest includes cloud computing, information assurance, knowledge management, and risk management. Dr. Karadsheh has published nine articles in refereed journals and international conference proceedings. He has 21 years of experience in planning, installation, troubleshooting, and designing local area networks and operating systems for small to medium-size sites. Dr. Karadsheh has provided technical edits/reviews for several major publishing companies, including Pearson Education and Cengage Learning, and evaluates the research proposals. He holds A+ and Security Certified Network professional certifications.

Dedication

This book is dedicated to my son AJ, who has been wonderful and supportive in all of my books.

Acknowledgments

The creation of a book is not a simple process and requires the talents and dedication from many people to make it happen. With this in mind, I would like to thank the folks at Pearson for their commitment to this project.

Specifically, I would like to say thanks to Betsy Brown for overseeing the project and keeping things moving. A special thanks to Dayna Isley for outstanding editing and focus. Also, thanks to Dr. Karadsheh, who worked tirelessly technically editing this book and fact checking it.

We Want to Hear from You!

As the reader of this book, *you* are our most important critic and commentator. We value your opinion and want to know what we're doing right, what we could do better, what areas you'd like to see us publish in, and any other words of wisdom you're willing to pass our way.

As an associate publisher for Pearson, I welcome your comments. You can email or write me directly to let me know what you did or didn't like about this book—as well as what we can do to make our books better.

Please note that I cannot help you with technical problems related to the topic of this book. We do have a User Services group, however, where I will forward specific technical questions related to the book.

When you write, please be sure to include this book's title and author as well as your name, email address, and phone number. I will carefully review your comments and share them with the author and editors who worked on the book.

Email: feedback@pearsonitcertification.com

Mail: David Dusthimer
            Associate Publisher
            Pearson Certification
            800 East 96th Street
            Indianapolis, IN 46240 USA

Reader Services

Visit our website and register this book at www.pearsonitcertification.com/register for convenient access to any updates, downloads, or errata that might be available for this book.

Introduction

It has been more than 6 years since the publication of the original edition of this book. A great deal has happened in the world of computer security since that time. This edition is updated to include newer information, updated issues, and revised content.

The real question is who is this book for. This book is a guide for any computer-savvy person. That means system administrators who are not security experts or anyone who has a working knowledge of computers and wishes to know more about cyber crime and terrorism could find this book useful. However, the core audience will be students who wish to take a first course in security but may not have a thorough background in computer networks. The book is in textbook format, making it ideal for introductory computer security courses that have no specific prerequisites. That lack of prerequisites means that people outside the normal computer science and computer information systems departments could also avail themselves of a course based on this book. This might be of particular interest to law enforcement officers, criminal justice majors, and even business majors with an interest in computer security.

As was previously mentioned, this book is intended as an introductory computer security book. In addition to the numerous end notes, the appendices will guide you to a plethora of additional resources. There are also review questions and practice exercises with every chapter.

This book is not a cookbook for hackers. You will see exactly how hackers target a system and get information about it. You will also see step-by-step instructions on how to use some password cracking utilities and some network scanning utilities. You will also be given a reasonably in depth explanation of various hacking attacks. However, you won't see a specific step-by-step recipe for executing an attack.

This book assumes that you are a competent computer user. That means you have used a computer at work and at home, are comfortable with email and web browsers, and know what words like *RAM* and *USB* mean. For instructors considering this as a textbook, that means that students will have had some basic understanding of PCs, but need not have had formal computer courses. For this reason, there is a chapter on basic networking concepts to get you up to speed. For readers with more knowledge, such as system administrators, you will find some chapters of more use to you than others. Feel free to simply skim any chapter that you feel is too elementary for you.

Chapter 1

Introduction to Computer Security

Chapter Objectives

After reading this chapter and completing the exercises, you will be able to do the following:

- Identify the top threats to a network: security breaches, denial of service attacks, and malware
- Assess the likelihood of an attack on your network
- Define key terms such as *cracker*, *sneaker*, *firewall*, and *authentication*
- Compare and contrast perimeter and layered approaches to network security
- Use online resources to secure your network

Introduction

It's hard to find a facet of modern life that does not involve a computer system, at least on some level. Online purchases, debit cards, and automatic bill pay are standard parts of modern life. Some retailers are using computerized automatic checkout. It is even likely that you have taken a class online, and you may even be using this textbook for a class you are currently taking online. You can, in fact, buy this book online. I personally purchase most of the books I read online.

Because so much of our business is transacted online, a great deal of personal information is stored in computers. Medical records, tax records, school records, and more are all stored in computer databases. This leads to some very important questions:

1. How is information safeguarded?
2. What are the vulnerabilities to these systems?
3. What steps are taken to ensure that these systems and data are safe?

FYI: Where Is the Internet Going?

Recently there have been more expansions to Internet technology and Internet use. Such expansions include increased transmission speeds, a wider use of wireless Internet, and the growing phenomenon of online education. Do you think that we will reach a point where all aspects of our lives have some Internet component? Have we already reached that point?

Recent news stories don't offer encouraging answers to these questions. The media gives a lot of attention to dramatic virus attacks, hackers, and other interesting Internet phenomena. Even the most technically naïve person cannot go more than a few weeks without hearing of some new virus or some hacking incident.

In spite of daily horror stories, however, many people (including some law enforcement professionals and trained computer professionals) lack an adequate understanding about the reality of these threats. Clearly the media will focus attention on the most dramatic computer security breaches, not necessarily giving an accurate picture of the most plausible threat scenarios. It is not uncommon to even encounter the occasional system administrator whose knowledge of computer security is inadequate.

This chapter outlines current dangers, describes the most common types of attacks on your personal computer and network, teaches you how to speak the lingo of both hackers and security professionals, and outlines the broad strokes of what it takes to secure your computer and your network.

In this book, you will learn how to secure both individual computers and entire networks. You will also find out how to secure data transmission, and you will complete an exercise to find out about your region's laws regarding computer security. Perhaps the most crucial discussion in this chapter is what attacks are commonly attempted and how they are perpetrated. In this first chapter we set the stage for the rest of the book by outlining what exactly the dangers are and introducing you to the terminology used by both network security professionals and hackers. All of these topics are explored more fully in subsequent chapters.

How Seriously Should You Take Threats to Network Security?

The first step in understanding computer and network security is to formulate a realistic assessment of the threats to those systems. You will need a clear picture of the dangers in order to adequately prepare a defense. There seem to be two extreme attitudes regarding computer security. The first group assumes there is no real threat. Subscribers to this belief feel that there is little real danger to computer systems, and that much of the negative news is simply unwarranted panic. They often believe taking only minimal security precautions should ensure the safety of their systems. The prevailing sentiment is, if our organization has not been attacked so far, we must be secure. If decision makers subscribe to this point of view, they tend to push a *reactive* approach to security. They will wait to address security issues until an incident occurs—the proverbial "closing the barn door after the horse has already gotten out." If you are fortunate, the incident will have only minor impact on your organization and will serve as a much needed wakeup call. If you are unfortunate, then your organization may face serious and possible catastrophic consequences. One major goal of this book is to encourage a proactive approach to security.

People who subscribe to the opposite viewpoint overestimate the dangers. They tend to assume that talented, numerous hackers are an imminent threat to your system. They may believe that any teenager with a laptop can traverse highly secure systems at will. Such a worldview makes excellent movie plots, but it is simply unrealistic. The reality is that many people who call themselves hackers are less knowledgeable than they think they are. These people have a low probability of being able to compromise any system that has implemented even moderate security precautions.

This does not mean that skillful hackers do not exist, of course. However, they must balance the costs (financial, time) against the rewards (ideological, monetary). "Good" hackers tend to target systems that yield the highest rewards. If a hacker doesn't perceive your system as beneficial to these goals, he is less likely to expend the resources to compromise your system. It is also important to understand that real intrusions into a network take time and effort. Hacking is not the dramatic process you see in movies. I often teach courses in hacking and penetration testing, and students are usually surprised to find that the process is actually a bit tedious and requires patience.

Both extremes of attitudes regarding the dangers to computer systems are inaccurate. It is certainly true that there are people who have the understanding of computer systems and the skills to compromise the security of many, if not most, systems. A number of people who call themselves hackers, though, are not as skilled as they claim to be. They have ascertained a few buzzwords from the Internet and may be convinced of their own digital supremacy, but they are not able to affect any real compromises to even a moderately secure system.

The truly talented hacker is no more common than the truly talented concert pianist. Consider how many people take piano lessons at some point in their lives. Now consider how many of those ever truly become virtuosos. The same is true of computer hackers. Keep in mind that even those who do possess the requisite skill need to be motivated to expend the time and effort to compromise your system.

A better way to assess the threat level to your system is to weigh the attractiveness of your system to potential intruders against the security measures in place.

Keep in mind, too, that the greatest external threat to any system is not hackers, but malware and denial of service attacks. Malware includes viruses, worms, Trojan horses, and logic bombs. And beyond the external attacks, there is the issue of internal problems due to malfeasance or simple ignorance.

Identifying Types of Threats

Most attacks can be categorized as one of six broad classes:

- **Malware:** This is a generic term for software that has a malicious purpose. It includes virus attacks, worms, adware, Trojan horses, and spyware. This is the most prevalent danger to your system.

- **Security breaches:** This group of attacks includes any attempt to gain unauthorized access to your system. This includes cracking passwords, elevating privileges, breaking into a server… all the things you probably associate with the term *hacking*.

- **Denial of service (DoS) attacks:** These are designed to prevent legitimate access to your system.

- **Web attacks:** This is any attack that attempts to breach your website. Two of the most common such attacks are SQL injection and cross-site scripting.

- **Session hijacking:** These attacks are rather advanced, and involve an attacker attempting to take over a session.

- **DNS poisoning:** This type of attack seeks to compromise a DNS server so that users can be redirected to malicious websites, including phishing websites.

This section offers a broad description of each type of attack. Later chapters go into greater detail with each specific attack, how it is accomplished, and how to avoid it.

Malware

Malware is a generic term for software that has a malicious purpose. This section discusses three types of malware: viruses, Trojan horses, and spyware. Trojan horses and viruses are the most widely encountered.

According to Symantec (makers of Norton antivirus and other software products), a *virus* is "a small program that replicates and hides itself inside other programs, usually without your knowledge" (Symantec, 2003). A computer virus is similar to a biological virus; both are designed to replicate and spread. The most common method for spreading a virus is using the victim's email account to spread the virus to everyone in their address book. Some viruses don't actually harm the system itself, but *all* of them cause network slowdowns due to the heavy network traffic caused by the virus replication.

The *Trojan horse* gets its name from an ancient tale. The city of Troy was besieged for an extended period of time. The attackers could not gain entrance, so they constructed a huge wooden horse and one night left it in front of the gates of Troy. The next morning the residents of Troy saw the horse and assumed it to be a gift, so they rolled the wooden horse into the city. Unbeknownst to them, several soldiers where hidden inside the horse. That evening the soldiers left the horse, opened the city gates, and let their fellow attackers into the city. An electronic Trojan horse works the same way, appearing to be benign software but secretly downloading a virus or some other type of malware onto your computer from within.

Another category of malware currently on the rise is *spyware*. Spyware is simply software that literally spies on what you do on your computer. Spyware can be as simple as a *cookie*—a text file that your browser creates and stores on your hard drive—that a website you have visited downloads to your machine and uses to recognize you when you return to the site. However, that flat file can then be read by the website or by other websites. Any data that the file saves can be retrieved by any website, so your entire Internet browsing history can be tracked.

A *logic bomb* is software that lays dormant until some specific condition is met. That condition is usually a date and time. When the condition is met, then the software does some malicious act such as deleting files, altering system configuration, or perhaps releasing a virus.

Another form of spyware, called a *key logger*, records all of your keystrokes. Some key loggers also take periodic screenshots of your computer. Data is then either stored for later retrieval by the person who installed the key logger or is sent immediately back via email. We will discuss specific types of key loggers later in this book.

Compromising System Security

Next we will look at attacks that breach your system's security. This activity is what is commonly referred to as *hacking*, though that is not the term hackers themselves use. We will delve into appropriate terminology in just a few pages; however, it should be noted at this point that *cracking* is the appropriate word for intruding into a system without permission, usually with malevolent intent. Any attack that is designed to breach your security, either via some operating system flaw or any other means, can be classified as cracking.

Social engineering is a technique for breaching a system's security by exploiting human nature rather than technology. This was the path that the famous hacker Kevin Mitnick most often used. Social engineering uses standard con techniques to get users to give up the information needed to gain access to a target system (Lemos, 2000). The way this method works is rather simple: The perpetrator gets preliminary information about a target organization and leverages it to obtain additional information from the system's users.

Following is an example of social engineering in action. Armed with the name of a system administrator, you might call someone in the business's accounting department and claim to be one of the company's technical support personnel. Mentioning the system administrator's name would help validate that claim, allowing you to ask questions in an attempt to ascertain more details about the system's specifications. A savvy intruder might even get the accounting person to say a username and password. As you can see, this method is based on how well the prospective intruder can manipulate people and actually has little to do with computer skills.

The growing popularity of wireless networks gave rise to new kinds of attacks. One such activity is *war-driving*. This type of attack is an offshoot of *war-dialing*. With war-dialing, a hacker set up a computer to call phone numbers in sequence until another computer answered to try to gain entry to its system. War-driving is much the same concept, applied to locating vulnerable wireless networks. In this scenario, the hacker simply drives around trying to locate wireless networks (Poulsen, 2001). Many people forget that their wireless network signal often extends as much as 100 feet (thus, past walls). At the 2004 DefCon convention for hackers, there was a war-driving contest where contestants drove around the city trying to locate as many vulnerable wireless networks as they could (BlackBeetle, 2004).

Denial of Service Attacks

In a *denial of service* (DoS), the attacker does not actually access the system. Rather, he or she simply blocks access from legitimate users (CERT, 2003). One common way to do prevent legitimate service is to flood the targeted system with so many false connection requests, that the system cannot respond to legitimate requests. DoS is probably the most common attack on the Web.

Web Attacks

By their nature, web servers have to allow communications. Oftentimes, websites allow users to interact with the website. Any part of a website that allows for user interaction is also a potential point for attempting a web-based attack. SQL injections involve entering SQL (Structured Query Language) commands into login forms (username and password text fields) in an attempt to trick the server into executing those commands. The most common purpose is to force the server to log the attacker on, even though the attacker does not have a legitimate username and password. While SQL injection is just one type of web attack, it is the most common.

Session Hijacking

Session hijacking can be rather complex to perform. For that reason, it is not a very common form of attack. Simply put, the attacker monitors an authenticated session between the client machine and the server, and takes that session over. We will explore specific methods of how this is done later in this book.

DNS Poisoning

Most of your communication on the Internet will involve DNS, or Domain Name Service. DNS is what translates the domain names you and I understand (like www.ChuckEasttom.com) into IP addresses that computers and routers understand. DNS poisoning uses one of several techniques to compromise that process and redirect traffic to an illicit site, often for the purpose of stealing personal information.

Assessing the Likelihood of an Attack on Your Network

How likely are these attacks? What are the real dangers facing you as an individual or your organization? What are the most likely attacks, and what are your vulnerabilities? Let's take a look at what threats are out there and which ones are the most likely to cause you or your organization problems.

At one time, the most likely threat to individuals and large organizations was the computer virus. And it is still true that in any given month, several new virus outbreaks will be documented. This situation means that new viruses are being created all the time—and old ones are still out there. However, there are other very common attacks, such as spyware. Spyware is fast becoming as big a problem, even bigger than viruses.

After viruses, the most common attack is unauthorized usage of computer systems. Unauthorized usage includes everything from DoS attacks to outright intrusion of your system. It also includes internal employees misusing system resources. A recent survey by the Computer Security Institute of 223 computer professionals showed over $445 million in losses due to computer security breaches. In 75% of the cases, an Internet connection was the point of attack, while 33% of the professionals cited the location as their internal systems. A rather astonishing 78% of those surveyed detected employee abuse of systems/Internet (Computer Security Institute, 2002). This statistic means that in any organization, one of the chief dangers might be its own employees. A 2007 study by Jeffery Johnson and Zolt Ugray, of Utah State University, showed similar problems.

Basic Security Terminology

Before you embark on the rest of this chapter and this book, it is important to know some basic terminology. The security and hacking terms in this section are merely an introduction to computer security terminology, but they are an excellent starting point to help you prepare for learning more about computer security. Additional terms will be introduced throughout the text and listed in the Glossary at the end of this book.

The world of computer security takes its vocabulary from both the professional security community and the hacker community.

Hacker Slang

You probably have heard the term *hacker* used in movies and in news broadcasts. Most people use it to describe any person who breaks into a computer system. In the hacking community, however, a hacker is an expert on a particular system or systems, a person who simply wants to learn more about the system. Hackers feel that looking at a system's flaws is the best way to learn about that system. For example, someone well versed in the Linux operating system who works to understand that system by learning its weaknesses and flaws would be a hacker.

This process does often mean seeing if a flaw can be exploited to gain access to a system. This "exploiting" part of the process is where hackers differentiate themselves into three groups:

- A white hat hacker, upon finding some flaw in a system, will report the flaw to the vendor of that system. For example, if they were to discover some flaw in Red Hat Linux, they would then email the Red Hat company (probably anonymously) and explain exactly what the flaw is and how it was exploited. White hat hackers are often hired specifically by companies to do penetration tests. The EC Council even has a certification test for white hat hackers, the Certified Ethical Hacker test.

- A black hat hacker is the person normally depicted in the media. Once she gains access to a system, her goal is to cause some type of harm. She might steal data, erase files, or deface websites. Black hat hackers are sometimes referred to as crackers.

■ A gray hat hacker is normally a law-abiding citizen, but in some cases will venture into illegal activities.

Regardless of how hackers view themselves, intruding on any system is illegal. This means that technically speaking all hackers, regardless of the color of the metaphorical hat they may wear, are in violation of the law. However, many people feel that white hat hackers actually perform a service by finding flaws and informing vendors before those flaws are exploited by less ethically inclined individuals.

Script Kiddies

A hacker is an expert in a given system, as with any profession it includes its share of frauds. So what is the term for someone who calls himself or herself a hacker but lacks the expertise? The most common term for this sort of person is *script kiddy* (Raymond, 1993). The name comes from the fact that the Internet is full of utilities and scripts that one can download to perform some hacking tasks. Many of these tools have an easy-to-use graphical user interface that allows someone with very little if any skill to operate the tool. A classic example is the Low Earth Orbit Ion Cannon tool for executing a DoS attack. Someone who downloads such a tool without really understanding the target system is considered a script kiddy. A significant number of the people you are likely to encounter who call themselves hackers are, in reality, mere script kiddies.

Ethical Hacking: Sneakers

When and why would someone give permission to another party to hack his system? The most common answer is in order to assess system vulnerabilities. This employee, commonly called a *sneaker*, legally breaks into a system in order to assess security deficiencies, such as portrayed in the 1992 film *Sneakers*, starring Robert Redford, Dan Aykroyd, and Sidney Poitier. More and more companies are soliciting the services of such individuals or firms to assess their vulnerabilities.

Anyone hired to assess the vulnerabilities of a system should be both technically proficient and ethical. Run a criminal background check, and avoid those people with problem pasts. There are plenty of legitimate security professionals available who know and understand hacker skills but have never committed security crimes. If you take the argument that hiring convicted hackers means hiring talented people to its logical conclusion, you could surmise that obviously the person in question is not as good a hacker as they would like to think, because they were caught.

Most importantly, giving a person with a criminal background access to your systems is on par with hiring a person with multiple DWI convictions to be your driver. In both cases, you are inviting problems and perhaps assuming significant civil liabilities.

Also some review of their qualifications is clearly in order. Just as there are people who claim to be highly skilled hackers yet are not, there are those who will claim to be skilled sneakers yet lack the skills truly needed. You would not want to inadvertently hire a script kiddy who thinks she is a sneaker. Such a person might then pronounce your system quite sound when, in fact, it was simply a lack of skills that prevented the script kiddy from successfully breaching your security. Later in this book, in

Chapter 11, "Network Scanning and Vulnerability Scanning," we discuss the basics of assessing a target system. In Chapter 11 we also discuss the qualifications you should seek in any consultant you might hire for this purpose.

Phreaking

One specialty type of hacking involves breaking into telephone systems. This subspecialty of hacking is referred to as *phreaking*. The *New Hacker's Dictionary* actually defines phreaking as "the action of using mischievous and mostly illegal ways in order to not pay for some sort of telecommunications bill, order, transfer, or other service" (Raymond, 2003). Phreaking requires a rather significant knowledge of telecommunications, and many phreakers have some professional experience working for a phone company or other telecommunications business. Often this type of activity is dependent upon specific technology required to compromise phone systems, more than simply knowing certain techniques.

Professional Terms

Most hacker terminology, as you may have noticed, is concerned with the activity (phreaking) or the person performing the activity (sneaker). In contrast, security professional terminology describes defensive barrier devices, procedures, and policies. This is quite logical because hacking is an offensive activity centered on attackers and attack methodologies, whereas security is a defensive activity concerning itself with defensive barriers and procedures.

Security Devices

The most basic security device is the *firewall*. A firewall is a barrier between a network and the outside world. Sometimes a firewall takes the form of a standalone server, sometimes a router, and sometimes software running on a machine. Whatever its physical form, a firewall filters traffic entering and exiting the network. A *proxy server* is often used with a firewall to hide the internal network's IP address and present a single IP address (its own) to the outside world.

Firewalls and proxy servers guard the perimeter by analyzing traffic (at least inbound and in many cases outbound as well) and blocking traffic that has been disallowed by the administrator. These two safeguards are often augmented by an *intrusion-detection system* (IDS). An IDS simply monitors traffic, looking for suspicious activity that might indicate an attempted intrusion.

Security Activities

In addition to devices, we have activities. *Authentication* is the most basic security activity. It is merely the process of determining if the credentials given by a user or another system (such as a username and password) are authorized to access the network resource in question. When you log in with your username and password, the system will attempt to authenticate that username and password. If it is authenticated, you will be granted access.

Another crucial safeguard is *auditing*, which is the process of reviewing logs, records, and procedures to determine if these items meet standards. This activity will be mentioned in many places throughout this book and will be a definite focus in a few chapters.

The security and hacking terms that we have just covered are only an introduction to computer security terminology, but they provide an excellent starting point that will help you prepare for learning more about computer security. Additional terms will be introduced throughout the text as needed and compiled in the Glossary at the end of the book.

Concepts and Approaches

The approach you take toward security influences all subsequent security decisions and sets the tone for the entire organization's network security infrastructure. Before we delve into various network security paradigms, let us take a moment to examine a few concepts that should permeate your entire thinking about security.

The first concept is the *CIA triangle*. This does not refer to clandestine operating involving the Central Intelligence Agency; rather it is a reference to the three pillars of security: confidentiality, integrity, and availability. When you are thinking about security, your thought processes should always be guided by these three principles. First and foremost, are you keeping the data confidential? Does your approach help guarantee the integrity of data? And does your approach still make the data readily available to authorized users?

Another important concept to keep in mind is *least privileges*. This literally means that each user or service running on your network should have the least number of privileges/access required to do their job. No one should be granted access to anything unless it is absolutely required for their job. In military and intelligence circles this is referred to as "need to know."

Network security paradigms can be classified by either the scope of security measures taken (perimeter, layered) or how proactive the system is.

In a *perimeter security approach*, the bulk of security efforts are focused on the perimeter of the network. This focus might include firewalls, proxy servers, password policies, or any technology or procedure to make unauthorized access of the network less likely. Little or no effort is put into securing the systems within the network. In this approach the perimeter is secured, but the various systems within that perimeter are often vulnerable.

There are additional issues regarding perimeter security that include physical security. That can include fences, closed-circuit TV, guards, locks, and so on, depending on the security needs of your organization.

The perimeter approach is clearly flawed, so why do some companies use it? A small organization might use the perimeter approach if they have budget constraints or inexperienced network administrators. A perimeter method might be adequate for small organizations that do not store sensitive data, but it rarely works in a larger corporate setting.

A *layered security approach* is one in which not only is the perimeter secured, but individual systems within the network are also secured. All servers, workstations, routers, and hubs within the network are secure. One way to accomplish this is to divide the network into segments and secure each segment as if it were a separate network, so if the perimeter security is compromised, not all the internal systems are affected. This is the preferred method whenever possible.

You should also measure your security approach by how proactive/reactive it is. This is done by gauging how much of the system's security infrastructure and policies is dedicated to preventive measures and how much of the security system is designed to respond to attack. A passive security approach takes few or no steps to prevent an attack. A dynamic or proactive defense is one in which steps are taken to prevent attacks before they occur.

One example of this defense is the use of intrusion-detection systems (IDS), which work to detect attempts to circumvent security measures. These systems can tell a system administrator that an attempt to breach security has been made, even if that attempt is not successful. IDS can also be used to detect various techniques intruders use to assess a target system, thus alerting a network administrator to the potential for an attempted breach before the attempt is even initiated.

In the real world, network security is usually not completely in one paradigm or another; it is usually a hybrid approach. Networks generally include elements of both security paradigms. The two categories also combine. One can have a network that is predominantly passive but layered, or one that is primarily perimeter but proactive. It can be helpful to consider approaches to computer security along a Cartesian coordinate system, as illustrated in Figure 1.1, with the x axis representing the level of passive-active approaches and the y axis depicting the range from perimeter to layered defense.

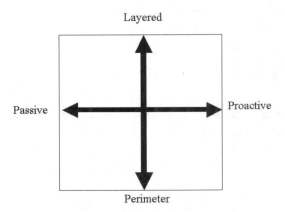

FIGURE 1.1   The security approach guide.

The most desirable hybrid approach is a layered paradigm that is dynamic, which is the upper-right quadrant of the figure.

How Do Legal Issues Impact Network Security?

An increasing number of legal issues affect how one approaches computer security. If your organization is a publicly traded company, a government agency, or does business with either one, there may be legal constraints regarding your network security. Even if your network is not legally bound to these security guidelines, it's useful to understand the various laws impacting computer security. You may choose to apply them to your own security standards.

One of the oldest pieces of legislation in the United States that affects computer security is the Computer Security Act of 1987 (100th Congress, 1987). It requires government agencies to identify sensitive systems, conduct computer security training, and develop computer security plans. This law was a vague mandate ordering federal agencies in the United States to establish security measures, but did not specify any standards.

This legislation established a legal mandate to enact specific standards, paving the way for future guidelines and regulations. It also helped define terms, such as what information is considered "sensitive." This quote is found in the legislation itself:

> The term 'sensitive information' means any information, the loss, misuse, or unauthorized access to or modification of which could adversely affect the national interest or the conduct of Federal programs, or the privacy to which individuals are entitled under section 552a of title 5, United States Code (the Privacy Act), but which has not been specifically authorized under criteria established by an Executive order or an Act of Congress to be kept secret in the interest of national defense or foreign policy. (100th Congress, 1987)

This definition of the word *sensitive* should be kept in mind because it is not just social security information or medical history that must be secured.

When considering what information needs to be secure, simply ask this question: Would the unauthorized access or modification of this information adversely affect your organization? If the answer is yes, then you must consider that information sensitive and in need of security precautions.

Another more specific federal law that applied to mandated security for government systems is OMB Circular A-130 (specifically, Appendix III). This document required that federal agencies establish security programs containing specified elements. It also described requirements for developing standards for computer systems and for records held by government agencies.

Most states have specific laws regarding computer security, such as legislation like the Computer Crimes Act of Florida, the Computer Crime Act of Alabama, and the Computer Crimes Act of Oklahoma. If you're responsible for network security, you might find yourself part of a criminal investigation. This could be an investigation into a hacking incident or employee misuse of computer resources. A list of computer crime laws (organized by state) can be found at http://law.findlaw.com/state-laws/computer-crimes/.

> (**CAUTION**)
>
> ### Privacy Laws
>
> It is also critical to keep in mind that any law that governs privacy (such as the Health Insurance Portability and Accountability Act of 1996, HIPAA) also has a direct impact on computer security. If your system is compromised, and thus data that is covered under any privacy statute is compromised, you may need to prove that you exercised due diligence in protecting that data. If it can be shown that you did not take proper precautions, you might be found civilly liable.

Online Security Resources

As you read this book, and when you move out into the professional world, you will have frequent need for additional security resources. Appendix B includes a more complete list of resources, but this section highlights a few of the most important ones you may find useful now.

CERT

The *Computer Emergency Response Team* (CERT, www.cert.org) is sponsored by Carnegie-Mellon University. CERT was the first computer incident-response team, and it is still one of the most respected in the industry. Anyone interested in network security should visit the site routinely. On the website you will find a wealth of documentation, including guidelines for security policies, cutting-edge security research, and more.

Microsoft Security Advisor

Because so many computers today run Microsoft operating systems, another good resource is the Microsoft Security Advisor website: www.microsoft.com/security/default.mspx. This site is a portal to all Microsoft security information, tools, and updates. If you use any Microsoft software, then it is advised that you visit this website regularly.

F-Secure

The F-Secure corporation maintains a website at www.f-secure.com. This site is, among other things, a repository for detailed information on virus outbreaks. Here you will not only find notifications about a particular virus but you will also find detailed information about the virus. This information includes how the virus spreads, ways to recognize the virus, and frequently, specific tools for cleaning an infected system of a particular virus.

SANS Institute

The SANS Institute website (www.sans.org) is a vast repository of security-related documentation. On this site you will find detailed documentation on virtually every aspect of computer security you can imagine. The SANS Institute also sponsors a number of security research projects and publishes information about those projects on their website.

Summary

Network security is a complex and constantly evolving field. Practitioners must stay on top of new threats and solutions and be proactive in assessing risk and protecting their networks. The first step to understanding network security is to become acquainted with the actual threats posed to a network. Without a realistic idea of what threats might affect your systems, you will be unable to effectively protect them. It is also critical that you acquire a basic understanding of the terminology used by both security professionals and those who would seek to compromise your security.

Test Your Skills

MULTIPLE CHOICE QUESTIONS

1. One extreme viewpoint about computer security is what?

    A. The federal government will handle security.

    B. Microsoft will handle security.

    C. There are no imminent dangers to your system.

    D. There is no danger if you use Linux.

2. Before you can formulate a defense for a network you need what?

    A. Appropriate security certifications

    B. A clear picture of the dangers to be defended against

    C. To finish this textbook

    D. The help of an outside consultant

3. Which of the following is not one of the three major classes of threats?

    A. Attempts to intrude on the system

    B. Online auction fraud

    C. Denial of service attacks

    D. A computer virus

4. What is a computer virus?

    A. Any program that is downloaded to your system without your permission

    B. Any program that self-replicates

    C. Any program that causes harm to your system

    D. Any program that can change your Windows Registry

5. What is spyware?

   A. Any software that monitors your system

   B. Only software that logs keystrokes

   C. Any software used to gather intelligence

   D. Only software that monitors what websites you visit

6. What is a sneaker?

   A. A person who hacks a system without being caught

   B. A person who hacks a system by faking a legitimate password

   C. A person who hacks a system to test its vulnerabilities

   D. A person who is an amateur hacker

7. What is the term for hacking a phone system?

   A. Telco-hacking

   B. Hacking

   C. Cracking

   D. Phreaking

8. What is malware?

   A. Software that has some malicious purpose

   B. Software that is not functioning properly

   C. Software that damages your system

   D. Software that is not properly configured for your system

9. What is war-driving?

   A. Driving and seeking a computer job

   B. Driving while using a wireless connection to hack

   C. Driving looking for wireless networks to hack

   D. Driving and seeking rival hackers

10. When a hacking technique uses persuasion and deception to get a person to provide information to help them compromise security, this is referred to as what?

   A. Social engineering

   B. Conning

   C. Human intel

   D. Soft hacking

11. What is the most common threat on the Internet?

    A. Auction fraud

    B. Hackers

    C. Computer viruses

    D. Illegal software

12. What are the three approaches to security?

    A. Perimeter, layered, hybrid

    B. High security, medium security, low security

    C. Internal, external, and hybrid

    D. Perimeter, complete, none

13. An intrusion-detection system is an example of which of the following?

    A. Proactive security

    B. Perimeter security

    C. Hybrid security

    D. Good security practices

14. Which of the following is the most basic security activity?

    A. Authentication

    B. Firewalls

    C. Password protection

    D. Auditing

15. The most desirable approach to security is one that is which of the following?

    A. Perimeter and dynamic

    B. Layered and dynamic

    C. Perimeter and static

    D. Layered and static

16. According to a recent survey of 223 computer professionals prepared by the Computer Security Institute, which of the following was cited as an issue by more of the respondents?

    A. Internal systems

    B. Employee abuse

    C. Routers

    D. Internet connection

17. Which of the following type of privacy law affects computer security?

    A. Any state privacy law

    B. Any privacy law applicable to your organization

    C. Any privacy law

    D. Any federal privacy law

18. The first computer incident-response team is affiliated with what university?

    A. Massachusetts Institute of Technology

    B. Carnegie-Mellon University

    C. Harvard University

    D. California Technical University

19. Which of the following is the best definition of the term *sensitive information*?

    A. Any information that has impact on national security

    B. Any information that is worth more than $1,000

    C. Any information that if accessed by unauthorized personnel could damage your organization in any way

    D. Any information that is protected by any privacy laws

20. Which of the following is a major resource for detailed information on a computer virus?

    A. The MIT Virus Library

    B. The Microsoft Virus Library

    C. The F-Secure Virus Library

    D. The National Virus Repository

EXERCISES

EXERCISE 1.1: How Many Virus Attacks Have Occurred This Month?

1. Using some website resource, such as www.f-secure.com, look up recent computer virus outbreaks.

2. How many virus outbreaks have occurred in the past 7 days?

3. Write down how many outbreaks there have been in the past 30 days, 90 days, and 1 year.

4. Are virus attacks increasing in frequency?

EXERCISE 1.2: **Learning about Cookies as Spyware**

1. Get an idea of what kind of information cookies store. You might find the following websites helpful:

   http://computercops.biz/article3911.html

   www.ctc-solutions.co.uk/internet_security_2.html

   www.howstuffworks.com/cookie1.htm

2. Write a brief essay explaining in what way cookies can invade privacy.

EXERCISE 1.3: **Hacker Terminology**

1. Use the *Hacker's Dictionary* at www.hackersdictionary.com/html/index.html to define the following hacker terms:

   A. Alpha geek

   B. Grok

   C. Red Book

   D. Wank

EXERCISE 1.4: **Using Security Resources**

1. Using one of the preferred web resources listed in this chapter, find three policy or procedure documents from that resource.

2. List the documents you selected.

3. Write a brief essay explaining why those particular documents are important to your organization's security.

EXERCISE 1.5: **Learning About the Law**

1. Using the Web, journals, books, or other resources, find out if your state or territory has any laws specific to computer security. You might find the following websites helpful:

   www.usdoj.gov/criminal/cybercrime/cclaws.html

   www.pbs.org/wgbh/pages/frontline/shows/hackers/blame/crimelaws.html

   www.ncsl.org/programs/lis/cip/viruslaws.htm

   www.cybercrime.gov/

2. List three laws that you find, with a brief description of each. The list can be a simple one, noting the pertinent laws in your region. Describe each one with one or two sentences.

PROJECTS

PROJECT 1.1: Learning About a Virus

1. Using web resources from Appendix B and sites such as www.f-secure.com, find a virus that has been released in the past 6 months.

2. Research how the virus spread and the damage it caused.

3. Write a brief (half to one page) paper on this virus. Explain how the virus worked, how it spread, and any other essential information you can find.

PROJECT 1.2: Considering the Law (a group project)

Write a description of a computer law that you would like to have passed, along with specifications as to its implementation, enforcement, and justification.

PROJECT 1.3: Recommending Security

1. Using the Web, journals, or books, locate security recommendations from any reputable source, such as the SANS Institute. Any of the sites mentioned in the "Online Security Resources" section of this chapter would be a good choice.

2. List five of those recommendations.

3. Explain why you agree or disagree with each one.

Case Study

In this case study we will consider a network administrator for a small, family-oriented video store. The store is not part of a chain of stores and has a very limited security budget. It has five machines for employees to use to check out movies and one server on which to keep centralized records. That server is in the manager's office. The administrator takes the following security precautions:

1. Each machine is upgraded to Windows XP, with the personal firewall turned on.

2. Antivirus software was installed on all machines.

3. A tape backup is added to the server, and tapes are kept in a file cabinet in the manager's office.

4. Internet access to employee machines is removed.

Now consider these questions:

1. What did these actions accomplish?

2. What additional actions might you recommend?

Chapter $\big|$ 2

Networks and the Internet

Chapter Objectives

After reading this chapter and completing the exercises, you will be able to do the following:

- Identify each of the major protocols used in network communication (for example, FTP and Telnet), and what use you can make of each
- Understand the various connection methods and speeds used on networks
- Compare and contrast a hub and switch
- Identify what a router is and its use
- Understand how data is transmitted over a network
- Explain how the Internet works and the use of IP addresses and URLs
- Recount a brief history of the Internet
- Use network utilities such as these: `ping`, `IPConfig`, and `tracert`
- Describe the OSI model of network communication and the use of MAC addresses

Introduction

To be able to manage network security, you will need knowledge about how computer networks operate. Those readers who already have a strong working knowledge of network operations may choose to skim this chapter, or perhaps give it a quick read as a review. For other readers new to computer networking, studying this chapter will give you a basic introduction to how networks and the Internet work, including a history of the Internet. This understanding of networks and the Internet will be crucial to your comprehension of later topics presented in this book.

We will begin by examining the basic technologies, protocols, and methods used for networks and the Internet to communicate. Then we will take a look at the history of the Internet. This information forms the background knowledge you will need to understand various cyber attacks, and how they are defended against. In the exercises at the end of the chapter, you will be able to practice using some protective methods, such as IPConfig, tracert, and ping.

Network Basics

Getting two or more computers to communicate and transmit data is a process that is simple in concept but complex in application. Consider all the factors involved. First you will need to physically connect the computers. This connection (although sometimes accomplished by infrared light) usually requires either a cable that plugs into your computer or wireless connection. The cable then is plugged either directly to another computer, or is plugged into a device that will, in turn, connect to several other computers.

Of course, wireless communication is being used with more frequency, and wireless connecting, obviously, doesn't require a cable. However, even wireless communication relies on a physical device to transmit the data. There is a card in most modern computers called a *network interface card*, or NIC. If the connection is through a cable, the part of the NIC that is external to the computer has a connection slot that looks like a telephone jack, only slightly bigger. Wireless networks also use a NIC; but rather than having a slot for a cable to connect to, the wireless network simply uses radio signals to transmit to a nearby wireless router or hub. Wireless routers, hubs, and NICs must have an antenna to transmit and receive signals. These devices are connective devices that will be explained in detail later in this chapter

The Physical Connection: Local Networks

As mentioned, cables are one of the ways that computers are connected to each other. The cable connection used with traditional NICs (meaning not wireless) is an RJ-45 connection. (*RJ* is short for Registered Jack—which is an international industry standard.) In contrast to the computer's RJ-45 jacks, standard telephone lines use RJ-11 jacks. The biggest difference between jacks involves the number of wires in the connector, also called the terminator. Phone lines have four wires, whereas RJ-45 connectors have eight.

If you look on the back of most computers or the connection area of a laptop, you will probably find two ports that, at first glance, look like phone jacks. One of the two ports is probably for a traditional modem and accepts a standard RJ-11 jack. The other port is larger and accepts an RJ-45 jack. Not all computers come with a NIC, but most modern computers do.

This standard connector jack must be on the end of the cable. The cable used in most networks today is a Category 5 cable—abbreviated as Cat 5 cable. (Note that Cat 6 cable is becoming more prevalent with high-speed networks.) Table 2.1 summarizes the various categories of cable and their uses.

TABLE 2.1   Cable Types and Uses

Category	Specifications	Uses
1	Low-speed analog (less than 1MHz)	Telephone, doorbell
2	Analog line (less than 10MHz)	Telephone
3	Up to 16MHz or 100 Mbps (megabits per second)	Voice transmissions
4	Up to 20MHz/100Mbps	Data lines, Ethernet networks
5	100 MHz/100Mbps	Most common type of network cable
6	1000 Mbps	Very high-speed networks
7	100 GBPS	The latest and fastest

The type of cable used in connecting computers is also often referred to as unshielded twisted-pair cable (UTP). In UTP, the wires in the cable are in pairs, twisted together without any additional shielding. As you can see in Table 2.1, each subsequent category of cable is somewhat faster and more robust than the last. It should be noted that although Cat 4 can be used for networks, it almost never is used for that purpose, as it is simply slower, less reliable, and an older technology. You will usually see Cat 5 cable and, increasingly, Cat 6. You should note that we are focusing on UTP because that is what is found most often. There are other types of cable such as shielded twisted pair (STP), but they are not nearly as common as UTP.

FYI: Cable Speed

Category 6 cable is for the new Gigabit Ethernet. Cat 5 cable works at speeds of up to 100Mbps, whereas Cat 6 works at 1000Mbps. Cat 6 is widely available and has been for several years. However, for Cat 6 to truly function properly, you need hubs/switches, and NICs that also transmit at gigabit speeds; thus, the spread of gigabit Ethernet has been much slower than many analysts expected. We will discuss hubs, switches, NICs, and other hardware in more detail later in this chapter.

As shown in Table 2.1, a key specification is speed, measured in mbps, or megabits per second. You are probably already aware that ultimately everything in the computer is stored in a binary format—namely, in the form of a 1 or a 0. These units are called bits. It takes 8 bits, which equals 1 byte, to represent a single character such as a letter, number, or carriage return. Remember that the data specification for each cable is the maximum that the cable can handle. A Cat 5 cable can transmit up to 100 mega (million) bits per second. This is known as the bandwidth of the cable. If multiple users are on a network, all sending data, that traffic uses up bandwidth rather quickly. Any pictures transmitted also use a lot of bandwidth. Simple scanned-in photos can easily reach 2 megabytes (2 million bytes, or 16 million bits) or much more. And streaming media, such as video, is perhaps the most demanding on bandwidth.

If you simply want to connect two computers to each other, you can have the cable go directly from one computer to the other. You would have to use a crossover cable, but you could connect two computers directly. But what do you do if you wish to connect more than one computer? What if you have 100 computers that you need to connect on a network? There are three devices that can help you to accomplish this task: the hub, the switch, and the router. These each use Cat 5 or Cat 6 cable with RJ-45 connectors and are explained in the following sections.

The Hub

The simplest connection device is the *hub*. A hub is a small box-shaped electronic device into which you can plug network cables. It will have four or more (commonly up to 24) RJ-45 jacks, each called a *port*. A hub can connect as many computers as it has ports. (For example, an 8-port hub can connect eight computers.) You can also connect one hub to another; this strategy is referred to as "stacking" hubs. Hubs are quite inexpensive and simple to set up; just plug in the cable. However, hubs have a downside. If you send a packet (a unit of data transmission) from one computer to another, a copy of that packet is actually sent out from every port on the hub. All these copies leads to a lot of unnecessary network traffic. This occurs because the hub, being a very simple device, has no way of knowing where a packet is supposed to go. Therefore, it simply sends copies of the packet out all of its ports. While you may go to your favorite electronic store and buy something called a "hub," true hubs no longer exist. What you are really getting is a switch, which we will discuss next.

Repeater

A repeater is a device used to boost signal. Basically if your cable needs to go further than the maximum length (which is 100 meters for UTP), then you need a repeater. There are two types of repeater: amplifier and signal. Amplifier repeaters simply boost the entire signal they receive, including any noise. Signal repeaters regenerate the signal, and thus don't rebroadcast any noise.

The Switch

The next connection device option is the *switch*. A switch is basically an intelligent hub; it works and looks exactly like a hub, with one significant difference. When a switch receives a packet, it will send that packet only out the port for the computer to which it needs to go. A switch is essentially a hub that is able to determine where a packet is being sent. How this determination is made is explained in the "Data Transmission" section.

The Router

Finally, if you wish to connect two or more networks together, you use a *router*. A router is similar in concept to a hub or switch, as it does relay packets; but it is far more sophisticated. You can program most routers and control how they relay packets. Most routers have interfaces allowing you to configure them. The more robust routers also offer more programming possibilities. The specifics of how you program the router are different from vendor to vendor, and there are entire books written specifically on just programming routers. It is not possible to cover specific router programming techniques in this book; however, you should be aware that most routers are programmable allowing you to change how they route traffic. Also, unlike using a hub or switch, the two networks connected by a router are still separate networks.

Faster Connection Speeds

The explanation above covers the connections between computers on a local network, but surely there are faster connection methods? Well, there are; in fact, your Internet service provider or the company for which you work probably has a much faster connection to the Internet. Table 2.2 summarizes the most common high-speed connection types and their speeds.

TABLE 2.2   Internet Connection Types

Connection Type	Speed	Details
DS0	64Kbps	Standard phone line.
ISDN	128Kbps	Two DS0 lines working together to provide a high-speed data connection.
T1	1.54Mbps	Twenty-four DS0 lines working as one. Twenty-three carry data, and one carries information about the other lines. This type of connection has become common for schools and businesses.
T3	43.2Mbps	672 DS0 lines working together. This method is the equivalent of 28 T1 lines.
OC3	155Mbps	All OC lines are optical and do not use traditional phone lines. OC3 lines are quite fast and very expensive. They are often found at telecommunications companies.
OC12	622Mbps	The equivalent of 336 T1 lines, or 8,064 phone lines.
OC48	2.5Gbps	The equivalent of four OC12 lines.

It is common to find T1 connection lines in many locations. A cable modem can sometimes achieve speeds comparable to a T1 line. Note that cable modems were not listed on the chart, simply because their actual speeds vary greatly depending on a variety of circumstances including how many people in your immediate vicinity are using the same cable modem provider. You are not likely to encounter the OC lines unless you work in telecommunications.

Data Transmission

We've seen, briefly, the physical connection methods; but how is data actually transmitted? To transmit data, a packet is sent. The basic purpose of a cable is to transmit packets from one machine to another. It does not matter whether that packet is a part of a document, video, an image, or just some internal signal from the computer. So what, exactly, is a packet? As we discussed earlier, everything in a computer is ultimately stored as 1s and 0s, called bits, which are grouped into sets of eight, called a byte. A *packet* is a certain number of bytes divided into a header and a body. The header is 20 bytes at the beginning of the packet that tells you where the packet is coming from, where it is going, and more. The body contains the actual data, in binary format, that you wish to send. The aforementioned routers and switches work by reading the header portion of any packets that come to them. This process is how they determine where the packet should be sent.

Protocols

There are different types of network communications for different purposes. The different types of network communications are called *protocols*. A protocol is, essentially, an agreed-upon method of communication. In fact, this definition is exactly how the word *protocol* is used in standard, noncomputer usage too. Each protocol has a specific purpose and normally operates on a certain port. (Ports are discussed in more detail below.) Some of the most important, and most commonly used, protocols are listed in Table 2.3.

TABLE 2.3 TCP/IP Protocols

Protocol	Purpose	Port
FTP (File Transfer Protocol)	For transferring files between computers.	20 and 21
TFTP (Trivial File Transfer Protocol)	A quicker but less-reliable form of FTP.	69
Telnet	Used to remotely log on to a system. You can then use a command prompt or shell to execute commands on that system. Popular with network administrators.	23
SMTP (Simple Mail Transfer Protocol)	Sends email.	25
WhoIS	A command that queries a target IP address for information.	43
DNS (Domain Name Service)	Translates URLs into Web addresses.	53
HTTP (Hypertext Transfer Protocol)	Displays web pages.	80
POP3 (Post Office Protocol version 3)	Retrieves email.	110
NNTP (Network News Transfer Protocol)	Used for network news groups (Usenet newsgroups). You can access these groups over the Web via www.google.com by selecting the Groups tab.	119
NetBIOS	An older Microsoft protocol that is for naming systems on a local network.	137, 138, 139
IRC (Internet Relay Chat)	Used for chat rooms.	194
ICMP (Internet Control Message Protocol)	These are simply packets that contain error messages, informational messages, and control messages.	No specific port

Each of these protocols will be explained in more detail, as needed, in later chapters of this book. You should also note that this list is not complete, as there are dozens of other protocols; but these are the basic protocols we will be discussing in this book. All of these protocols are part of a suite of protocols referred to as *TCP/IP* (Transmission Control Protocol/Internet Protocol). But no matter the particular protocol being used, all communication on networks takes place via packets, and those packets are transmitted according to certain protocols, depending on the type of communication that is occurring.

Ports

You may be wondering what a port is, especially since we've already talked about the ports that are the connection locations on the back of your computer, such as a serial port, a parallel port, or RJ-45 and RJ-11 ports. A *port*, in networking terms, is a handle—a connection point. It is a numeric designation for a particular pathway of communications. All network communication, regardless of the port used, comes into your computer via the connection on your NIC.

So, the picture we've drawn of networks, to this point, is one of machines connected to each other via cables, and perhaps to hubs, switches, or routers. These networks transmit binary information in packets using certain protocols and ports.

How the Internet Works

Now that you have a basic idea of how computers communicate with each other over a network, it is time to discuss how the Internet works. The Internet is essentially a large number of networks that are connected to each other. Therefore, the Internet works exactly the same way as your local network. It sends the same sort of data packets, using the same protocols. These various networks are simply connected into main transmission lines called *backbones*. The points where the backbones connect to each other are called *network access points (NAPs)*. When you log on to the Internet, you probably use an *Internet service provider (ISP)*. That ISP has a connection either to the Internet backbone or to yet another provider that has a backbone. So, logging on to the Internet is a process of connecting your computer to your ISP's network, which is, in turn, connected to one of the backbones on the Internet.

IP Addresses

With tens of thousands of networks and millions of individual computers communicating and sending data, a predictable problem arises. That problem is ensuring that the data packets go to the correct computer. This task is accomplished in much the same way as traditional "snail" letter mail is delivered to the right person: via an address. With network communications, this address is a special one, referred to as an "IP" address. An IP address can be IP version 4 or version 6.

IPv4

An *IP address* is a series of four values, separated by periods. (An example would be 107.22.98.198.) Each of the three-digit numbers must be between 0 and 255; thus an address of 107.22.98.466 would not be a valid one. These addresses are actually four binary numbers; you just see them in decimal format. Since each of these numbers is really just a decimal representation of 8 bits, they are often referred to as octets. So there are four octets in an IP v4 address. Recall that a byte is 8 bits (1s and 0s), and an 8-bit binary number converted to decimal format will be between 0 and 255. So you don't have to do the math yourself, I will tell you that this rule means there are a total of over 4.2 billion possible IP addresses. You should not be concerned, however, that we will run out of new IP addresses soon. There are methods already in place (which are discussed below) to extend the use of addresses.

> ### FYI: Converting Binary
>
> For those readers not familiar with converting decimal to binary, there are several methods, one of which is shown below. You should be aware that the computer will do this for you in the case of IP addresses, but here's one way—and perhaps the simplest—this is done:
>
> Divide repeatedly by 2, using "remainders" rather than decimal places, until you get down to 1. For example, convert decimal 31 to binary:
>
> 31/2 = 15 Remainder 1
>
> 15/2 = 7 Remainder 1
>
> 7/2 = 3 Remainder 1
>
> 3/2 = 1 Remainder 1
>
> 1/2 = 0 Remainder 1
>
> Now read the remainders from bottom to top: The binary equivalent is 11111.

The IP addresses come in two groups: public and private. The public IP addresses are for computers connected to the Internet. No two public IP address can be the same. However, a private IP address, such as one on a private company network, only has to be unique in that network. It does not matter if other computers in the world have the same IP address, because this computer is never connected to those other worldwide computers. Often network administrators use private IP addresses that begin with a 10, such as 10.102.230.17.

It should also be pointed out that often an ISP will buy a pool of public IP addresses and assign them to you when you log on. An ISP might own 1,000 public IP address and have 10,000 customers. Because all 10,000 customers will not be online at the same time, the ISP simply assigns an IP address to a customer when he logs on, and the ISP un-assigns the IP address when the customer logs off.

The address of a computer tells you a lot about that computer. The first byte (or the first decimal number) in an address tells you to what class of network that machine belongs. Table.2.4 summarizes the five network classes.

TABLE 2.4   Network Classes

Class	IP Range for the First Byte	Use
A	0–126	Extremely large networks. No Class A network IP addresses are left. All have been used.
B	128–191	Large corporate and government networks. All Class B IP addresses have been used.
C	192–223	The most common group of IP addresses. Your ISP probably has a Class C address.
D	224–247	These are reserved for multicasting (transmitting different data on the same channel).
E	248–255	Reserved for experimental use.

These five classes of networks will become more important later in this book (or should you decide to study networking on a deeper level). Observe Table 2.4 carefully, and you probably will discover that the IP range of 127 was not listed. This omission is because that range is reserved for testing. The IP address of 127.0.0.1 designates the machine you are on, regardless of that machine's assigned IP address. This address is often referred to as the *loopback address*. That address will be used often in testing your machine and your NIC. We will examine its use a bit later in this chapter, in the section on network utilities.

These particular classes are important as they tell you what part of the address represents the network and what part represents the node. For example, in a Class A address, the first octet represents the network, the remaining three represent the node. In a Class B address, the first two octets represent the network and the second two represent the node. And finally, in a Class C address, the first three octets represent the network, the last represents the node.

There are also some very specific IP addresses and IP address ranges you should be aware of. The first, as previously mentioned, is 127.0.0.1, or the loopback address. It is another way of referring to the network interface card of the machine you are on.

Private IP addresses are another issue to be aware of. Certain ranges of IP addresses have been designated for use within networks. These cannot be used as public IP addresses, but can be used for internal workstations and servers. Those IP addresses are:

- 10.0.0.10 to 10.255.255.255

- 172.16.0.0 to 172.31.255.255

- 192.168.0.0 to 192.168.255.255

Subnetting and CIDR

We have already discussed IP version 4 network addresses; now let's turn our attention to subnetting. If you are already familiar with this topic, feel free to skip this section. For some reason this topic tends to give networking students a great deal of trouble. So we will begin with a conceptual understanding. Subnetting is simply chopping up a network in to smaller portions. For example, if you have a network using the IP address 192.168.1.X (x being whatever the address is for the specific computer), then you have allocated 255 possible IP addresses. What if you want to divide that into two separate sub networks? Subnetting is how you do that.

More technically, the subnet mask is a 32-bit number that is assigned to each host to divide the 32-bit binary IP address into network and node portions. You also cannot just put in any number you want. The first value of a subnet mask must be 255; the remaining three values can be 255, 254, 252, 248, 240, or 224. Your computer will take your network IP address and the subnet mask and use a binary AND operation to combine them.

It may surprise you to know that you already have a subnet mask even if you have not been subnetting! If you have a Class C IP address, then your network subnet mask is 255.255.255.0. If you have a Class B IP address, then your subnet mask is 255.255.0.0. And finally, if it is Class A, your subnet mask is 255.0.0.0.

Now think about these numbers in relationship to binary numbers. The decimal value 255 converts to 11111111 in binary. So you are literally "masking" the portion of the network address that is used to define the network, and the remaining portion is used to define individual nodes. Now if you want fewer than 255 nodes in your subnet, then you need something like 255.255.255.240 for your subnet. If you convert 240 to binary, it is 11110000. That means the first three octets and the first 4 bits of the last octet define the network. The last 4 bits of the last octet define the node. That means you could have as many as 1111 (in binary) or 15 (in decimal) nodes on this subnetwork. This is the basic essence of subnetting.

CIDR

Subnetting only allows you to use certain, limited subnets. Another approach is CIDR, or classless interdomain routing. Rather than define a subnet mask, you have the IP address followed by a slash and a number. That number can be any number between 0 and 32, which results in IP addresses like these:

192.168.1.10/24 (basically a Class C IP address)

192.168.1.10/31 (much like a Class C IP address with a subnet mask)

When you use this, rather than having classes with subnets, you have variable-length subnet masking (VLSM) that provides classless IP address. This is the most common way to define network IP addresses today.

IPv6

You have probably heard talk of IP version 6, or IPv6, as an extension of IPv4. Essentially, IP version 4 is limited to 4.2 billion IP addresses. Even with the use of private IP addresses, we will run out of available IP addresses. Think of all the computers, printers, routers, servers, smart phones, tablets, etc., all connected to the Internet. IP version 6 was designed to alleviate this problem. And if you looked around in the network settings described in the last section, you probably saw the option to enable IPv6. IPv6 utilizes a 128-bit address (instead of 32), so there is no chance of running out of IP addresses in the foreseeable future. IPv6 also utilizes a hex numbering method in order to avoid long addresses such as 132.64.34.26.64.156.143.57.1.3.7.44.122.111.201.5. The hex address format will appear in the form of 3FFE:B00:800:2::C, for example.

There is no subnetting in IPv6. Instead, it only uses CIDR. Network portion is indicated by a slash followed by the number of bits in the address that are assigned to the network portion, such as

/48

/64

There is a loopback address for IPv6, and it can be written as ::/128. Other differences between IPv4 and IPv6 are described here:

- Link/machine-local.

  IPv6 version of IPv4's APIPA or Automatic Private IP Addressing. So if the machine is configured for dynamically assigned addresses, and cannot communicate with a DHCP server, it assigns itself a generic IP address. DHCP or Dynamic Host Configuration Protocol is used to dynamically assign IP addresses within a network.

IPV6 link/machine-local IP addresses all start with fe80::. So if your computer has this address, that means it could not get to a DHCP server and therefore made up its own generic IP address.

- Site/network-local.

  IPv6 version of IPv4 private address. In other words these are real IP addresses, but only work on this local network. They are not routable on the Internet.

  All site/network-local IP addresses begin with FE and have C to F for the third hexadecimal digit: FEC, FED, FEE, or FEF.

- DHCPv6 uses the Managed Address Configuration Flag (M flag).

  When set to 1, device should use DHCPV6 to obtain a stateful IPv6 address.

- Other stateful configuration flag (O flag).

  When set to 1, device should use DHCPv6 to obtain other TCP/IP configuration settings. In other words, it should use the DHCP server to set things like the IP address of the gateway and DNS servers.

- M flag

  This indicates that the machine should use DHCPv6 to retrieve an IP address.

This is the essence of IPv6. You still have all the same utilities you used with IPv4. However, there is a number 6 after the `ping` or `traceroute`, so if your computer has IPv6 enabled, you can use the following:

ping6 www.yahoo.com

We will be discussing `ping`, `traceroute`, and other commands later in this chapter.

Uniform Resource Locators

After you connect to your ISP, you will, of course, want to visit some websites. You probably type names, rather than IP addresses, into your browser's address bar. For example, you might type in www.chuckeasttom.com to go to my website. Your computer, or your ISP, must translate the name you typed in (called a *uniform resource locator [URL]*) into an IP address. The DNS protocol, mentioned in Table 2.3, handles this translation process. So you are typing in a name that makes sense to humans, but your computer is using a corresponding IP address to connect. If that address is found, your browser sends a packet (using the HTTP protocol) to port 80. If that target computer has software that listens and responds to such requests (like web server software such as Apache or Microsoft Internet Information Server), then the target computer will respond to your browser's request and communication will be established. This method is how web pages are viewed.

If you have ever received an Error 404: File Not Found, what you are seeing is that your browser received back a packet (from the web server) with error code 404, denoting that the page you requested could not be found. There are a series of error messages that the web server can send back to your web browser, indicating different situations. Many of these problems the browser handles itself, and you never see the error message. All error messages in the 400 series are *client errors*. This term means something is wrong on your side, not the web server. Messages in the 500 series are *server errors*, which means there is a problem on the web server. The 100 series messages are simply informational; 200 series messages indicate success (you usually do not see these, the browser simply processes them); and 300 series messages are redirectional, meaning the page you are seeking has moved and your browser is then directed to the new location.

Email works the same way as visiting websites. Your email client will seek out the address of your email server. Then your email client will use either the POP3 protocol to retrieve your incoming email or the SMTP protocol to send your outgoing email. Your email server (probably at your ISP or your company) will then try to resolve the address you are sending to. If you send something to chuck@chuckeasttom.com, your email server will translate that email address into an IP address for the email server at yahoo.com, and your server will send your email there. Note that there are newer email protocols available, but POP3 is still the most commonly used.

Many readers are probably familiar with chat rooms. A chat room, like the other methods of communication we have discussed, works with packets. You first find the address of the chat room; then you connect. The difference here is that your computer's chat software is constantly sending packets back and forth, unlike email, which only sends and receives when you tell it to (or on a predetermined time interval).

Remember that a packet has a header section and that header section contains your IP address and the destination IP address that you are going to (as well as other information). This packet structure will become important as we proceed through this book.

History of the Internet

At this point, you should have a basic understanding of how networks and the Internet work, as well as some familiarity with IP addresses, protocols, and packets. It is also helpful to know the history of the Internet, as many find that this overview helps put all of the material learned thus far into historical perspective.

The Internet traces its roots to the Cold War. One positive thing that can be said about the Cold War is that it was a time of significant investment in science and technology. In 1957, after the Soviet Union launched the Sputnik satellite, the U.S. government formed the Advanced Research Projects Agency (ARPA) within the Defense Department. ARPA's sole purpose was to fund and facilitate research into technology. Obviously, this aim would include weapons technology, but the total focus would also include communications technology.

In 1962, a study by the Rand Corporation proposed devising a communication method wherein data was sent in packets between locations. If a packet was lost, the originator of the message would automatically resend the message. This idea was a precursor to the Internet communication methodologies that would eventually arise.

In 1968, ARPA commissioned the construction of ARPANET, a simple Internet web of four points (called *nodes*): UCLA, Stanford, UC Berkley, and the University of Utah. Although no one knew it at the time, this small web was the birth of what would become the Internet. At this point, ARPANET had only these four nodes connected.

The year 1972 was a milestone for the development of the Internet, in more than one sense. That year ARPA was renamed DARPA, the Defense Advanced Research Projects Agency. Also that year, Ray Tomlinson invented the first email program. At this point, four years after the birth of ARPANET, there were 23 hosts on the network. (A *host* is a machine with data on it, to which you can connect; for example, a web server is a host.)

The following year, 1973, would mark the birth of the TCP/IP protocol, which allowed the various computers to communicate in a uniform fashion, regardless of their hardware or operating system.

In 1974, Vince Cerf published a paper on the TCP protocol, and for the first time in computer history, used the term *Internet*. In 1976, Ethernet cable was developed (the same cabling we use today), and DARPA began to require the use of TCP/IP protocol on its network. This year also marked the beginning of widespread distribution of the UNIX operating system. The development of UNIX and the Internet would go hand in hand for many years to come. By this time, 8 years after the birth of ARPANET, there were 111 hosts on the network.

In 1979, a major development occurred: the birth of Usenet newsgroups. These groups are essentially bulletin boards open to the entire world. (Today you can access these groups via newsgroup reader software, or via the Web by navigating to www.google.com and selecting Groups. There are thousands of newsgroups devoted to every topic imaginable.) Just 2 years later, the National Science Foundation (NSF) created CSNET for universities and research centers that were not part of ARPANET. That same year, Cerf proposed connecting CSNET and ARPANET. By1981, the University of Wisconsin had created DNS (Domain Name System) so that people could find nodes on the network via a name rather than the actual IP address. At this point (1981), there were 562 hosts on the network.

The early 1980s saw enormous growth in the early Internet. DARPA divided its ARPANET into military and nonmilitary segments, thus allowing more people to use the nonmilitary segment. And the NSF introduced the T1 line (a very fast connection). In 1986, the Internet Engineering Task Force (IETF) was formed to oversee the creation of standards for the Internet and Internet protocols. By this time, the Internet consisted of 2,308 hosts.

A pivotal year for Internet development turned out to be1990. That year, Tim Berners-Lee, working at CERN laboratories in Europe, developed the *Hypertext Transfer Protocol (HTTP)* and gave the world its very first web pages. Via the http protocol and the *Hypertext Markup Language (HTML)*, people could publish ideas on the Internet for anyone (with a connection) to view. By 1990, there were over 300,000 hosts on the Internet. (Fast-forward to 2004; Tim Berners-Lee receives the first Millennium Prize for contributions to technology. He is widely regarded as the father of the *World Wide Web [WWW]*.)

Internet growth and activity exploded in the 1990s. In 1992, CERN released the invention of web pages to the world at large. In 1993, the first graphical web browser, named Mosaic, was invented. By 1994, Pizza Hut began taking orders via web pages. The Internet has continued to grow; today, there are millions of websites around the world. Every organization has a site, from university departments, government agencies, corporations, schools, religions, to nearly any group you can imagine. And many individuals have personal websites, as well. Lots of you will use the Web for banking, shopping, information, and entertainment. Additionally, you likely use email on a daily basis. (By the way, I primarily use email for communication, so that is the best way to contact me if you wish: chuck@chuckeasttom.com.) The Internet has become a virtual "living level" of interaction in our society. What company does not have a website? What movie release does not have a website? What political candidate does not have a website? In just over three decades, the Internet has become an integral part of our society.

Basic Network Utilities

Later in this book, you will use information and techniques that are based, in part, on certain techniques anyone can perform on her own machine. There are network utilities that you can execute from a command prompt (Windows) or from a shell (UNIX/Linux). Many readers are already familiar with Windows, so the text's discussion will execute the commands and discuss them from the Windows command prompt perspective. However, it must be stressed that these utilities are available in all operating systems. In this section, you will read about IPConfig, ping, and tracert utilities.

IPConfig

The first step in studying networks is get information about your own system. To accomplish this fact-finding mission, you will need to get to a command prompt. In Windows XP, go to the Start menu, select All Programs (in Windows Vista or 7), then choose Accessories. You will then see an option called Command Prompt. (For Windows 2000 users, the process is identical, except the first option is simply called Programs rather than All Programs.) Next, type in **ipconfig**. (You could input the same command in UNIX or Linux by typing in **ifconfig** once inside the shell.) After typing ipconfig and pressing the Enter key, you should see something much like what is shown in Figure 2.1.

```
Command Prompt                                              _ □ ×
Microsoft Windows XP [Version 5.1.2600]
<C> Copyright 1985-2001 Microsoft Corp.

C:\Documents and Settings\Owner>ipconfig

Windows IP Configuration

Ethernet adapter Local Area Connection:

        Connection-specific DNS Suffix  . : comcast.net
        IP Address. . . . . . . . . . . . : 67.166.236.163
        Subnet Mask . . . . . . . . . . . : 255.255.255.128
        Default Gateway . . . . . . . . . : 67.166.236.129

C:\Documents and Settings\Owner>
```

FIGURE 2.1   IPConfig.

This command gives you some information about your connection to a network (or to the Internet). Most importantly, you find out your own IP address. The command also has the IP address for your default gateway, which is your connection to the outside world. Running the IPConfig command is a first step in determining your system's network configuration. Most commands that this book will mention, including IPConfig, have a number of parameters, or flags, that can be passed to the commands to make the computer behave in a certain way. You can find out what these commands are by typing in the command, followed by a space, and then typing in hyphen question mark, -?. Figure 2.2 shows the results of this method for the IPConfig command.

FIGURE 2.2   IPConfig help.

As you can see in Figure 2.2, there a number of options you might use to find out different details about your computer's configuration. The most commonly used method would probably be the IPConfig/all, shown in Figure 2.3. You can see that this option gives you much more information. For example, IPConfig/all gives the name of your computer, when your computer obtained its IP address, and more.

Ping

Another commonly used command is ping. ping is used to send a test packet, or echo packet, to a machine to find out if the machine is reachable and how long the packet takes to reach the machine. This useful diagnostic tool can be employed in elementary hacking techniques. In Figure 2.4 you see a ping command executed on www.yahoo.com.

```
Command Prompt                                                    - □ ×

C:\Documents and Settings\Owner>ipconfig /all

Windows IP Configuration

        Host Name . . . . . . . . . . . . : HAL9000
        Primary Dns Suffix  . . . . . . . :
        Node Type . . . . . . . . . . . . : Hybrid
        IP Routing Enabled. . . . . . . . : No
        WINS Proxy Enabled. . . . . . . . : No

Ethernet adapter Local Area Connection:

        Connection-specific DNS Suffix  . : comcast.net
        Description . . . . . . . . . . . : Realtek RTL8139 Family PCI Fast Ethe
rnet NIC
        Physical Address. . . . . . . . . : 00-40-CA-47-BF-23
        Dhcp Enabled. . . . . . . . . . . : Yes
        Autoconfiguration Enabled . . . . : Yes
        IP Address. . . . . . . . . . . . : 67.166.236.163
        Subnet Mask . . . . . . . . . . . : 255.255.255.128
        Default Gateway . . . . . . . . . : 67.166.236.129
        DHCP Server . . . . . . . . . . . : 12.242.18.34
        DNS Servers . . . . . . . . . . . : 63.240.76.198
                                            204.127.199.8
        Lease Obtained. . . . . . . . . . : Sunday, November 23, 2003 1:31:43 AM

        Lease Expires . . . . . . . . . . : Thursday, November 27, 2003 1:31:43
AM

C:\Documents and Settings\Owner>
```

FIGURE 2.3   IPConfig/all.

```
Command Prompt                                                    - □ ×

C:\Documents and Settings\Owner>ping www.yahoo.com

Pinging www.yahoo.akadns.net [216.109.118.71] with 32 bytes of data:

Reply from 216.109.118.71: bytes=32 time=42ms TTL=49
Reply from 216.109.118.71: bytes=32 time=43ms TTL=49
Reply from 216.109.118.71: bytes=32 time=44ms TTL=49
Reply from 216.109.118.71: bytes=32 time=42ms TTL=49

Ping statistics for 216.109.118.71:
    Packets: Sent = 4, Received = 4, Lost = 0 (0% loss),
Approximate round trip times in milli-seconds:
    Minimum = 42ms, Maximum = 44ms, Average = 42ms

C:\Documents and Settings\Owner>
```

FIGURE 2.4   Ping.

This figure tells you that a 32-byte echo packet was sent to the destination and returned. The TTL item (Time To Live) shows how many intermediary steps, or hops, the packet should take to the destination before giving up. Remember that the Internet is a vast conglomerate of interconnected networks. Your packet probably won't go straight to its destination; it will take several hops to get there. As with IPConfig, you can type in **ping -?** to find out various ways you can refine your ping.

Tracert

The final command we will examine in this chapter is the tracert command. This command is a more or less "ping deluxe." tracert not only tells you if the packet got to its destination and how long it took, but also it tells you all the intermediate hops it took to get there. This utility will prove very useful to you later in this book. Figure 2.5 illustrates a tracert to www.yahoo.com. (This same command can be executed in Linux or UNIX, but there it is called traceroute rather than tracert.)

```
Command Prompt                                                    _ □ x

C:\Documents and Settings\Owner>tracert www.yahoo.com

Tracing route to www.yahoo.akadns.net [216.109.118.73]
over a maximum of 30 hops:

  1     8 ms     9 ms     8 ms  10.180.228.1
  2     7 ms    29 ms     8 ms  12.244.113.33
  3     9 ms     9 ms     9 ms  12.244.73.10
  4     9 ms    10 ms     9 ms  gbr5-p80.dlstx.ip.att.net [12.123.17.26]
  5     9 ms    10 ms     8 ms  tbr1-p012401.dlstx.ip.att.net [12.122.12.65]
  6     9 ms     8 ms     8 ms  ggr2-p300.dlstx.ip.att.net [12.123.17.81]
  7    10 ms     9 ms    10 ms  att-gw.dc.genuity.net [192.205.32.114]
  8     9 ms     8 ms    10 ms  so-1-2-0.bbr2.Dallas1.Level3.net [209.244.15.165
]
  9    40 ms    41 ms    41 ms  so-1-2-0.bbr1.Washington1.Level3.net [64.159.0.1
38]
 10    41 ms    40 ms    39 ms  ge-7-0.ipcolo1.Washington1.Level3.net [64.159.18
.3]
 11    43 ms    44 ms    51 ms  unknown.Level3.net [63.210.59.254]
 12    43 ms    42 ms    45 ms  v130.bas1-m.dcn.yahoo.com [216.109.120.142]
 13    42 ms    42 ms    43 ms  p10.www.dcn.yahoo.com [216.109.118.73]

Trace complete.

C:\Documents and Settings\Owner>_
```

FIGURE 2.5   Tracert.

With tracert, you can see (in milliseconds) the IP addresses of each intermediate step listed and how long it took to get to that step. Knowing the steps required to reach a destination can be very important, as you will find later in this book.

Certainly there are other utilities that can be of use to you when working with network communications. However, the three we just examined are the core utilities. These three (IPConfig, ping, and tracert) are absolutely essential to any network administrator, and you should commit them to memory.

Other Network Devices

There are other devices involved in networking that work to protect your computer from the outside world, some of which were briefly mentioned in Chapter 1. Now we will review a couple of them in a bit more detail. The two most common are the firewall and the proxy server. A *firewall* is essentially a barrier between your network and the rest of the Internet. A personal computer (PC) can be used as a firewall; in many cases, a special router can function as a firewall. Firewalls use different techniques to protect your network, but the most common strategy is packet filtering. In a packet-filtering firewall, each incoming packet is examined. Only those packets that match the criteria you set are allowed through. (Commonly, only packets using certain types of protocols are allowed through.) Many operating systems, such as Windows (all versions since XP), and many Linux distributions, include basic packet-filtering software with the operating system.

The second very common type of defensive device is a *proxy server*. A proxy server will almost always be another computer. You might see the same machine used as both a proxy server and a firewall. A proxy server's purpose is quite simple: it hides your entire network from the outside world. People trying to investigate your network from the outside will see only the proxy server. They will not see the actual machines on your network. When packets go out of your network, their headers are changed so that the packets have the return address of the proxy server. Conversely, the only way you can access the outside world is via the proxy server. A proxy server combined with a firewall is basic network security. It would frankly be negligent to ever run a network that did not have a firewall and proxy server. In a later chapter, we will examine firewalls in more detail.

Advanced Network Communications Topics

These subjects are not absolutely required for you to understand this book, but they will give you a broader understanding of networks in general. If you have any intention of delving into network security on a professional level, then you will need this information—and much more.

The OSI Model

Let's begin with the *OSI model*, or Open Systems Interconnection model. This model is a description of how networks communicate. It describes the various protocols and activities, and it tells how the protocols and activities relate to each other. This model is divided into seven layers, as shown in Table 2.5, and was originally developed by the International Standards Organization (ISO) in the 1980s.

TABLE 2.5　The OSI Model

Layer Number	Layer	Description	Protocols
7	Application	This layer interfaces directly to the application and performs common application services for the application processes.	POP, SMTP, DNS, FTP, etc.

Layer Number	Layer	Description	Protocols
6	Presentation	The presentation layer relieves the application layer of concern regarding syntactical differences in data representation within the end-user systems.	
5	Session	The session layer provides the mechanism for managing the dialogue between end-user application processes.	NetBIOS
4	Transport	This layer provides end-to-end communication control.	TCP, UDP
3	Network	This layer routes the information in the network.	IP, Address Resolution Protocol, Internet Control Message Protocol
2	Data Link	This layer describes the logical organization of data bits transmitted on a particular medium. Data link is divided into two sublayers: the Media Access Control layer (MAC) and the Logical Link Control layer (LLC).	Serial Line Internet Protocol, Point-to-Point Protocol
1	Physical	This layer describes the physical properties of the various communications media, as well as the electrical properties and interpretation of the exchanged signals. In other words, the physical layer is the actual NIC, Ethernet cable, and so forth. This layer is where bits are translated into voltages, and vice versa.	None

Many networking students memorize this model. It's good to at least memorize the names of the seven layers and to understand basically what they each do. From a security perspective, the more you understand about network communications, the more sophisticated your defense can be. The most important thing for you to understand is that this model describes a hierarchy of communication. One layer will only communicate with the layer directly above it, or below it.

Media Access Control (MAC) Addresses

MAC addresses are unique addresses for an NIC. (MAC is also a sublayer of the data link layer of the OSI model.) Every NIC in the world has a unique address that is represented by a 6-byte hexadecimal number, and an Address Resolution Protocol (ARP) is used to convert IP addresses to MAC addresses. When you type in a web address, the DNS protocol is used to translate that into an IP address; then the ARP protocol will translate that IP address into a specific MAC address of an individual NIC.

This brings us to how DNS is accomplished; or rather, how does a URL get translated into an IP address? How does the computer know what IP goes with what URL? There are servers set up just to do this task, called *DNS servers*. If you are on a corporate network, you probably have a DNS server on your network. If not, then your ISP has one. These servers maintain a table of IP-to-URL entries. From time to time there are transfers of DNS data, called *zone transfers*, that allow one DNS server to send its changes to another. Across the Internet, there are root DNS servers that are maintained with centralized data for all registered URL/IP addresses.

Summary

This chapter cannot make you a networking expert. However, you should now have a basic understanding of how networks and the Internet work. Before you move on to subsequent chapters, you should make certain you completely understand basic hardware like switches, NICs, routers, and hubs. You should also be familiar with the basic protocols presented in this chapter. It is important that you be comfortable with the utilities presented. It is strongly suggested that you experiment with these utilities extensively. It is also important that you be comfortable with the basics of the OSI model. Many students struggle with it at first, but at least make sure you have a general understanding of it before you move on to Chapter 3, "Cyber Stalking, Fraud, and Abuse."

This material will be critical in later chapters. If you are new to this material, you should thoroughly study this chapter before continuing. In the exercises at the end of this chapter, you will be able to practice using IPConfig, tracert, and ping.

Test Your Skills

MULTIPLE CHOICE QUESTIONS

1. What type of cable do most networks use?

    A. Net cable

    B. Category 3 cable

    C. Phone cable

    D. Category 5 cable

2. The connector used with network cables is called what?

    A. RJ-11

    B. RJ-85

    C. RJ-12

    D. RJ-45

3. The cable used in networks is also referred to as what?

    A. Unshielded twisted pair

    B. Shielded twisted pair

    C. Unshielded untwisted pair

    D. Shielded untwisted pair

4. The simplest device for connecting computers is called what?

    A. NIC

    B. Interface

    C. Hub

    D. Router

5. What is a NIC?

    A. Network interface card

    B. Network interaction card

    C. Network interface connector

    D. Network interaction connector

6. A device used to connect two or more networks together is a what?

    A. Switch

    B. Router

    C. Hub

    D. NIC

7. A T1 line sends data at what speed?

    A. 100Mbps

    B. 1.54Mbps

    C. 155Mbps

    D. 56.6Kbps

8. How big is a TCP packet header?

    A. The size is dependent on the data being sent.

    B. The size is always 20 bytes.

    C. The size is dependent on the protocol being used.

    D. The size is always 40 bytes.

9. A protocol that translates web addresses into IP addresses is called what?

    A. DNS

    B. TFTP

    C. DHCP

    D. SMTP

10. What protocol is used to send email, and on what port does it work?

   A. SMTP, port 110

   B. POP3, port 25

   C. SMTP, port 25

   D. POP3, port 110

11. What protocol is used for remotely logging on to a computer?

   A. Telnet

   B. HTTP

   C. DNS

   D. SMTP

12. What protocol is used for web pages, and what port does it work on?

   A. HTTP, port 21

   B. HTTP, port 80

   C. DHCP, port 80

   D. DHCP, port 21

13. The point where the backbones of the Internet connect is called what?

   A. Connectors

   B. Routers

   C. Network access points

   D. Switches

14. Which of the following is not a valid IP address?

   A. 127.0.0.1

   B. 295.253.254.01

   C. 127.256.5.2

   D. 245.200.11.1

15. What class would the IP address of 193.44.34.12 be?

   A. A

   B. B

   C. C

   D. D

16. The IP address of 127.0.0.1 always refers to your what?

    A. Nearest router

    B. ISP

    C. Self

    D. Nearest NAP

17. Internet addresses of the form www.chuckeasttom.com are called what?

    A. User-friendly web addresses

    B. Uniform resource locators

    C. User-accessible web addresses

    D. Uniform address identifiers

18. Which U.S. government agency created the distributed network that formed the basis for the Internet?

    A. Advanced Research Projects Agency

    B. Central Intelligence Agency

    C. NASA

    D. Department of Energy

19. Which of the following was one of the three universities involved in the original distributed network setup by a government agency?

    A. Berkeley

    B. Harvard

    C. MIT

    D. Princeton

20. Vince Cerf invented what?

    A. The World Wide Web

    B. Email

    C. TCP

    D. The first computer virus

21. Tim Berners-Lee invented what?

    A. The World Wide Web

    B. Email

    C. TCP

    D. The first computer virus

22. Which utility gives you information about your machine's network configuration?

    A. Ping

    B. IPConfig

    C. Tracert

    D. MyConfig

23. The TCP protocol operates at what layer of the OSI model?

    A. Transport

    B. Application

    C. Network

    D. Data link

24. Which layer of the OSI model is divided into two sublayers?

    A. Data link

    B. Network

    C. Presentation

    D. Session

25. A unique hexadecimal number that identifies your network card is called what?

    A. A NIC address

    B. A MAC address

    C. A NIC ID

    D. A MAC ID

EXERCISES

EXERCISE 2.1: Using IPConfig

1. Open your command prompt or DOS Prompt. (Go to Start > All Programs > Accessories > Command Prompt [DOS prompt in Windows 98].)

2. Type in **ipconfig**.

3. Use the IPConfig command to find out information about your computer.

4. Write down your computer's IP address, default gateway, and subnet mask.

EXERCISE 2.2: **Using Tracert**

1. Open your command prompt or DOS prompt.

2. Type in **tracert www.chuckeasttom.com**.

3. Note what hops your computer takes to get to www.chuckeasttom.com.

4. Then try the same process with www.whitehouse.gov and www.prenhall.com.

5. Did you notice that the first few hops are the same? Write down what hops are taken to reach each destination, and what hops are the same. Then briefly describe why you think some of the intermediate steps are the same for different destinations.

EXERCISE 2.3: **NSLOOKUP**

The command NSLOOKUP is not mentioned in this chapter. But if you are comfortable with ping, tracert, and IPConfig, this command will be easy to learn.

1. Go to the command prompt

2. Type **nslookup www.chuckeasttom.com**.

3. Note that this command gives you the actual name of the server, as per the hosting company's naming conventions; its IP address; and any aliases under which that server operates.

EXERCISE 2.4: **More about IPConfig**

1. Open your command prompt or DOS prompt.

2. Use the -? flag on the IPConfig command to find out what other options you have with these commands. You should notice a number of options, including /all, /renew, and others.

3. Now try ipconfig /all . What do you see now that you didn't see when you simply used ipconfig in Exercise 1?

EXERCISE 2.5: **More about Ping**

1. Open your command prompt or DOS prompt.

2. Use the -? flag on the ping command and find out what other options you have with these commands. You should notice several additional options, such as -w, -t, -n, -i.

3. Try a simple ping of www.chuckeasttom.com.

4. Try the option ping -n 2 www.chuckeasttom.com, then try ping -n 7 www.chuckeasttom.com. What differences do you notice?

PROJECTS

PROJECT 2.1: Learning about DNS

1. Using web resources, look up the DNS protocol. You may find the following websites to be of help:

   www.freesoft.org/CIE/Topics/75.htm

   www.dns.net/dnsrd/docs/whatis.html

   www.webfavor.com/tips/DNS.html

2. Look up these facts: Who invented this protocol? What is its purpose? How is it used?

3. Write a brief paper describing what the protocol does. Mention a bit about who invented it, when, and how it works.

PROJECT 2.2: Learning about Your System

1. Find out if your organization (for example, your school or business) uses switches, hubs, or both. Why does your group use these? You can find out by simply asking the network administrator or the help desk. Make sure you tell them that you are seeking this information for a class project.

2. Write a brief paper explaining your findings, and any changes you would make if you could. For example, if your organization uses only hubs, would you change that method? If so, why?

PROJECT 2.3: Learning about NetStat

1. At the command prompt, type **netstat**. Notice the information it provides you. You should be seeing any IP addresses or server names that are currently connected to your computer. If you are using a home computer, you will need to log on to your Internet service provider to see anything.

> **CAUTION**
>
> ### Stopping NetStat
>
> Note that with many versions of Windows, for the next steps you will need to use the Control-Break key combination to stop netstat before starting it again with a new option.

- Now type in **netstat -?** to see options with this command. You should see -a, -e, and others.

- Now type in **netstat –a** and note the information you see.

- Finally, try **netstat –e**. What do you see now?

Chapter | **3**

Cyber Stalking, Fraud, and Abuse

Chapter Objectives

After reading this chapter and completing the exercises, you will be able to do the following:

- Know the various types of Internet investment scams and auction frauds
- Know specific steps one can take to avoid fraud on the Internet
- Have an understanding of what identity theft is and how it is done
- Know specific steps that can be taken to avoid identity theft
- Understand what cyber stalking is, and be familiar with relevant laws
- Know how to configure a web browser's privacy settings
- Know what laws apply to these computer crimes

Introduction

In every new frontier, a criminal element is bound to emerge. In times past, the high seas gave rise to pirates, and America's wild west produced gangs of outlaws. The Internet is no different than any other frontier; it has its share of outlaws. Besides hacking and virus creation, both mentioned in Chapter 1, "Introduction to Computer Security," there are other dangers. Fraud is one of the most common dangers of the Internet. As more people utilize the Internet as a conduit for commerce, there arises a greater opportunity for fraud. Fraud has been a part of life for as long as civilization has existed; in past centuries "snake oil" salesmen roamed the country selling face cures and elixirs. The Internet makes such fraud even easier. In fact, many experts would consider fraud to be the most prevalent danger on the Internet. There are multiple reasons for the popularity of Internet fraud among con artists. First, committing an Internet fraud does not require the technical expertise that hacking and virus creation require. Second, there are a great number of people engaging in various forms of online commerce, and this large amount of business creates a great many opportunities for fraud.

There are many avenues for fraud on the Internet. In this chapter, we will explore what the various major types of fraud are, what the law says, and what you can do to protect yourself. Fortunately for some readers, this particular chapter is not particularly technical, because most Internet fraud does not rely on in-depth technological expertise. Internet fraud merely uses the computer as a venue for many of the same fraud schemes that have been perpetrated throughout history.

How Internet Fraud Works

There are a variety of ways that a fraud can be perpetrated via the Internet. The Securities and Exchange Commission lists several types of Internet fraud on their website;[1] we will briefly discuss each of those and others, but it is not possible for us to cover every variation of each fraud scheme that has been used on the Internet. Such an undertaking would not only fill an entire book, but also possibly several volumes. What we can do is to cover the more common scams, and try to extrapolate some general principles that you can apply to any potential fraud. If you use these specific cases to extrapolate some general principles, then you should be prepared to avoid most fraud schemes.

Investment Offers

Investment offers are nothing new. Even some legitimate stockbrokers make their living by cold calling, the process of simply calling people (perhaps from the phone book), and trying to get them to invest in a specific stock. This practice is employed by some legitimate firms, but it is also a favorite con game for perpetrators of fraud. The Internet has allowed investment offers—both genuine and fraudulent—to be more easily disseminated to the general public. Most readers are probably familiar with investment offers flooding their inbox on a daily basis. Some of these email notifications entice you to become directly involved with a particular investment plan; other emails offer seemingly unbiased information from investors, free of charge. (Unfortunately, much of this advice is not as unbiased as it might appear to be.) While legitimate online newsletters can help investors gather valuable information, keep in mind that some online newsletters are fraudulent.

Common Schemes

One of the more common schemes involves sending out an email that suggests that you can make an outrageous sum of money with a very minimal investment. Perhaps the most famous of these schemes has been the Nigerian fraud. In this scenario, an email is sent to a number of random email addresses. Each one contains a message purporting to be from a relative of some deceased Nigerian doctor or government official. The deceased person will be someone you would associate with significant social standing, thus increasing the likelihood that you would view the offer more favorably. The offer goes like this: A person has a sum of money he wishes to transfer out of his country, and for security reasons, he cannot use normal channels. He wishes to use your bank account to "park" the funds temporarily. If you will allow him access to your account, you will receive a hefty fee. If you do agree to this arrangement, you will receive, via normal mail, a variety of very official-looking documents, enough to convince most casual observers that the arrangement is legitimate. You will then be asked to advance some money to cover items such as taxes and wire fees. Should you actually send any money, you will have lost the money you advanced and you will never hear from these individuals again. The U.S. Secret Service has a bulletin issued detailing this particular fraud scheme.[2]

Now consider this investment scam, and variations of it, from a logical point of view. If you had large sums of money you needed to transfer, would you send it to a person in a foreign country, someone you had never met? Wouldn't you be worried that the recipient would cash out her account and take the next plane to Rio? If a person needs to transfer money internationally, why doesn't he just transfer the money to an account in the Bahamas? Or cash out the account and send it via Federal Express or United Parcel Service to a storage facility in the United States? The point is that there are many ways a person could get money out of a country without trusting some stranger he has never seen before. That fact alone should indicate to you that this offer is simply not legitimate. This concept is the first general principle you should derive concerning fraud. In any offer, consider the point of view of the person offering it. Does it sound as if he is taking an inordinately large risk? Does the deal seem oddly biased in your favor? Put yourself in his position. Would you engage in the deal if you where in his position? If not, then this factor is a sign that the deal might not be what it seems.

Investment Advice

Such blatant fraud schemes are not the only investment pitfall on the Internet. Some companies pay the people who write online newsletters to recommend their stocks. While this activity isn't actually illegal, U.S. federal securities laws do require the newsletters to disclose that they where paid to proffer this advice. Such laws are in place because when the writers are recommending any product, their opinion might be swayed by the fact that compensation is being provided to them for that opinion. Many online investment newsletters do not disclose that they are actually being paid to recommend certain stocks. This situation means that the "unbiased" stock advice you are getting could actually be quite biased. Rather than getting the advice of an unbiased expert, you may be getting a paid advertisement. This pitfall is one of the most common traps of online investment advice, more common than the blatant frauds.

Sometimes these online stock bulletins can be part of a wider scheme, often called a pump and dump. A classic pump and dump is rather simple. The con artist takes a stock that is virtually worthless and purchases large amounts of the stock. The con artist then artificially inflates the value,[3] in several ways. One common method is to begin circulating rumors on various Internet bulletin boards and chat rooms that the stock is about to go up significantly. Often it is suggested by the trickster that the company has some new innovative product due to come out in the next few weeks. Another method is to simply push the stock on as many people as possible. The more people vying to buy a stock, the higher its price will rise. If both methods are combined, it is possible to take a worthless stock and temporarily double or triple its value. The perpetrator of the fraud has already purchased volumes of the stock, at a very low price, before executing this scheme. When the stock goes as high as she thinks it can, she then dumps her stock and takes the money. In a short time, and certainly by the time the company's next quarterly earnings report is released, the stock returns to its real value. This sort of scheme has been very popular in the past several decades; thus, you should always be wary of such "insider" information. If a person is aware that Company X is about to release an innovative new product that will drive her stock value up, why would she share that information with total strangers?

The U.S. Securities and Exchange Commission lists several tips for avoiding such scams:[4]

1. Consider the source. Especially if you are not well versed in the market, make sure you accept advice only from well-known and reputable stock analysts.

2. Independently verify claims. Do not simply accept someone else's word about anything.

3. Research. Read up on the company, the claims about the company, its stock history, and so forth.

4. Beware of high-pressure tactics. Legitimate stock traders do not pressure customers into buying. They help customers pick stocks that customers want. If you are being pressured, that is an indication of potential problems.

5. Be skeptical. A healthy dose of skepticism can save you a lot of money. Or, as the saying goes, "If it's too good to be true, it probably isn't."

6. Make sure you thoroughly research any investment opportunity.

The truth is that these types of fraud depend on the greed of the victim. It is not my intent to blame victims of fraud, but it is important to realize that if you allow avarice to do your thinking for you, you are a prime candidate to be a victim of fraud. Your 401K or IRA may not earn you exorbitant wealth overnight, but they are steady and relatively safe. (No investment is completely safe.) If you are seeking ways to make large sums of money with minimal time and effort, then you are an ideal target for perpetrators of fraud.

In Practice

Practically speaking, the recommended way to handle online investments is to only participate in them if you initiated the discussion with a reputable broker. This would mean you would never respond to or participate in any investment offer that was sent to you via email, online ads etc. You would only participate in investments that you initiated with well-known brokers. Usually such brokers are traditional investment firms with long-standing reputations that now simply offer their services online. It is also important to check out any broker with the Securities and Exchange Commission (SEC).

Auction Frauds

Online auctions, such as eBay, can be a wonderful way to find merchandise at very good prices. I routinely use such auctions to purchase goods. However, any auction site can be fraught with peril. Will you actually get the merchandise you ordered? Will it be "as advertised"? Most online auctions are legitimate, and most auction websites take precautions to limit fraud on their website. But problems still occur. In fact, the U.S. Federal Trade Commission[5] (FTC) lists the following four categories of online auction fraud:

- Failure to send the merchandise

- Sending something of lesser value than advertised

- Failure to deliver in a timely manner

- Failure to disclose all relevant information about a product or terms of the sale

The first category, failure to deliver the merchandise, is the most clear-cut case of fraud and is fairly simple. Once you have paid for an item, no item arrives. The seller simply keeps your money. In organized fraud, the seller will simultaneously advertise several items for sale, collect money on all the auctions, and then disappear. If he or she has planned this well, the entire process was done with a fake identification, using a rented mailbox and anonymous email service. The person then walks away with the proceeds of the scam.

The second category of fraud, delivering an item of lesser value than the one advertised, can become a gray area. In some cases, it is outright fraud. The seller advertises something about the product that simply is not true. For example, the seller might advertise a signed copy of the first printing of a famous author's book, but then instead ship you a fourth printing with either no autograph, or one that is unverified. However, in other cases of this type of problem, it can simply be that the seller is overzealous, or frankly mistaken. The seller might claim his baseball was signed by a famous athlete, but not be aware himself that the autograph is a fraud.

This problem is closely related to the fourth item on the FTC list, failure to disclose all relevant facts about the item. For example, a book might be an authentic first printing and autographed, but be in such poor physical condition as to render it worthless. This fact may or may not be mentioned in advance by the seller. Failure to be forthcoming with all the relevant facts about a particular item might be the result of outright fraud or simply of the seller's ignorance. The FTC also lists failure to deliver the product on time as a form of fraud. It is unclear whether or not that is fraud in many cases, or merely woefully inadequate customer service.

The Federal Trade Commission and Auction Fraud

The FTC also lists three other areas of bidding fraud that are growing in popularity on the Internet. From the FTC website:[5]

- *Shill bidding,* when fraudulent sellers (or their "shills") bid on the seller's items to drive up the price.

- *Bid shielding,* when fraudulent buyers submit very high bids to discourage other bidders from competing for the same item. The fake buyers then retract their bids so that people they know can get the item at a lower price.

■ *Bid siphoning*, when con artists lure bidders off legitimate auction sites by offering to sell the "same" item at a lower price. Their intent is to trick consumers into sending money without proffering the item. By going off-site, buyers lose any protections the original site may provide, such as insurance, feedback forms, or guarantees.

Shill Bidding

Shill bidding has been probably the most common of these three auction frauds. It is not very complex. If the perpetrator is selling an item at an auction site, she will also create several fake identities. She will use these fake identities to bid on the item and thus drive the price up. It is very difficult to detect if such a scheme is in operation. However, a simple rule of thumb on auctions is to decide, before you start bidding, what your maximum price is. And then, under no circumstances, do you exceed that price, by even one penny.

Bid Shielding

While shill bidding may be difficult to combat, bid shielding can be addressed fairly easily by the proprietors of the auction site. Many of the major auction sites, such as eBay, have taken steps to prevent bid shielding. The most obvious is to revoke bidding privileges for bidders who back out after they have won an auction. So if a person puts in a very high bid to keep others away, then at the last moment retracts his bid, he might lose his ability to be on that auction site.

Bid Siphoning

Bid siphoning is a less-common practice. In this scheme, the perpetrator places a legitimate item up for bid on an auction site. But then, in the ad for that item, she provides links to sites that are not part of the auction site. The unwary buyer who follows those links might find himself on an alternative site that is a "setup" to perpetrate some sort of fraud.

All of these tactics have a common aim: to subvert the normal auction process. The normal auction process is an ideal blend of capitalism and democracy. Everyone has an equal chance to obtain the product in question, if he or she is willing to outbid the other shoppers. The buyers themselves set the price of the product, based on the value they perceive the product to have. In my opinion, auctions are an excellent vehicle for commerce. However, unscrupulous individuals will always attempt to subvert any process for their own goals.

Identity Theft

Identity theft is a growing problem and a very troubling one. The concept is rather simple, though the process can be complex, and the consequences for the victim can be quite severe. The idea is simply for one person to take on the identity of another. This is usually attempted to make purchases; but identity theft can be done for other reasons, such as obtaining credit cards in the victim's name, or even driver's licenses. If the perpetrator obtains a credit card in someone else's name, then he can purchase products and the victim of this fraud is left with debts she was not aware of and did not authorize.

In the case of getting a driver's license in the victim's name, this fraud might be attempted to shield the perpetrator from the consequences of his or her own poor driving record. For example, a person might get your driving information to create a license with his or her own picture. Perhaps the criminal in this case has a very bad driving record and even warrants out for immediate arrest. Should the person be stopped by law enforcement officers, he or she can then show the fake license. When the police officer checks the license, it is legitimate and has no outstanding warrants. However, the ticket the criminal receives will be going on your driving record, because it is your information on the driver's license. It is also unlikely that the perpetrator of that fraud will actually pay the ticket, so at some point you—whose identity was stolen—will receive notification that your license has been revoked for failure to pay a ticket. Unless you can then prove, with witnesses, that you were not at the location the ticket was given at the time it was given, you may have no recourse but to pay the ticket, in order to reestablish your driving privileges.

The U.S. Department of Justice defines identity theft in this manner:[6]

> "*Identity theft* and *identity fraud* are terms used to refer to all types of crime in which someone wrongfully obtains and uses another person's personal data in some way that involves fraud or deception, typically for economic gain."

The advent of the Internet has made the process of stealing a person's identity even easier than it used to be. Many states now have court records and motor vehicle records online. In some states, a person's social security number is used for the driver's license number. So if a criminal gets a person's social security number, he or she can look up that person's driving record, perhaps get a duplicate of the person's license, find out about any court records concerning that person, and on some websites, even run the person's credit history. Later in this book, we will examine using the Internet as an investigative tool. Like any tool, it can be used for benign or malevolent purposes. The same tools you can use to do a background check on a prospective employee can be used to find out enough information to forge someone else's identity.

FYI: Alternate Means of Identity Theft

There are other means for a perpetrator to conduct identity theft that do not involve the Internet. A ring of criminals in the Dallas-Fort Worth metroplex were working with waiters in restaurants. When the waiter took your credit card or debit card to pay for the meal, they would also use a small hand held device (kept hidden in a pocket) to scan in your credit card information. They would then give this information to the identity theft ring, who could either make online purchases or use that information to produce fake credit cards with your name and account data. This is a new twist on identity theft. The only way to avoid this sort of danger is to never use your credit or debit card unless it is going to be processed right there in front of you. Do not let someone take your card out of your site to process it.

Phishing

One of the more common ways to accomplish identity theft is via a technique called phishing, which is the process of trying to induce the target to provide you with personal information. For example the attacker might send out an email purporting to be from a bank, and telling recipients that there is a problem with their bank account. The email then directs them to click on a link to the bank website where they can login and verify their account. However, the link really goes to a fake website set up by the attacker. When the target goes to that website and enters his information, he will have just given his username and password to the attacker.

Many end users today are aware of these sorts of tactics and avoid clicking on email links. But unfortunately, not everyone is so prudent, and this attack still is effective. It is also the case that the attackers have come up with new ways of phishing. One of these methods is called cross-site scripting. If a website allows users to post content that other users can see (such as a product review) the attacker then posts, but instead of posting a review or other legitimate content, they post a script (i.e., JavaScript or something similar). Now when other users visit that web page, instead of loading a review or comment, it will load the attacker's script. That script may do any number of things, but it is common for the script to redirect the end user to a phishing website. If the attacker is clever, the phishing website looks identical to the real one, and end users are not aware they have been redirected. Cross-site scripting can be prevented by web developers filtering all user input.

Cyber Stalking

Stalking in general has received a great deal of attention in the past few years. The primary reason is that stalking has often been a prelude to violent acts, including sexual assault and homicide. For this reason, many states have passed a variety of antistalking laws. However, stalking has expanded into cyberspace. What is cyber stalking? It is using the Internet to harass another person; or, as the U.S. Department of Justice[7] puts it:

> "Although there is no universally accepted definition of *cyber stalking*, the term is used in this report to refer to the use of the Internet, e-mail, or other electronic communications devices to stalk another person. Stalking generally involves harassing or threatening behavior that an individual engages in repeatedly, such as following a person, appearing at a person's home or place of business, making harassing phone calls, leaving written messages or objects, or vandalizing a person's property. Most stalking laws require that the perpetrator make a credible threat of violence against the victim; others include threats against the victim's immediate family; and still others require only that the alleged stalker's course of conduct constitute an implied threat. While some conduct involving annoying or menacing behavior might fall short of illegal stalking, such behavior may be a prelude to stalking and violence and should be treated seriously."

If someone uses the Internet to harass, threaten, or intimidate another person, then the perpetrator is guilty of cyber stalking. The most obvious example is sending threatening email. The guidelines on what is considered "threatening" can vary a great deal from jurisdiction to jurisdiction. But a good rule of thumb is that if the email's content would be considered threatening in normal speech, then it will probably be considered a threat if sent electronically. Other examples of cyber stalking are less clear. If you request that someone quit emailing you, yet they continue to do so, is that a crime? Unfortunately, there is no clear answer on that issue. The truth is that it may or may not be considered a crime, depending on such factors as the content of the emails, the frequency, the prior relationship between you and the sender, as well as your jurisdiction.

Real Cyber Stalking Cases

The following three cases, also from the Department of Justice website,[7] illustrate cases of cyber stalking. Examining the facts in these cases might help you to get an idea of what legally constitutes cyber stalking.

1. In the first successful prosecution under California's new cyber stalking law, prosecutors in the Los Angeles District Attorney's Office obtained a guilty plea from a 50-year-old former security guard who used the Internet to solicit the rape of a woman who rejected his romantic advances. The defendant terrorized his 28-year-old victim by impersonating her in various Internet chat rooms and online bulletin boards, where he posted, along with her telephone number and address, messages that she fantasized being raped. On at least six occasions, sometimes in the middle of the night, men knocked on the woman's door saying they wanted to rape her. The former security guard pleaded guilty in April 1999 to one count of stalking and three counts of solicitation of sexual assault. He faces up to six years in prison.

2. A local prosecutor's office in Massachusetts charged a man who, using anonymous re-mailers, allegedly engaged in a systematic pattern of harassment of a co-worker, which culminated in an attempt to extort sexual favors from the victim under threat of disclosing past sexual activities to the victim's new husband.

3. An honors graduate from the University of San Diego terrorized five female university students over the Internet for more than a year. The victims received hundreds of violent and threatening emails, sometimes receiving four or five messages a day. The graduate student, who has entered a guilty plea and faces up to six years in prison, told police he committed the crimes because he thought the women were laughing at him and causing others to ridicule him. In fact, the victims had never met him.

Clearly, using the Internet to harass people is just as serious a crime as harassing them in person. This problem has even extended to workplace issues. For example, court cases have upheld that unwanted email pornography can be construed as sexual harassment. If an employee complains about unwanted email, the employer has a duty to at least attempt to ameliorate the situation. This attempt can be as simple as installing a very inexpensive spam blocker (software that tries to limit or eradicate unwanted email). However, if the employer takes no steps whatsoever to correct the problem, that reticence may be seen by a court as contributing to a hostile work environment. As previously stated, if the stalking act would constitute as harassment in person, then it would be considered harassment in cyberspace. *Black's Law Dictionary*[8] defines *harassment* as follows:

"A course of conduct directed at a specific person that causes substantial emotional distress in such person and serves no legitimate purpose."

"Words, gestures, and actions that tend to annoy, alarm, and abuse (verbally) another person."

Usually law enforcement officials will need some credible threat of harm in order to pursue harassment complaints. In simple terms, this situation means that if you are in an anonymous chat room and someone utters some obscenity, that act probably will not be considered harassment. However, if you receive specific threats via email, those threats would probably be considered harassment.

Laws about Internet Fraud

Over the past several years, various legislatures (in the United States and in other countries) have passed laws defining *Internet fraud* and stating the proscribed punishments. In many cases, existing laws against fraud and harassment are applicable to the Internet as well; however, some legislators have felt that cyber crime warranted its own distinct legislation.

Identity theft has been the subject of various state and federal laws. Most states now have laws against identity theft.[9] This crime is also covered by federal law. In 1998, the federal government passed 18 U.S.C. 1028, also known as The Identity Theft and Assumption Deterrence Act of 1998. This law made identity theft a federal crime.[10] Throughout the United States, federal law now covers identity theft, and in many states identity theft is also covered by state law.

Many states specifically prohibit cyber stalking; and in general, existing anti-stalking laws can be applied to the Internet. In 2001, in California a man was convicted of cyber stalking under existing antistalking statutes.[11] Other countries also have existing antistalking laws that can be applied to cyber stalking as well. Canada has had a comprehensive antistalking law since 1993. Unfortunately, there are many similar cases. Just a few include the following:

- From 2010, there is the case of Joseph Medico (70 years old), who met a 16-year-old girl at his church. Mr. Medico followed the girl to her car and tried to talk her into going to dinner with him and then back to his home. When she rejected his advances, he began calling and texting her several times a day. His activities escalated until the girl reported the activities and Mr. Medico was arrested for stalking.

- In 2008 Shawn Michael Hutchinson, 20, posted threats and nude pictures of a former girlfriend. His threats included statements such as "'I told you that if I saw you with David that would be the end of you. That's not a threat, it's a promise."

One nation that has decided to crack down hard on cyber criminals is Romania. Some experts have described Romanian cyber crime law as the strictest in the world.[12] However, what is most interesting about Romanian law is how specific it is. The crafters of this legislation went to some effort to very specifically define all the terms used in the legislation. This specificity is very important in order to avoid defendants finding loopholes in laws. Unfortunately, the Romanian government only took such measures after media sources around the world identified their country as a "Citadel for Cyber Crime." The country's reactive approach to cyber crime is probably not the best solution.

The University of Dayton School of Law has an entire website devoted to cyber crime.[13] The school has some rather extensive links on cyber crime, cyber stalking, and other Internet-based crimes. As we move forward in the twenty-first century, one can expect to see more law schools with courses dedicated to cyber crime.

An interesting phenomenon has begun in the past few years: the emergence of attorneys who specialize in cyber crime cases. The fact that there are lawyers who specialize in this area of law is a strong indicator that Internet crime is becoming a growing problem in modern society.

Protecting Yourself against Cyber Crime

Now that you know about the various frauds that are prevalent on the Internet and have looked at the relevant laws, you might be wondering what you can do to protect yourself. There are several specific steps you can take to minimize the chances of being the victim of Internet crime. There are also some clear guidelines on how you should handle the situation, should you become a victim.

Protecting against Investment Fraud

To protect yourself against investment fraud, follow these guidelines:

1. Only invest with well-known, reputable brokers.

2. If it sounds too good to be true, then avoid it.

3. Ask yourself why this person is informing you of this great investment deal. Why would a complete stranger decide to share some incredible investment opportunity with you?

4. Remember that even legitimate investment involves risk, so never invest money that you cannot afford to lose.

Protecting against Identity Theft

When the issue is identity theft, your steps are clear:

1. Do not provide your personal information to anyone if it is not absolutely necessary. This rule means that when communicating on the Internet with anyone you do not personally know, do not reveal anything about yourself; not your age, occupation, real name, nothing.

2. Destroy documents that have personal information on them. If you simply throw away bank statements and credit card bills, then someone rummaging through your trash can get a great deal of personal data. You can obtain a paper shredder from an office supply store or many retail department stores for less than $20. Shred these documents before disposing of them. This rule may not seem like it is related to computer security, but information gathered through nontechnical means can be used in conjunction with the Internet to perpetrate identity theft.

3. Check your credit frequently. Many websites, including www.consumerinfo.com, allow you to check your credit and even get your beacon score for a nominal fee. I check my credit twice per year. If you see any items you did not authorize, that is a clear indication that you might be a victim of identity theft.

4. If your state has online driving records, then check yours once per year. If you see driving infractions that you did not commit, this evidence is a clear sign that your identity is being used by someone else. In an upcoming chapter on cyber detective work, we will explore in detail how to obtain such records online, often for less than $5.

To summarize, the first step in preventing identity theft is restricting the amount of personal information you make available. The next step is simply monitoring your credit and driving records so that you will be aware if someone attempts to use your identity.

Another part of protecting your identity is protecting your privacy in general. That task means preventing others from gaining information about you that you don't explicitly provide them. That preventative method includes keeping websites from gathering information about you without your knowledge. Many websites store information about you and your visit to their site in small files called *cookies*. These cookie files are stored on your machine. The problem with cookies is that any website can read any cookie on your machine, even ones that the website you are currently visiting did not create. So if you visit one website and it stores items like your name, the site you visited, and the time you where there, then another website could potentially read that cookie and know where you have been on the Internet. One of the best ways to stop cookies you don't want is anti-spyware software. We will discuss such software in more detail in a later chapter. Right now, let's see how to change your Internet settings to help reduce exposures to your privacy.

Secure Browser Settings

If you are using Microsoft Internet Explorer, you can go to Tools and use the drop-down menu; then select Options. You will then see a screen much like the one shown in Figure 3.1. You can then select the third tab, labeled Privacy.

When you select that Privacy tab, you will see the screen shown in Figure 3.2. Notice the sliding bar on the left that lets you select various levels of general protection against cookies. It is recommended that you select Medium High as your level.

Note the Advanced button at the bottom of the screen. This button allows you to block or allow individual websites from creating cookies on your computer's hard drive. Altering cookie settings on your machine is just one part of protecting your privacy, but it is an important part.

You probably also want to ensure that you have selected the In Private browsing option, also shown in Figure 3.2.

If you are working with Firefox, the process is similar. You select Tools from the drop-down menu, then select Options. You will then see the screen shown in Figure 3.3.

FIGURE 3.1   Internet Explorer options.

FIGURE 3.2   Internet Explorer privacy options.

FIGURE 3.3   Firefox options.

Notice the Privacy option and you will see a screen much like the one shown in Figure 3.4.

FIGURE 3.4   Firefox privacy.

As you can see from Figure 3.4, there are a number of privacy settings for you to select, and they are self-explanatory. You can also select the Security tab and see the screen in Figure 3.5.

FIGURE 3.5   Firefox security.

I recommend selecting High Security. Also, I would only allow first-party cookies. Third-party cookies are notorious for behaving in ways that violate user privacy. We will discuss cookies and spyware in much more detail in a later chapter, but the simple steps just examined can go a long way toward helping to secure your privacy.

Dealing with auction fraud involves a different set of precautions; here are four good ideas.

1. Only use reputable auction sites. The most well-known site is eBay, but any widely known, reputable site will be a safer gamble. Such auction sites tend to take precautions to prevent fraud and abuse.

2. If it sounds too good to be true, don't bid.

3. Some sites actually allow you to read feedback other buyers have provided on a given seller. Read the feedback, and only work with reputable sellers.

4. When possible use a separate credit card, one with a low limit, for online auctions. That way, should your credit card be compromised, your liability is limited. Using your debit card is simply inviting trouble.

Online auctions can be a very good way to get valuable merchandise at low prices. However one must exercise some degree of caution when using these services.

Protecting yourself from online harassment also has its own guidelines:

1. If you use chat rooms, discussion boards, and so forth, do not use your real name. Set up a separate email account with an anonymous service, such as Yahoo!, Gmail, or Hotmail. Then use that account and a fake name online. This makes it very hard for an online stalker to trace back to you personally.

2. If you are the victim of online harassment, keep all the emails in both digital and printed format. Use some the investigative techniques we will explore later in this book to try and identify the perpetrator. If you are successful, then you can take the emails and the information on the perpetrator to law enforcement officials.

3. Do not, in any case, ignore cyber stalking. According to the Working to Halt Online Abuse website,[14] 19% of cyber stalking cases escalate to stalking in the real world.

It is not the intent of this chapter or of this book to make you frightened about using the Internet. My family routinely uses the Internet for entertainment, commerce, and informational purposes. One simply needs to exercise some caution when using the Internet.

Summary

Clearly, fraud and identity theft are very real and growing problems. In our modern age of instant access to information and online purchasing, it is critical that every person take steps to protect themselves against this issue. Individuals must work to protect their privacy, using steps outlined in this chapter. It is also imperative for law enforcement officers to obtain the skills needed to investigate and solve these sorts of cyber crimes.

Cyber stalking is one area that is often new to both civilians and law enforcement. It is very important that both groups have a clear understanding of what is, and is not, cyber stalking. Unfortunately, cyber stalking cases can escalate into real-world violence.

Test Your Skills

MULTIPLE CHOICE

1. The most common Internet investment fraud is known as what?

   A. The Nigerian fraud

   B. The Manhattan fraud

   C. The pump and dump

   D. The bait and switch

2. What is the most likely problem with unsolicited investment advice?

   A. You might not earn as much as claimed.

   B. The advice might not be truly unbiased.

   C. The advice might not be from a legitimate firm.

   D. You might lose money.

3. Artificially inflating a stock in order to sell it at a higher value is referred to as what?

   A. Bait and switch

   B. The Nigerian fraud

   C. Pump and dump

   D. The Wall Street fraud

4. What is the top rule for avoiding Internet fraud?

   A. If it seems too good to be true, it probably is.

   B. Never use your bank account numbers.

   C. Only work with people who have verifiable email addresses.

   D. Don't invest in foreign deals.

5. Which of the following is not one of the Security and Exchange Commission's tips for avoiding investment fraud?

   A. Don't invest online.

   B. Consider the source of the offer.

   C. Always be skeptical.

   D. Always research the investment.

6. What are the four categories of auction fraud?

   A. Failure to send, failure to disclose, sending to wrong address, failure to deliver

   B. Failure to send, failure to disclose, sending something of lesser value, failure to deliver

   C. Failure to disclose, sending something to wrong address, failure to send, failure to deliver

   D. Failure to disclose, sending something of lesser value, failure to send, sending something of greater value

7. A seller bidding on his or her own item to drive up the price is referred to as what?

   A. Bid siphoning

   B. Bid shielding

   C. Shill bidding

   D. Ghost bidding

8. Submitting a fake but very high bid to deter other bidders is referred to as what?

   A. Bid siphoning

   B. Bid shielding

   C. Shill bidding

   D. Ghost bidding

9. Identity theft is most often attempted in order to accomplish what goal?

   A. To make illicit purchases

   B. To discredit the victim

   C. To avoid criminal prosecution

   D. To invade privacy

10. According to the U.S. Department of Justice, identity theft is generally motivated by what?

   A. Malicious intent

   B. Personal hostility towards the victim

   C. Economic gain

   D. Thrill seeking

11. Why is cyber stalking a serious crime?

    A. It is frightening to the victim.

    B. It can be a prelude to violent crime.

    C. It is using interstate communication.

    D. It can be a prelude to identity theft.

12. What is cyber stalking?

    A. Any use of the Internet to send or post threats

    B. Any use of electronic communications to stalk a person

    C. Only use of email to send threats

    D. Only the use of email to stalk a person

13. What will law enforcement officials usually require of the victim in order to pursue harassment allegations?

    A. A verifiable threat of death or serious injury

    B. A credible threat of death or serious injury

    C. A verifiable threat of harm

    D. A credible threat of harm

14. If you are posting anonymously in a chat room and another anonymous poster threatens you with assault or even death, is this person's post harassment?

    A. Yes, any threat of violence is harassment.

    B. Probably not, because both parties are anonymous, so the threat is not credible.

    C. Yes, chat room threats are no different than threats in person.

    D. Probably not, because making a chat room threat is not the same as making a threat in person.

15. What must exist for cyber stalking to be illegal in a state or territory?

    A. Specific laws against cyber stalking in that state or territory.

    B. Specific laws against cyber stalking in that nation.

    C. Nothing; existing stalking laws can apply.

    D. Nothing; existing international cyber stalking laws apply.

16. What is the first step in protecting yourself from identity theft?

    A. Never provide any personal data about yourself unless absolutely necessary.

    B. Routinely check your records for signs of identity theft.

    C. Never use your real name on the Internet.

    D. Routinely check for spyware on your computer.

17. What can you do on your local computer to protect your privacy?

    A. Install a virus scanner.

    B. Install a firewall.

    C. Set your browser's security settings.

    D. Set your computer's filter settings.

18. What is a cookie?

    A. A piece of data that web servers gather about you.

    B. A small file made that contains data and then is stored on your computer.

    C. A piece of data that your web browser gathers about you.

    D. A small file made that contains data and then is stored on the web server.

19. Which of the following is not an efficient method of protecting yourself from auction fraud?

    A. Only use auctions for inexpensive items.

    B. Only use reputable auction sites.

    C. Only work with well-rated sellers.

    D. Only bid on items that seem realistic.

20. The top rule for chat room safety is what?

    A. Make certain you have antivirus software installed.

    B. Never use your real name or any real personally identifying characteristics.

    C. Only use chat rooms that encrypt transmissions.

    D. Use chat rooms that are sponsored by well-known websites or companies.

21. Why is it useful to have a separate credit card dedicated to online purchases?

    A. If the credit card number is used illegally, you will limit your financial liability.

    B. You can keep better track of your auction activities.

    C. If you are defrauded, you can possibly get the credit card company to handle the problem.

    D. You can easily cancel that single card, if you need to do so.

22. What percentage of cyber stalking cases escalate to real-world violence?

    A. Less than 1%

    B. 25%

    C. 90% or more

    D. About 19%

23. If you are a victim of cyber stalking, what should you do to assist the police?

    A. Nothing; it is their job and you should stay out of it.

    B. Attempt to lure the stalker into a public place.

    C. Keep electronic and hard copies of all harassing communications.

    D. Try to provoke the stalker into revealing personal information about himself or herself.

24. What is the top way to protect yourself from cyber stalking?

    A. Do not use your real identity online.

    B. Always use a firewall.

    C. Always use a virus scanner.

    D. Do not give out email addresses.

EXERCISES

EXERCISE 3.1: Setting Web Browser Privacy in Internet Explorer

1. This process was described in detail with images in the chapter, but we will walk through the process here:

    ▪ Select Tools from the drop-down menu at the top of Internet Explorer, then choose Internet Options.

    ▪ Select the third tab, which is labeled Privacy.

    ▪ Click the Advanced button.

    ▪ Set your browser to accept first party cookies, prompt for third-party cookies, and accept session cookies.

EXERCISE 3.2: Using Alternative Web Browsers

1. Download the Firefox browser from www.mozilla.org.

2. Set privacy and security settings.

EXERCISE 3.3: **Tracking in a Chat Room**

The purpose of this exercise is to grasp how easy it is to obtain personal information about someone from his or her online activities.

1. Enter any chat room. If you are not familiar with chat rooms or have not used them before, any of the following websites would make a good starting point for you:

    http://chat.icq.com/icqchat/

    www.aol.com/community/chat/allchats.html

    www.javachatrooms.net/

    www.chat-avenue.com/

2. Note those people who use their real names.

3. Note those people who reveal personal details.

4. Compile as much information as you can about posers in the chat room.

CAUTION

The purpose of this exercise is merely to show you how easy it is for someone to learn about another person from his or her online activities. In no case would you consider using this information to invade another person's privacy or to harass or embarrass another person.

PROJECTS

PROJECT 3.1: **Finding Out about Cyber Stalking and the Law**

1. Using the Web or other resources, find out what your state, country, or province's laws are regarding cyber stalking.

2. Write a brief paper describing those laws and what they mean. You may select to do a quick summary of several laws or a more in-depth examination of one law. If you choose the former, then simply list the laws and write a brief paragraph explaining what they cover. If you choose the latter option, then discuss the law's authors, why it was written, and possible ramifications of the law.

PROJECT 3.2: **Looking for Auction Fraud**

Go to any auction site and try to identify if there are any sellers you feel might be fraudulent. Write a brief paper explaining what about that seller indicated that he or she may not be dealing honestly.

PROJECT 3.3: **Examining Cyber Stalking Case Studies**

1. Using the Web, find a case of cyber stalking not mentioned in this chapter. You may find some of the following websites helpful:

   www.safetyed.org/help/stalking/

   www.cyber-stalking.net/

   www.technomom.com/harassed/index.shtml

2. Write a brief paper discussing this case, with particular attention to steps you think might have helped avoid or ameliorate the situation.

Case Study

Consider the case of an intrepid identity thief. The perpetrator, Jane, encounters the victim, John, online in a chat room. John is using his real first name, but only his last initial. However, over a series of online conversations between Jane and John, he does reveal personal details about his life (marital status, children, occupation, region he lives in, and so forth). Eventually, Jane offers John some piece of information, such as perhaps an investment tip, as a trick to get John's email address from him. Once she gets his email address, an email exchange begins outside of the chat room, wherein Jane purports to give John her real name, thus encouraging John to do the same. Of course, the perpetrator's name is fictitious, such as "Mary." But Jane now has John's real name, city, marital status, occupation, and so on.

Jane has a number of options she can try, but we will choose a simple one. She begins by using the phone book or the Web to get John's home address and phone number. She can then use this information to get John's social security number, in a variety of ways. The most straightforward would be to go through John's trash while he is at work. However, if John works in a large company, Jane can just call (or enlist someone to call), claiming to be John's wife or another close relative, wanting to verify personnel data. If Jane is clever enough, she may come away with John's social security number. Then it is a trivial matter (as we will see in Chapter 13, "Cyber Detective") to get John's credit report and to get credit cards in his name.

From this scenario, consider the following questions:

1. What reasonable steps could John have taken to protect his identity in the chat room?

2. What steps should any employer take to prevent being unwittingly complicit in identity theft?

Chapter Footnotes

1. The U.S. Securities and Exchange Commission. "Internet Fraud: How to Avoid Internet Investment Scams." Washington, D.C.: Author, November 15, 2001. Accessed April 2011: www.sec.gov/investor/pubs/cyberfraud.htm

2. The U.S. Secret Service. "Public Awareness Advisory Regarding '4-1-9' or 'Advance Fee Fraud' Schemes." Washington, D.C.: Author, 2002. Accessed April 2011: http://www.lbl.gov/IT/CIS/CITG/email/419-Fraud.html

3. The Fraud Bureau. "Pump and Dump Classic." Stock Scams 101. Ontario: Fraud Bureau Corporation, 1999. Accessed April 2011: www.fraudbureau.com/investor/101/article15.html

4. The U.S. Securities and Exchange Commission "Pump+Dump.con: Avoiding Stock Scams on the Internet." Washington, D.C.: Author, September 8, 2000. April 2011: www.sec.gov/investor/pubs/pump.htm

5. The U.S. Federal Trade Commission, Accessed April 2011: www.ftc.gov/bcp/edu/pubs/consumer/alerts/alt124.shtm

6. The U.S. Department of Justice Identity Theft web page, Accessed April 2011: www.justice.gov/criminal/fraud/websites/idtheft.html

7. The U.S. Department of Justice Cyber Stalking page. Accessed April 2011: www.usdoj.gov/criminal/cybercrime/cyberstalking.htm

8. *Blacks Law Dictionary*, 1999, West Publishing Company, 7th Edition.

9. The National Conference of State Legislatures. "State Computer Harassment or 'Cyberstalking' Laws." Denver and Washington, DC.: Author, 2004. Accessed April 2011: www.ncsl.org/programs/lis/cip/stalk99.htm

10. The Identity Theft and Deterrence Act of 1998, USC 1028

11. *The Minneapolis-St.Paul Star Tribune*, Accessed August 23, 2001: www.startribune.com/

12. Romanian Information Technology Initiative. Accessed April 2011: www.riti-internews.ro/cybercrime.htm

13. University of Dayton School of Law. Accessed November 2003: cybercrimes.net/

14. Working to Halt Online Abuse. Accessed April 2011: www.haltabuse.org/

## Chapter 4

Denial of Service Attacks

Chapter Objectives

After reading this chapter and completing the exercises, you will be able to do the following:

- Understand how denial of service (DoS) attacks are accomplished
- Know how certain DoS attacks work, such as SYN flood, Smurf, and DDoS
- Take specific measures to protect against denial of service attacks
- Know how to defend against specific DoS attacks

Introduction

By now you are aware, in a general way, of the dangers of the Internet and have also explored a few basic rules for protection on the Internet. In Chapter 3, "Cyber Stalking, Fraud, and Abuse," you were introduced to some fraud, stalking, and related crimes. It is now time to become more specific about how attacks on systems are conducted. In this chapter, we will examine one category of attack that might be used to cause harm to a target computer system. This chapter will describe for you, in depth, the workings of the *denial of service (DoS)* attack. This threat is one of the most common attacks on the Internet, so it is prudent for you to understand how it works and how to defend yourself against it. Further, in the exercises at the end of the book, you will practice stopping a DoS attack. In information security, the old adage that "knowledge is power" is not only good advice, but also an axiom upon which to build your entire security outlook.

Denial of Service

As was said in the introduction, one of the most common and simplest forms of attack on a system is a denial of service (DoS). This attack does not even attempt to intrude on your system or to obtain sensitive information; it simply aims to prevent legitimate users from accessing the system. This type of attack is fairly easy to execute. The basic concept requires a minimum of technical skill. It is based on the fact that any device has operational limits. For example, a truck can only carry a finite load or travel a finite distance. Computers are no different than any other machine; they, too, have limits. Any computer system, web server, or network can only handle a finite load. A workload for a computer system may be defined by the number of simultaneous users, the size of files, the speed of data transmission, or the amount of data stored. If you exceed any of those limits, the excess load will stop the system from responding. For example, if you can flood a web server with more requests than it can process, it will be overloaded and will no longer be able to respond to further requests (Webopedia, 2004). This reality underlies the DoS attack. Simply overload the system with requests, and it will no longer be able to respond to legitimate users attempting to access the web server.

> ### FYI: Buffer Overflows
>
> A denial of service attack is one of the most common attacks on a system. Another common type of attack is the buffer overflow. Which one is the leading form of attack is subject to debate among the experts. Regardless, understanding DoS attacks and how to thwart them is clearly an important component of system security. However, buffer-overflow attacks are becoming less common since modern operating systems and web servers are no longer susceptible to them. The only way to execute one is via a vulnerability in some application (perhaps an e-commerce application).

Illustrating an Attack

One simple way to illustrate this attack, especially in a classroom setting, involves the use of the `ping` command discussed in Chapter 2, "Networks and the Internet":

1. Start a web server service running on one machine (you can use Apache, IIS, or any web server).

2. Ask several people to open their browsers and key the IP address of that machine in the address bar. They should then be viewing the default website for that web server.

Now you can do a rather primitive denial of service attack on the system. Recall from Chapter 2 that typing in `ping /h` will show you all the options for the `ping` command. The `-l` option changes the size of the packet you can send. Remember that a TCP packet can be only of a finite size. Thus, you are going to set these packets to be almost as large as you can send. The `-w` option determines how many milliseconds the `ping` utility will wait for a response from the target. You are going to use `-0` so that the ping utility does not wait at all. Then the `-t` instructs the ping utility to keep sending packets until explicitly told to stop.

1. Open the command prompt in Windows XP/Vista/7 (that is the shell in UNIX/Linux).

2. Type in **ping <address of target machine goes here>–l 65000 –w 0 –t**. You will then see something very much like what is shown in Figure 4.1. Note that, in the figure, I am pinging the loop-back address for my own machine. You will want to substitute the address of the machine on which you are running the web server.

```
Command Prompt - ping 127.0.0.1 -l 65000 -w 0 -t                          _ □ ×

C:\>ping 127.0.0.1 -l 65000 -w 0 -t

Pinging 127.0.0.1 with 65000 bytes of data:

Reply from 127.0.0.1: bytes=65000 time<10ms TTL=128
Reply from 127.0.0.1: bytes=65000 time<10ms TTL=128
Reply from 127.0.0.1: bytes=65000 time<10ms TTL=128
Reply from 127.0.0.1: bytes=65000 time<10ms TTL=128
Reply from 127.0.0.1: bytes=65000 time<10ms TTL=128
Reply from 127.0.0.1: bytes=65000 time<10ms TTL=128
```

FIGURE 4.1   Ping from the command prompt.

What is happening at this point is that this single machine is continually pinging away at the target machine. Of course, just one machine in your classroom or lab that is simply pinging on your web server is not going to adversely affect the web server. However, you can now, one by one, get other machines in the classroom pinging the server in the same way. After each batch of three or four machines you add, try to go to the web server's default web page. After a certain threshold (certain number of machines pinging the server), it will stop responding to requests, and you will no longer be able to see the web page.

How many machines it will take to deny service depends on the web server you are using. In order to see this denial happen with as few machines involved as possible, you could use a very low-capacity PC as your web server. For example, running an Apache web server on a simple laptop running Windows 7 Home Edition, it can take about 15 machines each running about 10 different command windows simultaneously pinging to cause a web server to stop responding to legitimate requests. This strategy is, of course, counter to what you would normally select for a web server—no real web server would be running on a simple laptop with Windows 7 Home Edition. Likewise, actual DoS attacks use much more sophisticated methods. This simple exercise, however, should demonstrate for you the basic principle behind the DoS attack: Simply flood the target machine with so many packets that it can no longer respond to legitimate requests.

Generally, the methods used for DoS attacks are significantly more sophisticated than the illustration. For example, a hacker might develop a small virus whose sole purpose is to initiate a ping flood against a predetermined target. Once the virus has spread, the various machines that are infected with that virus, then begin their ping flood of the target system. This sort of denial of service is easy to do, and it can be hard to stop. A denial of service that is launched from several different machines is called a distributed denial of service (DDoS).

Common Tools Used for DoS

As with any of the security issues discussed in this book, you will find that hackers have at their disposal a vast array of tools with which to work. The DoS arena is no different. While it is certainly well beyond the scope of this book to begin to categorize or discuss all of these tools, a brief introduction to just a few of them will prove useful. The two tools discussed here, TFN and Stacheldraht, are typical of the types of tools that someone wishing to perform a DoS attack would utilize.

TFN and TFN2K

TFN, also known as Tribal Flood Network, and TFN2K are not tools that can be used to perform a DDoS. Both tools have been around for many years, and are still in use today. TFN2K is a newer version of TFN that supports both Windows Server (2003 and 2008) and UNIX platforms (and can easily be ported to additional platforms). It has some features that make detection more difficult than its predecessor, including sending decoy information to avoid being traced. Experts at using TFN2K can use the resources of a number of agents to coordinate an attack against one or more targets. Additionally, TFN and TFN2K can perform various attacks such as UDP flood attacks, ICMP flood attacks, and TCP SYN flood attacks (all discussed later in this chapter).

TFN2K works on two fronts. First, there is a command-driven client on the master system. Second, there is a daemon process operating on an agent system. The attack works like this:

1. The master instructs its agents to attack a list of designated targets.

2. The agents respond by flooding the targets with a barrage of packets.

With this tool, multiple agents, coordinated by the master, can work together during the attack to disrupt access to the target. Additionally, there are a number of "safety" features for the attacker that significantly complicates development of effective and efficient countermeasures for TFN2K.

- Master-to-agent communications are encrypted and may be mixed with any number of decoy packets.

- Both master-to-agent communications and the attacks themselves can be sent via randomized TCP, UDP, and ICMP packets.

- The master can falsify its IP address (spoof).

Stacheldraht

Stacheldraht, which is German for "barbed wire," is a DDoS attack tool that combines features of the Trinoo DDoS tool (another common tool) with the source code from the TFN DDoS attack tool. Like TFN2K, it adds encryption of communication between the attacker and the Stacheldraht masters. It also adds an automatic updating of the agents.

Stacheldraht can perform a variety of attacks including UDP flood, ICMP flood, TCP SYN flood, and Smurf attacks. It also detects and automatically enables source address forgery.

DoS Weaknesses

The weakness in any DoS attack, from the attacker's point of view, is that the flood of packets must be sustained. As soon as the packets stop sending, the target system is back up. A DoS/DDoS attack, however, is very often used in conjunction with another form of attack, such as disabling one side of a connection in TCP hijacking or preventing authentication or logging between servers.

If the hacker is using a distributed attack, as soon as the administrators or owners of the infected machines realize their machine is infected, they will take steps to remove the virus and thus stop the attack. If a hacker attempts to launch an attack from her own machine, she must be aware that each packet has the potential to be traced back to its source. This fact means that a single hacker using a DoS will almost certainly be caught by the authorities. For this reason, the DDoS is quickly becoming the most common type of DoS attack. The specifics of DDoS attacks will be discussed later in this chapter.

Specific DoS attacks

The basic concept for perpetrating a DoS attack is not complicated. The real problem for the attacker is performing the attack without being caught. The next few sections of this chapter will examine some specific types of DoS attacks and look at specific case studies. This information should help you gain a deeper understanding of this particular Internet threat.

TCP SYN Flood Attack

One popular version of the DoS attack is the *SYN flood*. This particular attack depends on the hacker's knowledge of how connections are made to a server. When a session is initiated between the client and server in a network using the TCP protocol, a packet is sent to the server with a 1-bit flag called a SYN flag set. SYN is short for synchronize. And this packet is literally asking the target server to please synchronize communications. The server will then allocate appropriate resources and then send to the client a packet with both the SYN (synchronize) and the ACK (acknowledge) flags set. The client machine is then supposed to respond with an ACK flag set. This is called the three-way handshake and is summarized as follows:

1. Client sends a packet with the SYN flag set.

2. Server allocates resources for the client and then responds with the SYN and ACK flags set.

3. Client responds with the ACK flag set.

There have been a number of well-known SYN flood attacks on web servers. The reason for the popularity of this attack type is that any machine that engages in TCP communication is vulnerable to it—and all machines connected to the Internet engage in TCP communications. Such communication is obviously the entire reason for web servers. The easiest way to block DoS attacks is via firewall rules. We will discuss firewalls in detail in Chapter 12, "Cyber Terrorism and Information Warfare." There are, however, several methods and techniques you can implement on individual servers to protect against these attacks. The basic defensive techniques are as follows:

- Micro blocks
- SYN cookies
- RST cookies
- Stack tweaking

Some of these methods require more technical sophistication than others. These methods will be discussed in general here. When you are entrusted with defending a system against these forms of attacks, you can select the methods most appropriate for your network environment and your level of expertise and examine it further at that time. The specifics of how to implement any of these methods will depend on the operating system that your web server is using. You will need to consult your operating system's documentation, or appropriate websites, in order to find explicit instruction on how to implement methods.

Micro Blocks

A *micro block* works by simply allocating a micro-record instead of allocating a complete connection object (an entire buffer segment) to the SYN object. In this way, an incoming SYN object can allocate as little as 16 bytes of space, making it significantly more difficult to flood a system.

SYN Cookies

As the name *SYN cookies* suggests, this method uses cookies, not unlike the standard cookies used on many websites. With this method, the system does not immediately create a buffer space in memory for the handshaking process. Rather, it first sends a *SYN+ACK* (the acknowledgment signal that begins the handshaking process). The SYN+ACK contains a carefully constructed cookie, generated as a hash that contains the IP address, port number, and other information from the client machine requesting the connection. When the client responds with a normal ACK (acknowledgment), the information from that cookie will be included, which the server then verifies. Thus, the system does not fully allocate any memory until the third stage of the handshaking process. This enables the system to continue to operate normally; typically, the only effect seen is the disabling of large windows. However, the cryptographic hashing used in SYN cookies is fairly resource intensive, so system administrators that expect a great deal of incoming connections may choose not to use this defensive technique.

RST Cookies

Another cookie method that is easier to implement than SYN cookies is the *RST cookie*. In this method, the server sends a wrong SYN+ACK back to the client. The client should then generate an RST packet telling the server that something is wrong. Because the client sent back a packet notifying the server of the error, the server now knows the client request is legitimate and can now accept incoming connections from that client in the normal fashion. This method has two disadvantages. It might cause problems with older Windows machines and/or machines that are communicating from behind firewalls.

Stack Tweaking

The method of *stack tweaking* involves altering the TCP stack on the server so that it will take less time to timeout when a SYN connection is left incomplete. Unfortunately, this protective method will just make executing a SYN flood against that target more difficult; to a determined hacker, the attack is still possible.

Smurf IP Attack

The Smurf attack is a very popular version of the DoS attack. An ICMP (Internet Control Message Protocol) packet is sent out to the broadcast address of the network. Since it is broadcast, it responds by echoing the packet out to all hosts on the network, who then send it to the spoofed source address. Also, the spoofed source address can be anywhere on the Internet, not just on the local subnet. If the hacker can continually send such packets, she will cause the network itself to perform a DoS attack on one or more of its member servers. This attack is clever and rather simple. The only problem for the hacker is getting the packets started on the target network. This task can be accomplished via some software, such as a virus or Trojan horse, that will begin sending the packets.

In a Smurf attack, there are three people/systems involved: the attacker, the intermediary (who can also be a victim), and the victim. The attacker first sends an ICMP echo request packet to the intermediary's IP broadcast addresses. Since this is sent to the IP broadcast address, many of the machines on the intermediary's network will receive this request packet and will send an ICMP echo reply packet back. If all the machines on a network are responding to this request, the network becomes congested and there can be outages.

The attacker impacts the third party—the intended victim—by creating forged packets that contain the spoofed source address of the victim. Therefore, when all the machines on the intermediary's network start replying to the echo request, those replies will flood the victim's network. Thus, another network becomes congested and could become unusable.

The Smurf attack is an example of the creativity that some malicious parties can employ. It is sometimes viewed as the digital equivalent of the biological process in an auto-immune disorder. With such disorders, the immune system attacks the patient's own body. In a Smurf attack, the network performs a DoS attack on one of its own systems. This method's cleverness illustrates why it is important that you attempt to work creatively and in a forward-thinking manner if you are responsible for system security in your network. The perpetrators of computer attacks are inventive and always coming up with new techniques. If your defense is less creative and clever than the attackers' defense, then it is simply a matter of time before your system is compromised.

There are several ways to protect your system against this problem. One is to guard against Trojan horses. More will be said about the Trojan horse attack in later chapters; however, having policies prohibiting employees from downloading applications will help. Also, having adequate virus scanners can go a long way in protecting your system from a Trojan horse and, thus, a Smurf attack. It is also imperative that you use a proxy server, which was discussed in Chapter 2. If the internal IP addresses of your network are not known, then it is more difficult to target one in a Smurf attack. Probably the best way to protect your system is to combine these defenses along with prohibiting directed broadcasts and patching the hosts to refuse to reply to any directed broadcasts.

UDP Flood Attack

UDP, as you will recall from Chapter 2, is a connectionless protocol that does not require any connection setup procedure prior to transferring data. In a *UDP flood attack*, the attacker sends a UDP packet to a random port on a target system. When the target system receives a UDP packet, it automatically determines what application is waiting on the destination port. In this case, since there is no application waiting on the port, the target system will generate an ICMP packet of "destination unreachable" and attempt to send it back to the forged source address. If enough UDP packets are delivered to ports on the target, the system will become overloaded trying to determine awaiting applications (which do not exist) and then generating and sending packets back.

ICMP Flood Attack

There are two basic types of *ICMP flood attacks*: floods and nukes. An ICMP flood is usually accomplished by broadcasting a large number of either pings or UDP packets. Like other flood attacks, the idea is to send so much data to the target system that it slows down. If it can be forced to slow down enough, the target will time out (not send replies fast enough) and be disconnected from the Internet. ICMP nukes exploit known bugs in specific operating systems. The attacker sends a packet of information that he knows the operating system on the target system cannot handle. In many cases, this will cause the target system to lock up completely.

The Ping of Death (PoD)

Recall from Chapter 2 that TCP packets are of limited size. In some cases, simply sending a packet that is too large can shut down a target machine. This action is referred to as the *ping of death (PoD)*. It works simply by overloading the target system. The hacker sends merely a single ping, but he does so with a very large packet and thus can shut down some machines.

This attack is quite similar to the classroom example discussed earlier in this chapter. The aim in both cases is to overload the target system and cause it to quit responding. PoD works to compromise systems that cannot deal with extremely large packet sizes. If successful, the server will actually shut down completely. It can, of course, be rebooted.

The only real safeguard against PoD is to ensure that all operating systems and software are routinely patched. This attack relies on vulnerabilities in the way a particular operating system (or application) handles abnormally large TCP packets. When such vulnerabilities are discovered, it is customary for the vendor to release a patch. The possibility of PoD is one reason, among many, why you must keep patches updated on all of your systems.

Teardrop Attack

In a *teardrop attack*, the attacker sends a fragmented message. The two fragments overlap in ways that make it impossible to reassemble them properly without destroying the individual packet headers. Therefore, when the victim attempts to reconstruct the message, the message is destroyed. This causes the target system to halt or crash. There are a number of variations on the basic teardrop attack that are available such as TearDrop2, Boink, targa, Nestea Boink, NewTear, and SYNdrop.

Land Attack

A *land attack* is probably the simplest in concept. The attacker sends a forged packet with the same source IP address and destination IP address (the target's IP address). The method is to drive the target system "crazy" by having it attempt to send messages to and from itself. The victim system will often be confused and will crash or reboot.

Echo/Chargen Attack

The character generator (chargen) service was designed primarily for testing purposes. It simply generates a stream of characters. In an *echo/chargen attack*, this service is abused by attackers who exhaust the target system's resources. The attacker accomplishes this by creating a spoofed network session that appears to come from that local system's echo service and which is pointed at the chargen service to form a "loop." This session will cause huge amounts of data to be passed in an endless loop. This constant looping causes a heavy load to the system. Alternately, if the spoofed session is pointed at a system's echo service, it will cause heavy network traffic that slows down the target's network.

Distributed Denial of Service (DDoS)

Another form of trickery is the *distributed denial of service attack (DDoS)*. As with all such denial attacks, it is accomplished by the hacker getting a number of machines to attack the target. However, this attack works a bit differently than other DoS attacks. Rather than getting computers to attack the target, one of the ways the hacker accomplishes a DDoS is to trick Internet routers into attacking a target. Another form of DDoS relies on compromised (zombie) hosts to simultaneously attack a given target with a large number of packets.

Recall from the discussion of ports in Chapter 2 that many of the routers on the Internet backbone communicate on port 179 (Gibson, 2002). They use Border Gateway Protocol to exchange routing information with each other. This attack exploits that communication line and gets routers to attack a target system. What makes this attack particularly wicked is that it does not require the routers in question to be compromised in any way. Instead, the hacker sends a stream of packets to the various routers requesting a connection. The packets have been altered so that they appear to come from the target system's IP address. The routers respond by initiating connections with the target system. What occurs then is a flood of connections from multiple routers, all hitting the same target system. This flood has the effect of rendering the system unreachable.

Real-World Examples

A good deal of time has been spent discussing the basics of how various DoS attacks are conducted. By now, you should have a firm grasp of what a DoS attack is and have a basic understanding of how it works. It is now time to begin discussing specific, real-world examples of such attacks. This section will take the theoretical knowledge you have gained and give you real-world examples of its application.

MyDoom

One of the most well publicized DoS attacks was the MyDoom attack. While this attack is a few years old, it is an excellent one to study. This threat was a classically distributed DoS attack. The virus/worm would email itself to everyone in your address book and then, at a preset time, all infected machines would begin a coordinated attack on www.sco.com (Network World, 2004). Estimates put the number of infected machines between 500,000 and 1 million. This attack was successful and promptly shut down the SCO website. It should be noted that well before the day that the DoS attack was actually executed, network administrators and home users were well aware of what MyDoom would do. There were also several tools available free of charge on the Internet for removing the virus/worm. However, it appears that many people did not take the steps necessary to clean their machines of this virus/worm.

What is interesting is that MyDoom is still causing problems. In July 2009, there was a DoS that utilized MyDoom as a back door to launch a DoS attack against South Korean and United States web servers.

FYI: Virus or Worm?

Definitions of the terms *virus* and *worm* are widely debated among the experts. And, depending upon the definition, what some would call a virus, others would call a worm. One general distinction that is accepted by many is that worms do not require direct human interaction to propagate, whereas viruses do. If you accept this definition, then both MyDoom and Slammer are worms. To avoid confusion on this issue, however, the term *virus/worm* will be used.

One thing that makes this attack so interesting is that it is clearly an example of domestic cyber terrorism (although it is certain that the creators of MyDoom would probably see it differently). (Cyber terrorism will be discussed further in Chapter 12, "Cyber Terrorism and Information Warfare.") For those readers who do not know the story, it will be examined here briefly. Santa Cruz Operations (SCO) makes a version of the UNIX operating system. Like most UNIX versions, their version is copyright protected. Several months before this attack, SCO began accusing certain Linux distributions of containing segments of SCO UNIX code. SCO sent demand letters to many Linux users demanding license fees. Many people in the Linux community viewed this request as simply an attempt to undermine the growing popularity of Linux, an open-source operating system. SCO went even further and filed suit against major companies that were distributing Linux (Software Patent Workgroup, 2003). This claim by SCO seemed unfounded to many legal and technology analysts. It was also viewed with great suspicion because SCO had close ties to Microsoft, which had been trying desperately to stop the growing popularity of Linux.

Many analysts feel that the MyDoom virus/worm was created by some individual (or group of individuals) who felt that the Santa Cruz Operations tactics were unacceptable. The hackers wished to cause economic harm to SCO and damage its public image. This probable motive makes this case clearly one of domestic economic terrorism: One group attacks the technological assets of another group based on an ideological difference. Prior to this virus/worm, there were numerous website defacements and other small-scale attacks that were part of ideological conflicts. However, this virus/worm was the first such attack to be so widespread and successful. This incident began a new trend in information warfare. As technology becomes less expensive and the tactics more readily available, you can expect to see an increase in this sort of attack in the coming years.

Anonymous Uses DoS

On December 8, 2010, the infamous hacker group Anonymous launched multiple DDoS attacks on various financial companies, including Mastercard.com, PayPal, Visa.com and PostFinance. These sites were brought down for over 16 hours. The attacks were launched because these sites refused to process donations for Wikileaks. The group Anonymous is a supporter of Wikileaks founder Julian Assange.

How to Defend against DoS Attacks

There is no guaranteed way to prevent all DoS attacks, just as there is no sure way to prevent any hacking attack. However, there are steps you can take to minimize the danger. Some methodologies, such as SYN cookies and RST cookies, have already been mentioned. In this section, a few of the steps you can take to make your system less susceptible to a DoS attack will be examined.

One of the first things for you to consider is how these attacks are perpetrated. They may be executed via ICMP packets that are used to send error messages on the Internet or are sent by the ping and traceroute utilities. If you have a firewall (and you absolutely should have one), then simply configuring it to refuse ICMP packets from outside your network will be a major step in protecting your network from DoS attacks. Since DoS/DDoS attacks can be executed via a wide variety of protocols, you can also configure your firewall to disallow any incoming traffic at all, regardless of what protocol or port it occurs on. This step may seem radical, but it is certainly a secure one.

In Practice

Blocking ICMP Packets

There are very few legitimate reasons (and, some would argue, no good reasons) for an ICMP packet from outside your network to enter your network. Thus, blocking such packets is very often used as one part of the strategy to defend against DoS attacks. Incidentally, that will also make it more difficult for an attacker to scan your network (as we will see in Chapter 12).

It is also possible to detect some threats from certain DoS tools, such as TFN2K, by using information tools like NetStat. Many of these tools can be configured to look for the SYN_RECEIVED state, which could indicate a SYN flood attack.

If your network is large enough to have internal routers, then you can configure those routers to disallow any traffic that does not originate with your network. In that way, should packets make it past your firewall, they will not be propagated throughout the network. You should also consider disabling directed IP broadcasts on all routers. This strategy will prevent the router from sending broadcast packets to all machines on the network, thus stopping many DoS attacks. Additionally, you can install a filter on the router to verify that external packets actually have external IP addresses and that internal IPs have internal IP addresses.

Because many distributed DoS attacks depend on "unwitting" computers being used as launch points, one way to reduce such attacks is to protect your computer against virus attacks and Trojan horses. This problem will be discussed in more detail in a later chapter, but for now, it is important that you remember three things:

- Always use virus-scanning software and keep it updated.

- Always keep operating system and software patches updated.

- Have an organizational policy stating that employees cannot download anything onto their machines unless the download has been cleared by the IT staff.

As previously stated, none of these steps will make your network totally secure from either being the victim of a DoS attack or being the launch point for one, but they will help reduce the chances of either occurring. A good resource for this topic is the SANS Institute website, at www.sans.org/dosstep/. This site has some good tips on how to prevent DoS attacks.

Summary

DoS attacks are among the most common attacks on the Internet. They are easy to perform, do not require a great deal of sophistication on the part of the perpetrator, and can have devastating effects on the target system. Only virus attacks are more common. (And, in some cases, the virus can be the source of the DoS attack.) In the exercises, you will practice stopping a DoS.

Test Your Skills

MULTIPLE CHOICE QUESTIONS

1. What is one of the most common and simplest attacks on a system?

    A. Denial of service

    B. Buffer overflow

    C. Session hacking

    D. Password cracking

2. Which of the following is not a valid way to define a computer's workload?

    A. Number of simultaneous users

    B. Storage capacity

    C. Maximum voltage

    D. Speed of network connection

3. What do you call a DoS launched from several machines simultaneously?

    A. Wide-area attack

    B. Smurf attack

    C. SYN flood

    D. DDoS attack

4. Leaving a connection half open is referred to as what?

    A. Smurf attack

    B. Partial attack

    C. SYN flood attack

    D. DDoS attack

5. What is the basic mechanism behind a DoS attack?

    A. Computers don't handle TCP packets well.

    B. Computers can only handle a finite load.

    C. Computers cannot handle large volumes of TCP traffic.

    D. Computers cannot handle large loads.

6. What is the most significant weakness in a DoS attack from the attacker's viewpoint?

    A. The attack is often unsuccessful.

    B. The attack is difficult to execute.

    C. The attack is easy to stop.

    D. The attack must be sustained.

7. What is the most common class of DoS attacks?

    A. Distributed denial of service

    B. Smurf attacks

    C. SYN floods

    D. Ping of death

8. What are three methods for protecting against SYN flood attacks?

    A. SYN cookies, RST cookies, and stack tweaking

    B. SYN cookies, DoS cookies, and stack tweaking

    C. DoS cookies, RST cookies, and stack deletion

    D. DoS cookies, SYN cookies, and stack deletion

9. Which attack mentioned in this chapter causes a network to perform a DoS on one of its own servers?

    A. SYN flood

    B. Ping of death

    C. Smurf attack

    D. DDoS

10. A defense that depends on a hash encryption being sent back to the requesting client is called what?

    A. Stack tweaking

    B. RST cookies

    C. SYN cookies

    D. Hash tweaking

11. What type of defense depends on sending the client an incorrect SYNACK?

    A. Stack tweaking

    B. RST cookies

    C. SYN cookies

    D. Hash tweaking

12. What type of defense depends on changing the server so that unfinished handshaking times out sooner?

    A. Stack tweaking

    B. RST cookies

    C. SYN cookies

    D. Hash tweaking

13. What type of attack is dependent on sending packets too large for the server to handle?

    A. Ping of death

    B. Smurf attack

    C. Slammer attack

    D. DDoS

14. What type of attack uses Internet routers to perform a DoS on the target?

    A. Ping of death

    B. Smurf attack

    C. Slammer attack

    D. DDoS

15. Which of the following is an example of a DDoS attack?

    A. MyDoom virus

    B. Bagle virus

    C. DoS virus

    D. Smurf virus

16. How can securing internal routers help protect against DoS attacks?

    A. Attacks cannot occur if your internal router is secured.

    B. Because attacks originate outside your network, securing internal routers cannot help protect you against DoS.

    C. Securing the router will only stop router-based DoS attacks.

    D. It will prevent an attack from propagating across network segments.

17. What can you do to your internal network routers to help defend against DoS attacks?

    A. Disallow all traffic that is not encrypted

    B. Disallow all traffic that comes from outside the network

    C. Disallow all traffic that comes from inside the network

    D. Disallow all traffic that comes from untrusted sources

18. Which of the following was rated by many experts to be the fastest growing virus on the Internet?

    A. MyDoom virus

    B. Bagle virus

    C. Slammer virus

    D. Smurf virus

19. What can you do with your firewall to defend against DoS attacks?

    A. Block all incoming traffic

    B. Block all incoming TCP packets

    C. Block all incoming traffic on port 80

    D. Block all incoming ICMP packets

20. Why will protecting against Trojan horse attacks reduce DoS attacks?

    A. Because many denial of service attacks are conducted by using a Trojan horse to get an unsuspecting machine to execute the DoS

    B. Because if you can stop a Trojan horse attack, you will also stop DoS attacks

    C. Because a Trojan horse will often open ports allowing a DoS attack

    D. Because a Trojan horse attacks in much the same way as a DoS attack

EXERCISES

EXERCISE 4.1: Executing a DoS

Note that Exercise 1 is best done in a laboratory setting where there are several machines available for this purpose.

1. Set up one machine (preferably a machine with very limited capacity) to run a small web server. (You can download Apache for free for either Windows or Linux from www.apache.org.)

2. Use the `ping` utility with various other computers to attempt to perform a simple DoS on that web server. This attempt is accomplished by getting other machines to begin a continuous ping of that target machine using the previously mentioned `ping` command of `ping -l 65000 -w0 -t <insert target address here>`.

3. You should only add one to three lab machines to the "attack" at a time. (Start with one, add on a few more, and then a few more.)

4. As you add more machines, time how long it takes for another machine to bring up the home page of the target server. Also note the threshold (when that server quits responding completely).

EXERCISE 4.2: Stopping SYN Flood Attacks

Note that this exercise is advanced. Some students may wish to work in groups.

1. Search the Web or your operating system's documentation for instructions on implementing either the RST cookie or the SYN cookie.

2. Follow those implementation instructions on either your own machine or on a machine designated by your instructor. The following websites might be of help to you in this matter.

Linux:

www.linuxjournal.com/article.php?sid=3554

Windows:

http://cr.yp.to/syncookies.html

www.securityfocus.com/infocus/1729

Both Linux and Windows:

www.securiteam.com/tools/6D00K0K01O.html

EXERCISE 4.3: Using Firewall Settings

This exercise is only for students with access to a lab firewall.

1. Use your firewall's documentation to see how to block ICMP packets.

2. Set your firewall to block those packets.

EXERCISE 4.4: Using Router Settings

This exercise is only for students with access to a lab router.

1. Use your router's documentation to see how to block all traffic not originating on your own network.

2. Set your router to block that traffic.

PROJECTS

PROJECT 4.1: Employing Alternative Defenses

1. Using the Web or another research tool, search for alternative means of defending against either general DoS attacks or a specific type of DoS attack. This can be any defense other than the ones already mentioned in this chapter.

2. Write a brief paper concerning this defense technique.

PROJECT 4.2: Defending Against Specific Denial of Service Attacks

1. Using the Web or other tools, find a DoS attack that has occurred in the last six months. You might find some resources at www.f-secure.com.

2. Note how that attack was conducted.

3. Write a brief explanation of how one might have defended against that specific attack.

PROJECT 4.3: Hardening the TCP Stack against DoS

Note that this project requires access to a lab machine. It is also a long project, requiring some research time on the part of the students.

1. Using manuals, vendor documentation, and other resources, find one method for altering TCP communications to help prevent DoS attacks. You may find the following websites helpful:

   http://support.microsoft.com/default.aspx?scid=kb;en-us;315669

   http://moat.nlanr.net/Software/TCPtune/

2. Using this information, implement one of these methods on your lab computer.

Case Study

Runa Singh is the network administrator in charge of network security for a medium-sized company. The firm already has a firewall, its network is divided into multiple segments separated by routers, and it has updated virus scanners on all machines. Runa wants to take extra precautions to prevent DoS attacks. She takes the following actions:

- She adjusts her firewall so that no incoming ICMP packets are allowed.
- She changes the web server so that it uses SYN cookies.

Now consider the following questions:

- Are there problems with any of her precautions? If so, what are the problems?
- What additional steps would you recommend to Runa?

## Chapter 5

Malware

Chapter Objectives

After reading this chapter and completing the exercises, you will be able to do the following:

- Understand viruses (worms) and how they propagate, including the Sobig and Sasser types
- Have a working knowledge of several specific virus outbreaks
- Understand how virus scanners operate
- Understand what a Trojan horse is and how it operates
- Have a working knowledge of several specific Trojan horse attacks
- Grasp the concept behind the buffer-overflow attack
- Have a better understanding of spyware and how it enters a system
- Defend against each of these attacks through sound practices, antivirus software, and antispyware software

Introduction

In Chapter 4, "Denial of Service Attacks," we examined the denial of service attack. It is a very common attack and one that can easily be perpetrated. In this chapter, you will continue your examination of security threats by learning about several other types of attacks. First, you will learn about virus outbreaks. Our discussion will focus on crucial information about how and why virus attacks work, including their deployment through Trojan horses. This chapter is not a "how to create your own virus" tutorial, but rather an introduction to the concepts underlying these attacks as well as an examination of some specific case studies.

This chapter will also explore buffer-overflow attacks, spyware, and several other forms of malware. Each of these brings a unique approach to an attack, and each needs to be considered when defending a system. Your ability to defend against such attacks will be enhanced by expanding your knowledge of how they work. In the exercises at the end of the chapter, you will have the opportunity to research preventative methods for viruses and to try out antivirus methods from McAfee and Norton.

Viruses

By definition, a computer virus is a program that self-replicates. Generally, a virus will also have some other unpleasant function, but the self-replication and rapid spread are the hallmarks of a virus. Often this growth, in and of itself, can be a problem for an infected network. The last chapter discussed the Slammer virus and the effects of its rapid, high-volume scanning. Any rapidly spreading virus can reduce the functionality and responsiveness of a network. Simply by exceeding the traffic load that a network was designed to carry, the network may be rendered temporarily nonfunctional. The infamous I Love You virus actually had no negative payload, but the shear volume of emails it generated bogged down many networks.

How a Virus Spreads

A virus will usually spread primarily in one of two ways. The first is to simply scan your computer for connections to a network, then copy itself to other machines on the network to which your computer has access. This is actually the most efficient way for a virus to spread. However, this method requires more programming skill than other methods. The more common method is to read your email address book and email itself to everyone in your address book. Programming this is a trivial task, which explains why it is so common.

The latter method is, by far, the most common method for virus propagation, and Microsoft Outlook may be the one email program most often hit with such virus attacks. The reason is not so much a security flaw in Outlook as it is the ease of working with Outlook. All Microsoft Office products are made so that a legitimate programmer who is writing software for a business can access many of the application's internal objects and thereby easily create applications that integrate the applications within the Microsoft Office suite. For example, a programmer could write an application that would access a Word document, import an Excel spreadsheet, and then use Outlook to automatically email the resulting document to interested parties. Microsoft has done a good job of making this process very easy, for it usually takes a minimum amount of programming to accomplish these tasks. Using Outlook, it takes less than five lines of code to reference Outlook and send out an email. This means a program can literally cause Outlook itself to send emails, unbeknownst to the user. There are numerous code examples on the Internet that show exactly how to do this, free for the taking. For this reason, it does not take a very skilled programmer to be able to access your Outlook address book and automatically send emails. Essentially, the ease of programming Outlook is why there are so many virus attacks that target Outlook.

While the overwhelming majority of virus attacks spread by attaching themselves to the victim's existing email software, some recent virus outbreaks have used other methods for propagation, such as their own internal email engine. Another virus propagation method is to simply copy itself across a network. Virus outbreaks that spread via multiple routes are becoming more common.

The method of delivering a payload can be rather simplistic and rely more on end-user negligence than on the skill of the virus writer. Enticing users to go to websites or open files they should not is a common method for delivering a virus and one that requires no programming skill at all. Regardless of the way a virus arrives at your doorstep, once it is on your system, it will attempt to spread and, in many cases, will also attempt to cause some harm to your system. Once a virus is on your system, it can do anything that any legitimate program can do. That means it could potentially delete files, change system settings, or cause other harm.

Recent Virus Examples

The threat from virus attacks cannot be overstated. While there are many web pages that give virus information, in my opinion, there are only a handful of web pages that consistently give the latest, most reliable, most detailed information on virus outbreaks. Any security professional will want to consult these sites on a regular basis. You can read more about any virus, past or current, at the following websites:

- www.f-secure.com/virus-info/virus-news/
- www.cert.org/nav/index_red.html
- http://securityresponse.symantec.com/
- http://vil.nai.com/vil/

The sections below will look at a few recent virus outbreaks (and some not so recent) and review how they operated and what they did.

W32/Netsky-P

This worm was first found in 2006 but is still going around in 2011. It is a fairly typical virus in that it spreads primarily through email, but also uses file sharing utilities to copy itself. It also copies itself to various directories and shared folders. In one interesting twist, it attempts to copy itself to C:\WINDOWS\FVProtect.exe. The name would make many people (including otherwise technically savvy people) think this program was actually part of some antivirus utility. It also copies itself to C:\WINDOWS\userconfig9x.dll. Again, it would appear to be a system file, thus making people less likely to delete it.

This is also a classic worm/virus in that the email it sends out had a fairly generic title and content that attempts to get the recipient to open the attachment. For example, the body of the message might say something like "Please see the attached file for details" or "Your file is attached."

Troj/Invo-Zip

This particular worm is a classic worm/Trojan horse. It was first reported in mid 2010. It is transmitted as a zip file attached to an email. The email claims that the zip file contains data related to an invoice, tax issue, or similar urgent paperwork. This is a classic example of attempting to entice the recipient to open the attachment. And in this case, the recipients most likely to be enticed would be businesspeople.

If the recipient does open the attachment, then he or she will have installed spyware on his machine that would first disable the firewall then start attempting to capture information including financial data, and even taking screenshots of the user's desktop.

MacDefender

This virus is very interesting for multiple reasons. First because it specifically targets Macintosh computers. Most experts have long agreed that Apple products remained relatively virus free simply because their products did not have enough market share to attract the attention of virus writers. It has long been suspected that if Apple garnered a greater market share, they would also begin to get more virus attacks. That has proven to be true.

This virus was first seen in the early months of 2011. It is embedded in some web pages and when a user visits those web pages, he or she is given a fake virus scan that tells the user that they have a virus and it needs to be fixed. The "fix" is actually downloading a virus. The point of the virus is to get end users to purchase the MacDefender "antivirus" product. This is the second reason this case is noteworthy. Fake antivirus attacks, also known as scareware, have been becoming increasingly common.

The Sobig Virus

This is obviously not a recent virus, as it was first found in 2003. However, it is an excellent virus to study. This virus is important to study because it received the most media attention and perhaps caused the most harm in 2003. The first interesting thing to study about this virus was how it spread. It spread utilizing a multimodal approach to spreading. This means that it used more than one mechanism to spread and infect new machines. It would copy itself to any shared drives on your network and it would email itself out to everyone in your address book. For these reasons, this virus was particularly virulent, and this is also why it is important to study.

FYI: Virulent Virus

The term *virulent* means essentially the same thing in reference to a computer virus as it does to a biological virus. It is a measure of how rapidly the infection spreads and how easily it infects new targets.

In the case of Sobig, if one person on a network was unfortunate enough to open an email containing the virus, not only would his machine be infected, but so would every shared drive on that network to which this person had access. However, Sobig, like most email-distributed virus attacks, had tell-tale signs in the email subject or title that could be used to identify the email as one infected by a virus. The email would have some enticing title such as "here is the sample" or "the document" to encourage you to be curious enough to open the attached file. The virus would then copy itself into the Windows System directory.

This particular virus spread so far and infected so many networks that the multiple copying of the virus alone was enough to bring some networks to a standstill. This virus did not destroy files or damage the system, but it generated a great deal of traffic that bogged down the networks infected by it. The virus itself was of moderate sophistication. Once it was out, however, many variants began to spring up, further complicating the situation. One of the effects of some variants of Sobig was to download a file from the Internet that would then cause printing problems. Some network printers would just start printing junk. The Sobig.E variant would even write to the Windows Registry, causing itself to be in the computer startup (F-Secure, 2003). These complex characteristics indicate that the creator knew how to access the Windows Registry, access shared drives, alter the Windows startup, and access Outlook.

This brings up the issue of virus variants and how they occur. In the case of a biological virus, mutations in the genetic code cause new virus strains to appear, and the pressures of natural selection allow some of these strains to evolve into entirely new species of viruses. Obviously, the biological method is not what occurs with a computer virus. With a computer virus, what occurs is that some intrepid programmer with malicious intent will get a copy of a virus (perhaps her own machine becomes infected) and will then reverse-engineer it. Since many virus attacks are in the form of a script attached to an email, unlike traditionally compiled programs, the source code of these attacks is readily readable and alterable. The programmer in question then simply takes the original virus code and introduces some change, then re-releases the variant. Frequently, the people who are caught for virus creation are actually the developers of the variants who lacked the skill of the original virus writer and therefore were easily caught.

The Mimail Virus

This is another older virus that is still worth studying. The Mimail virus did not receive as much media attention as Sobig, but it had its intriguing characteristics. This virus not only collected email addresses from your address book, but also from other documents on your machine (Gudmundsson, 2004). Thus, if you had a Word document on your hard drive and an email address was in that document, Mimail would find it. This strategy meant that Mimail would spread farther than many other viruses. Mimail had its own built-in email engine, so it did not have to "piggy back" off your email client. It could spread regardless of what email software you used.

These two variations from most virus attacks made Mimail interesting to people who study computer viruses. There are a variety of techniques that allow you to programmatically open and process files on your computer; however, most virus attacks do not employ them. The scanning of the document for email addresses indicates a certain level of skill and creativity on the part of the virus writer. In this author's opinion, Mimail was not the work of an amateur, but rather a person with professional-level programming skill.

The Bagle Virus

This is the last of the "historical viruses" that we will examine. It is noteworthy in that it combined email attachments along with the fake virus warning. The Bagle virus began to spread rapidly in the fourth quarter of 2003. The email it sent claimed to be from your system administrator. It would tell you that your email account had been infected by a virus and that you should open the attached file to get instructions. Once you opened the attached file, your system was infected. This virus was particularly interesting for several reasons. To begin with, it spread both through email and copying itself to shared folders. Second, it could also scan files on your PC looking for email addresses. Finally, it would disable processes used by antivirus scanners. In biological terms, this virus took out your computer's "immune system." The disabling of virus scanners is a new twist that indicates at least moderate programming skills on the part of the virus creator.

A Nonvirus Virus

Another new type of virus has been gaining popularity in the past few years, and that is the "nonvirus virus" or, put simply, a hoax. Rather than actually writing a virus, a hacker sends an email to every address he has. The email claims to be from some well-known antivirus center and warns of a new virus that is circulating. The email instructs people to delete some file from their computer to get rid of the virus. The file, however, is not really a virus but part of a computer's system. The jdbgmgr.exe virus hoax used this scheme (Rhode Island Soft Systems, Inc., 2003). It encouraged the reader to delete a file that was actually needed by the system. Surprisingly, a number of people followed this advice and not only deleted the file, but promptly emailed their friends and colleagues to warn them to delete the file from their machines.

FYI: The Morris Internet Worm

The Morris worm was one of the first computer worms ever to be distributed over the Internet. And it was certainly the first to gain any significant media attention.

Robert Tappan Morris, Jr., then a student at Cornell University, wrote this worm and launched it from an MIT system on November 2, 1988. Morris did not actually intend to cause any damage with the worm. Instead, he wanted the worm to reveal bugs in the programs it exploited in order to spread. However, bugs in the code allowed an individual computer to be infected multiple times, and the worm became a menace. Each additional "infection" spawned a new process on the infected computer. At a certain point, the high number of processes running on an infected machine slowed down the computer to the point of being unusable. At least 6,000 UNIX machines were infected with this worm.

Morris was convicted of violating the 1986 Computer Fraud and Abuse Act and was sentenced to a $10,000 fine, 3 years probation, and 400 hours of community service. But perhaps the greatest impact of this worm was that it led to the creation of the Computer Emergency Response Team (CERT). CERT is an organization hosted at Carnegie Mellon University (www.cert.org/) that is a repository for security bulletins, information, and guidelines. CERT is a source that any security professional should be familiar with.

Rules for Avoiding Viruses

You should notice a common theme with all virus attacks (except the hoax), which is that they want you to open some type of attachment. The most common way for a virus to spread is as an email attachment. This realization leads to some simple rules that will drastically reduce the odds of becoming infected with a virus.

- Use a virus scanner. McAfee and Norton (explored in the exercises at the end of this chapter) are the two most widely accepted and used virus scanners. However, Kaspersky and AVG are also good, reputable choices. Each costs about $30 per year to keep your virus scanner updated. Do it. Now each antivirus has its proponents and detractors—I won't delve into the opinions on which is better. For most users, any of the four major antivirus programs would be effective. I personally rotate which one I use periodically, just so I can stay familiar with all of them.

- If you are not sure about an attachment, do not open it.

- You might even exchange a code word with friends and colleagues. Tell them that if they wish to send you an attachment, they should put the code word in the title of the message. Without seeing the code word, you will not open any attachment.

- Do not believe "security alerts" that are sent to you. Microsoft does not send out alerts in this manner. Check the Microsoft website regularly, as well as one of the antivirus websites previously mentioned.

These rules will not make your system 100% virus proof, but they will go a long way toward protecting your system.

Trojan Horses

Recall from earlier chapters that *Trojan horse* is a term for a program that looks benign but actually has a malicious purpose. We have already seen viruses that are delivered via a Trojan horse. You might receive or download a program that appears to be a harmless business utility or game. More likely, the Trojan horse is just a script attached to a benign-looking email. When you run the program or open the attachment, it does something else other than or in addition to what you thought it would. It might

- Download harmful software from a website.

- Install a key logger or other spyware on your machine.

- Delete files.

- Open a back door for a hacker to use.

It is common to find combination virus plus Trojan horse attacks. In those scenarios, the Trojan horse spreads like a virus. The MyDoom virus opened a port on your machine that a later virus, doomjuice, would exploit, thus making MyDoom a combination virus and Trojan horse.

A Trojan horse could also be crafted especially for an individual. If a hacker wished to spy on a certain individual, such as the company accountant, he could craft a program specifically to attract that person's attention. For example, if he knew the accountant was an avid golfer, he could write a program that computed handicap and listed best golf courses. He would post that program on a free web server. He would then email a number of people, including the accountant, telling them about the free software. The software, once installed, could check the name of the currently logged-on person. If the logged-on name matched the accountant's name, the software could then go out, unknown to the user, and download a key logger or other monitoring application. If the software did not damage files or replicate itself, then it would probably go undetected for quite a long time. There have been a number of Trojan horses through the years. One of the earliest and most widely known was Back Orifice.

FYI: Virus or Worm?

As noted in the previous chapter, there is disagreement among the experts as to the distinction between a virus and a worm. Some experts would call MyDoom (as well as Sasser, which will be discussed later) a worm because it spread without human intervention. However, I would define a virus as any file that can self replicate, and a worm is any program that can propagate without human interference. This is also the most common definition you will find among security experts.

Such a program could be within the skill set of virtually any moderately competent programmer. This is one reason that many organizations have rules against downloading *any* software onto company machines. I am unaware of any actual incident of a Trojan horse being custom tailored in this fashion. However, it is important to remember that those creating virus attacks tend to be innovative people.

It is also important to note that creating a Trojan horse does not require programming skill. There are free tools on the Internet, such as EliteWrapper, that allow one to combine two programs together, one hidden and one not. So one could easily take a virus and combine it with, for example, a poker game. The end user would only see the poker game, but when it was run it would launch the virus.

Another scenario to consider is one that would be quite devastating. Without divulging programming details, the basic premise will be outlined here to illustrate the grave dangers of Trojan horses. Imagine a small application that displays a series of unflattering pictures of Osama Bin Laden. This application would probably be popular with many people in the United States, particularly people in the military, intelligence community, or defense-related industries. Now assume that this application simply sits dormant on the machine for a period of time. It need not replicate like a virus because the computer user will probably send it to many of his associates. On a certain date and time, the software connects to any drive it can, including network drives, and begins deleting all files. If such a Trojan horse were released "in the wild," within 30 days it would probably be shipped to thousands, perhaps millions, of people. Imagine the devastation when thousands of computers begin deleting files and folders.

This scenario is mentioned precisely to frighten you a little. Computer users, including professionals who should know better, routinely download all sorts of things from the Internet, such as amusing flash videos and cute games. Every time an employee downloads something of this nature, there is the chance of downloading a Trojan horse. One need not be a statistician to realize that if employees continue that practice long enough, they will eventually download a Trojan horse onto a company machine. If so, hopefully the virus will not be as vicious as the theoretical one just outlined here.

The Buffer-Overflow Attack

You have become knowledgeable about a number of ways to attack a target system: denial of service, virus, and Trojan horse. While these attacks are probably the most common, they are not the only methods. Another method of attacking a system is called a buffer-overflow (or buffer-overrun) attack. A buffer-overflow attack happens when one tries to put more data in a buffer than it was designed to hold (searchSecurity.com, 2004a). Any program that communicates with the Internet or a private network must take in some data. This data is stored, at least temporarily, in a space in memory called a buffer. If the programmer who wrote the application was careful, when you try to place too much information into a buffer, that information is then either simply truncated or outright rejected. Given the number of applications that might be running on a target system and the number of buffers in each application, the chances of having at least one buffer that was not written properly are significant enough to cause any prudent person some concern.

Someone who is moderately skilled in programming can write a program that purposefully writes more into the buffer than it can hold. For example, if the buffer can hold 1024 bytes of data and you try to fill it with 2048 bytes, the extra 1024 bytes is then simply loaded into memory. If that extra data is actually a malicious program, then it has just been loaded into memory and is thus now running on the target system. Or, perhaps the perpetrator simply wants to flood the target machine's memory, thus overwriting other items that are currently in memory and causing them to crash. Either way, the buffer overflow is a very serious attack.

Fortunately, buffer-overflow attacks are a bit harder to execute than a DoS or simple Microsoft Outlook script virus. To create a buffer-overflow attack, you must have a good working knowledge of some programming language (C or C++ is often chosen) and understand the target operating system/application well enough to know whether it has a buffer overflow weakness and how that weakness might be exploited.

It must be noted that modern operating systems and web servers are not susceptible to this attack. Windows 95 was quite susceptible, but it has been many years since a Windows operating system was susceptible. Certainly Windows 7 cannot be compromised with a buffer overflow. However, the same cannot be necessarily said for all the custom applications developed to run on various systems. It is always possible that an Internet-enabled application, including but not limited to web applications, might be susceptible to this attack.

Essentially, this vulnerability only exists if programmers fail to program correctly. If all programs truncate extra data, then a buffer overflow cannot be executed on that system. However, if the program does not check the boundaries of variables and arrays, and allows excess data to be loaded, then that system is vulnerable to a buffer overflow.

The Sasser Virus/Buffer Overflow

This is an older attack, but one that demonstrates the use of a buffer-overflow attack. Sasser is a combination attack in that the virus (or worm) spreads by exploiting a buffer overrun.

The Sasser virus spreads by exploiting a known flaw in a Windows system program. Sasser copies itself to the Windows directory as avserve.exe and creates a Registry key to load itself at startup. In that way, once your machine is infected, you will start the virus every time you start the machine. This virus scans random IP addresses, listening on successive TCP ports starting at 1068 for exploitable systems—that is, systems that have not been patched to fix this flaw. When one is found, the worm exploits the vulnerable system by overflowing a buffer in LSASS.EXE, which is a file that is part of the Windows operating system. That executable is a built-in system file and is part of Windows. Sasser also acts as an FTP server on TCP port 5554, and it creates a remote shell on TCP port 9996. Next, Sasser creates an FTP script named cmd.ftp on the remote host and executes that script. This FTP script instructs the target victim to download and execute the worm from the infected host. The infected host accepts this FTP traffic on TCP port 5554. The computer also creates a file named win.log on the C: drive. This file contains the IP address of the localhost. Copies of the virus are created in the Windows System directory as #_up.exe. Examples are shown here:

- c:\WINDOWS\system32\12553_up.exe
- c:\WINDOWS\system32\17923_up.exe
- c:\WINDOWS\system32\29679_up.exe

A side effect of this virus is that it causes your machine to reboot. A machine that is repeatedly rebooting without any other known cause may well be infected with the Sasser virus.

This is another case in which the infection can easily be prevented by several means. First, if you update your systems on a regular basis, your systems should not be vulnerable to this flaw. Second, if your network's routers or firewall block traffic on the ports mentioned (9996 and 5554), you will then prevent most of Sasser's damage. Your firewall should only allow in traffic on specified ports; all other ports should be shut down. In short, if you as the network administrator are aware of security issues and are taking prudent steps to protect the network, your network will be safe. The fact that so many networks were affected by this virus should indicate that not enough administrators are properly trained in computer security.

Spyware

In Chapter 1, "Introduction to Computer Security," spyware was mentioned as one of the threats to computer security. Using spyware, however, requires a great deal more technical knowledge on the part of the perpetrator than some other forms of malware. The perpetrator must be able to develop spyware for the particular situation or customize existing spyware for his needs. He must then be able to get the spyware on the target machine.

Spyware can be as simple as a cookie used by a website to record a few brief facts about your visit to that website, or spyware could be of a more insidious type, such as a key logger. Recall from Chapter 1 that key loggers are programs that record every keystroke you make on your keyboard; this spyware then logs your keystrokes to the spy's file. The most common use of a key logger is to capture usernames and passwords. However, this method can capture every username and password you enter and every document you type, as well as anything else you might type. This data can be stored in a small file hidden on your machine for later extraction or sent out in TCP packets to some predetermined address. In some cases, the software is even set to wait until after hours to upload this data to some server or to use your own email software to send the data to an anonymous email address. There are also some key loggers that take periodic screenshots from your machine, revealing anything that is open on your computer. Whatever the specific mode of operation, spyware is software that literally spies on your activities on a particular computer.

Legal Uses of Spyware

There are some perfectly legal uses for spyware. Some employers have embraced such spyware as a means of monitoring employee use of company technology. Many companies have elected to monitor phone, email, or web traffic within the organization. Keep in mind that the computer, network, and phone systems are the property of the company or organization, not of the employee. These technologies are supposedly only used for work purposes; therefore, company monitoring might not constitute any invasion of privacy. While courts have upheld this monitoring as a company's right, it is critical to consult an attorney before initiating this level of employee monitoring as well as to consider the potential negative impact on employee morale.

Parents can also elect to use this type of software on their home computer to monitor the activities of their children on the Internet. The goal is usually a laudable one—protecting their children from online predators. Yet, as with employees in a company, the practice may illicit a strong negative reaction from the parties being spied upon (namely, their children). Parents have to weigh the risk to their children versus what might be viewed as a breach of trust.

How Is Spyware Delivered to a Target System?

Clearly, spyware programs can track all activity on a computer, and that information can be retrieved by another party via a number of different methods. The real question is this: How does spyware get onto a computer system in the first place? The most common method is a Trojan horse. It is also possible that when you visit a certain website spyware may download in the background while you are simply perusing the website. Of course, if an employer (or parent) is installing the spyware, it can then be installed non-covertly in the same way that an organization would install any other application.

Obtaining Spyware Software

Given the many other utilities and tools that have been mentioned as available from the Internet, you probably will not be surprised to learn that you can obtain many spyware products for free, or at very low cost, on the Internet. You can check the Counterexploitation (www.cexx.org) website, shown in

Figure 5.1, for a lengthy list of known spyware products circulating on the Internet and for information about methods one can use to remove them. The Spyware Guide website (SpywareGuide, 2004) (www.spywareguide.com) lists spyware that you can get right off the Internet should you feel some compelling reason to spy on someone's computer activities. Figure 5.2 shows the categories of malware that are available from this site. Several key logger applications are listed on this site, as shown in Figure 5.3. These applications include well-known key loggers such as Absolute Keylogger, Tiny Keylogger, and TypO. Most can be downloaded for free or for a nominal charge from the Internet.

FIGURE 5.1   Counterexploitation website.

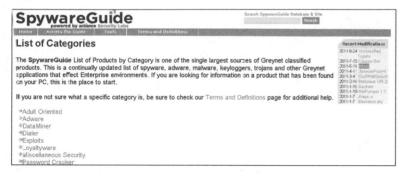

FIGURE 5.2   Malware categories at the Spyware Guide website.

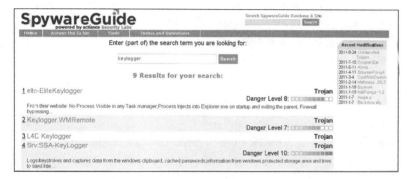

FIGURE 5.3   List of key loggers available through the Spyware Guide website.

Some well-known Trojan horses are also listed at this site (as shown in Figure 5.4), such as the 2nd Thought application that downloads to a person's PC and then blasts it with advertisements. This particular piece of spyware is one that downloads to your PC when you visit certain websites. It is benign in that it causes no direct harm to your system or files, nor does it gather sensitive information from your PC. However, it is incredibly annoying as it inundates your machine with unwanted ads. This sort of software is often referred to as adware. Frequently, these ads cannot be stopped by normal protective pop-up blockers because the pop-up windows are not generated by a website that you visit but rather by some rogue software running on your machine. Pop-up blockers only work to stop sites you visit from opening new windows. Websites use well-known scripting techniques to cause your browser to open a window, and pop-up blockers recognize these techniques and prevent the ad window from opening. However, if the adware launches a new browser instance, it bypasses the pop-up blocker's function.

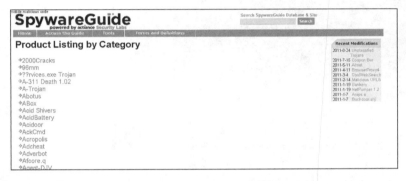

FIGURE 5.4   Trojan horses available at the Spyware Guide website.

Other Forms of Malware

In this and preceding chapters, the most prominent forms of malware have been discussed. There are, however, many other forms of attack. It is beyond the scope of this book to explore each of these, but you should be aware of the existence of these other forms of malware. Simply being aware can go a long way toward enabling you to defend your system efficiently. This section will touch upon just a few other forms of malware. You should reference the websites discussed in the end of chapter exercises and projects often so that you can stay up-to-date with all current forms of attack and defenses.

Rootkit

A rootkit is a collection of tools that a hacker uses to mask her intrusion and obtain administrator-level access to a computer or computer network. The intruder installs a rootkit on a computer after first obtaining user-level access, either by exploiting a known vulnerability or cracking a password. The rootkit then collects user IDs and passwords to other machines on the network, thus giving the hacker root or privileged access.

A rootkit may consist of utilities that also

- Monitor traffic and keystrokes

- Create a "back door" into the system for the hacker's use

- Alter log files

- Attack other machines on the network

- Alter existing system tools to circumvent detection

The presence of a rootkit on a network was first documented in the early 1990s. At that time, Sun and Linux operating systems were the primary targets for a hacker looking to install a rootkit. Today, rootkits are available for a number of operating systems and are increasingly difficult to detect on any network (searchSecurity.com, 2004b).

Malicious Web-Based Code

A malicious web-based code, also known as a web-based mobile code, simply refers to a code that is portable to all operating systems or platforms such as HTTP, Java, and so on. The "malicious" part implies that is it a virus, worm, Trojan horse, or some other form of malware. Simply put, the malicious code does not care what the operating system may be or what browser is in use. It infects them all blindly (Yakabovicz, 2003).

Where do these codes come from, and how are they spread? The first generation of the Internet was mostly indexed text files. However, as the Internet has grown into a graphical, multimedia user experience, programmers have created scripting languages and new application technologies to enable a more interactive experience. As with any new technology, programs written with scripting languages run the gamut from useful to poorly crafted to outright dangerous.

Technologies such as Java and ActiveX enable these buggy or untrustworthy programs to move to and execute on user workstations. (Other technologies that can enable malicious code are executables, JavaScript, Visual Basic Script, and plug-ins.) The Web acts to increase the mobility of code without differentiating between program quality, integrity, or reliability. Using available tools, it is quite simple to "drag and drop" code into documents that are subsequently placed on web servers and made available to employees throughout the organization or individuals across the Internet. If this code is maliciously programmed or just improperly tested, it can cause serious damage.

Not surprisingly, hackers have used these very useful tools to steal, alter, and erase data files as well as gain unauthorized access to corporate networks. A malicious code attack can penetrate corporate networks and systems from a variety of access points, including websites, HTML content in email messages, or corporate intranets. Figure 5.5 shows the rapid growth of mobile malicious code in recent years versus viruses.

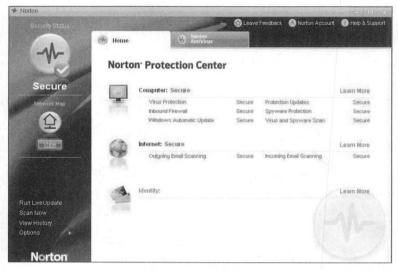

FIGURE 5.5   Growth of mobile malicious code.

Today, with literally billions of Internet users, new malicious code attacks can spread almost instantly through corporations. The majority of damage caused by malicious code happens in the first hours after a first-strike attack occurs—before there is time for countermeasures. The costs of network downtime or theft of IP make malicious code a top priority (finjan software, 2004).

Logic Bombs

A logic bomb is a type of malware that executes its malicious purpose when a specific criteria is met. The most common factor is date/time. For example a logic bomb might delete files on a certain date/time. An example is the case of Roger Duronio. In June 2006, Roger Duronio, a system administrator for UBS, was charged with using a logic bomb to damage the company's computer network. His plan was to drive the company stock down due to damage from the logic bomb and so he was charged with securities fraud. Duronio was later convicted and sentenced to 8 years and 1 month in prison and ordered to pay $3.1 million restitution to UBS.

Spam

Spam is something most readers are probably familiar with. It is unwanted email. Spam is email that is sent out to multiple parties, that is unsolicited. Often it is used for marketing purposes, but it can be used for much more malicious goals. For example, spam is a common way to spread a virus or worm. Spam is also used to send emails enticing recipients to visit phishing websites in order to steal the recipient's identity. Essentially, spam is, at best, an annoyance and, at worst, a vehicle for spyware, viruses, worms, and phishing attacks.

Detecting and Eliminating Viruses and Spyware

Antivirus Software

In this chapter, and throughout this book, the need for running virus–scanning software has been discussed. It is prudent at this point to provide you with some details on how virus scanners work and information on the major virus-scanning software packages. This information should help you better understand how a virus scanner might help protect your system and help you make intelligent decisions regarding the purchase and deployment of some antivirus solution.

A virus scanner can work in one of two ways. The first is to look for a signature (or pattern) that matches a known virus. This is why it is important to keep your virus software updated so that you have the most recent list of signatures with which to work.

The other way in which a virus scanner might check a given PC is to look at the behavior of an executable. If that program behaves in a way consistent with virus activity, the virus scanner may flag it as a virus. Such activity could include the following:

- Attempting to copy itself

- Attempting to access the address book of the system's email program

- Attempting to change Registry settings in Windows

Figure 5.6 shows the Norton AntiVirus software in action. You can see that the virus definitions are up-to-date, that the virus scanning is enabled, auto-protection is enabled, and the Internet worm protection is enabled as well. The other popular virus scanners have many of the same features.

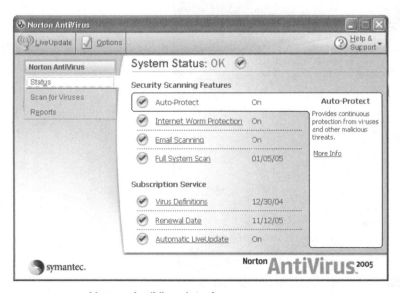

FIGURE 5.6   Norton AntiVirus interface.

Most antivirus software today offer additional features. Some of these features include warning the user of known phishing websites, detecting spyware as well as viruses, and even detecting likely phishing attempts. Any modern antivirus should be a comprehensive package, protecting against a variety of attacks, rather than just stopping viruses.

Antispyware Software

Fortunately, just as there are many different spyware applications available, there are likewise many different software applications on the market that are designed specifically to detect and remove spyware. These applications are also usually available at extremely low cost. You can often get a free trial version to use for a limited time so that you can make a more intelligent purchasing decision. Of course, the most prudent course of action you can take to avoid getting spyware on your machine is to never download anything from the Internet that does not come from a very well-known and trusted website. However, in an organizational environment, you cannot simply rely on your employees to do the right thing. It is prudent as the company's computer security expert to take steps yourself to prevent the employees from compromising your system security.

Some of the better known and more widely used antispyware applications include Spy Sweeper from www.webroot.com, Zero Spyware Removal from www.zerospyware.com, and Spector Pro from www.spectorsoft.com. All of these applications can be obtained for anywhere from $20 to $50, and many offer a free trial version. And most modern antivirus software either includes antispyware, or it can be added as an option.

Figure 5.7 shows the items found by running the WebRoot Spy Sweeper software on a system. These items can be selected for quarantine and removal.

FIGURE 5.7   Items recommended for removal by Spy Sweeper.

Figure 5.8 shows the summary results after all of the items found have been quarantined. Note that the number of files scanned, the number of items removed, the date the full sweep was performed, as well as additional information is all detailed on this summary page. Each of the antispyware applications would provide similar results and each contain similar options for sweeping a system.

FIGURE 5.8   Summary results of a system sweep.

Summary

Clearly, there are a number of ways to attack a target system: by denial of service, virus/worm, Trojan horse, buffer-overflow attacks, and spyware. Each type of attack comes in many distinct variations. It should be obvious by this point that securing your system is absolutely critical. In the upcoming exercises, you will try out the antivirus programs by Norton and McAfee. There are so many ways for a hacker to attack a system that securing your system can be a rather complex task.

Another theme that is driven home throughout this chapter is that many, if not most, attacks are preventable. The exercises ahead will give you practice in figuring out how to prevent the Sasser and Sobig virus. In most cases, prompt and regular patching of the system, use of antivirus tools, and blocking unneeded ports would prevent the attack. The fact that so many systems do get infected is an indication of the very real problem of network professionals who are not skilled in computer security.

Test Your Skills

MULTIPLE CHOICE QUESTIONS

1. Which of the following is the best definition of virus?

    A. Program that causes harm on your computer

    B. Program used in a DoS attack

    C. Program that slows down networks

    D. Program that self-replicates

2. What is the most common damage caused by virus attacks?

    A. Slowing down networks by the virus traffic

    B. Deleting files

    C. Changing the Windows Registry

    D. Corrupting the operating system

3. What is the most common way for a virus to spread?

    A. By copying to shared folders

    B. By email attachment

    C. By FTP

    D. By downloading from a website

4. Which of the following is the primary reason that Microsoft Outlook is so often a target for virus attacks?

   A. Many hackers dislike Microsoft.

   B. Outlook copies virus files faster.

   C. It is easy to write programs that access Outlook's inner mechanisms.

   D. Outlook is more common than other email systems.

5. Which of the following virus attacks used a multimodal approach?

   A. Slammer virus

   B. Mimail virus

   C. Sobig virus

   D. Bagle virus

6. What factor about the Sobig virus made it most intriguing to security experts?

   A. It spread in multiple ways.

   B. It deleted critical system files.

   C. It was difficult to protect against.

   D. It was very sophisticated.

7. What was most interesting to security experts about the Mimail virus?

   A. It spread more rapidly than other virus attacks.

   B. It spread in multiple ways.

   C. It grabbed email addresses from documents on the hard drive.

   D. It deleted critical system files.

8. Which of the following reasons most likely made the Bagle virus spread so rapidly?

   A. The email containing it claimed to be from the system administrator.

   B. It copied itself across the network.

   C. It was a sophisticated virus.

   D. It was particularly virulent.

9. What made the Bagle virus so dangerous?

   A. It changed Windows Registry settings.

   B. It disabled antivirus software.

   C. It deleted key system files.

   D. It corrupted the operating system.

10. Which of the following is a way that any person can use to protect against virus attacks?

  A. Set up a firewall

  B. Use encrypted transmissions

  C. Use secure email software

  D. Never open unknown email attachments

11. Which of the following is the safest way to send and receive attachments?

  A. Use a code word indicating the attachment is legitimate

  B. Only send spreadsheet attachments

  C. Use encryption

  D. Use virus scanners before opening attachments

12. Which of the following is true regarding emailed security alerts?

  A. You must follow them.

  B. Most companies do not send alerts via email.

  C. You can trust attachments on security alerts.

  D. Most companies send alerts via email.

13. Which of the following is something a Trojan horse might do?

  A. Open a back door for malicious software

  B. Change your memory configuration

  C. Change ports on your computer

  D. Alter your IP address

14. What is a buffer-overflow attack?

  A. Overflowing a port with too many packets

  B. Putting more email in an email system than it can hold

  C. Overflowing the system

  D. Putting more data in a buffer than it can hold

15. What virus exploited buffer overflows?

  A. Sobig virus

  B. Mimail virus

  C. Sasser virus

  D. Bagle virus

16. What can you do with a firewall to help protect against virus attacks?

   A. There is nothing you can do on the firewall to stop virus attacks.

   B. Shut down all unneeded ports.

   C. Close all incoming ports.

   D. None of the above.

17. A key logger is what type of malware?

   A. Virus

   B. Buffer overflow

   C. Trojan horse

   D. Spyware

18. Which of the following is a step that all computer users should take to protect against virus attacks?

   A. Purchase and configure a firewall

   B. Shut down all incoming ports

   C. Use nonstandard email clients

   D. Install and use antivirus software

19. What is the primary way a virus scanner works?

   A. By comparing files against a list of known virus profiles

   B. By blocking files that copy themselves

   C. By blocking all unknown files

   D. By looking at files for virus-like behavior

20. What other way can a virus scanner work?

   A. By comparing files against a list of known virus profiles

   B. By blocking files that copy themselves

   C. By blocking all unknown files

   D. By looking at files for virus-like behavior

Exercises

EXERCISE 5.1: Using Norton AntiVirus

1. Go to the Norton AntiVirus website (www.symantec.com/downloads) and download the trial version of their software.

2. Install and run their software.

3. Carefully study the application, noting features that you like and dislike.

EXERCISE 5.2: **Using McAfee AntiVirus**

1. Go to the McAfee antivirus website (http://us.mcafee.com/root/package.asp?pkgid=100&cid=9901) and download the trial version of their software.

2. Install and run their software.

3. Carefully study the application, noting features you like and dislike.

EXERCISE 5.3: **Preventing Sasser**

1. Using resources on the Web or in journals, carefully research the Sasser virus. You may find that www.f-secure.com and Symantec's virus information center at www.sarc.com/avcenter/ are helpful in this exercise.

2. Write a brief essay about how it spread, what damage it caused, and what steps could be taken to prevent it.

EXERCISE 5.4: **Preventing Sobig**

1. Using resources on the Web or in journals, carefully research the Sobig virus. You may find that www.f-secure.com and Symantec's virus information center at www.sarc.com/avcenter/ are helpful in this exercise.

2. Write a brief essay about how it spread, what damage it caused, and what steps could be taken to prevent it.

EXERCISE 5.5: **Learning about Current Virus Attacks**

1. Using resources on the Web or in journals, find a virus that has been spreading in the last 90 days. You may find that www.f-secure.com and Symantec's virus information center at www.sarc.com/avcenter/ are helpful in this exercise.

2. Write a brief essay about how it spread, what damage it caused, and what steps could be taken to prevent it.

EXERCISE 5.6: **Using Antispyware Software**

1. Go to Spy Sweeper website (www.webroot.com/downloads) and download the trial version of the software.

2. Install and run the Spy Sweeper software.

3. Carefully study the application, exploring the options and noting features that you like and dislike.

4. Repeat this process to download and explore Adaware software (which is available from a variety of websites).

5. Assess which of these two antispyware applications would work best for your computer system.

Projects

PROJECT 5.1: **Antivirus Policies**

This activity can also work as a group project.

Considering what you have learned in this chapter and in previous chapters, as well as using outside resources, write an antivirus policy for a small business or school. Your policy should include technical recommendations as well as procedural guidelines. You may choose to consult existing antivirus policy guidelines that you find on the Web to give you some ideas. The following websites may be of some help to you in this project:

- www.sans.org/resources/policies/Anti-virus_Guidelines.pdf
- http://irmc.state.nc.us/documents/approvals/1_VirusPolicy.pdf

However, you should not simply copy their antivirus policies. Rather, you should come up with your own.

PROJECT 5.2: **The Worst Virus Attacks**

Using resources on the Web, books, or journals, find a virus outbreak that you consider to have been the worst in history. Write a brief paper describing this attack, and explain why you think it is the worst. Was it widely spread? How quickly did it spread? What damage did it do?

PROJECT 5.3: **Why Write a Virus?**

A number of hypotheses have been formed regarding why people write a virus. These hypotheses range from the frankly conspiratorial to the academically psychological. Taking whatever position you feel is most likely, write a paper explaining why you think people take the time and effort to write a virus.

Case Study

Chiao Chien manages IT security for a school. Given the wide range of people who use the school's computers, it is difficult for Chien to prevent virus attacks. Chien has a reasonably good budget and has installed antivirus software on every machine. He also has a firewall that has all unneeded ports blocked, and there is a school policy prohibiting the downloading of any software from the Web. Consider the following questions:

- How secure do you think Chien's network is from virus attacks?
- What areas has Chien not secured?
- What recommendations would you make to Chien?

## Chapter 6

Techniques Used by Hackers

Chapter Objectives

After reading this chapter and completing the exercises, you will be able to do the following:

- Understand the basic methodology used by hackers
- Be familiar with some of the basic tools
- Understand the hacking mentality

Introduction

In the preceding five chapters, we have explored computer security and various security breaches. In this chapter we will be exploring the techniques that hackers use to commit computer crimes. Before we go any further, it is important that you realize that many hackers are not criminals. A hacker is a person who wants to understand a system, often by probing its weaknesses. There are even hackers that work for organizations, testing the organization's system security. This is called penetration testing. This is also often referred to as white hat hacking. The EC Council (www.eccouncil.org) even has a certification for this, the Certified Ethical Hacker. Then there are hobbyists, who simply like to probe systems, learning about them. There is a magazine for such people called *2600* (www.2600.com). However, there are people who use hacking techniques to breach systems to steal data, damage systems, or commit other cyber crimes. These people are usually referred to as black hat hackers or crackers.

The techniques presented in this chapter are not only presented to give the reader an understanding of how black hat hackers work, but also provide a method whereby a network administrator can perform a penetration test on his or her own network. By attempting some of these techniques on your network, you can assess your vulnerability. It should be pointed out that you should only do this once you are very comfortable with the techniques in this chapter, and only with permission from senior management.

Basic Terminology

Before we can delve into the world of hacking, we need to discuss the basic terminology used in this community. We have already introduced you to the term *white hat hacker*, one who uses hacking techniques for legal/ethical purposes. And we have discussed the term *black hat hacker* or *cracker*, one who uses hacking techniques for illegal techniques.

There are a few other terms you should be familiar with. A *gray hat hacker* is one who was previously a black hat hacker and turned into a white hat hacker (basically, a former criminal now turned ethical). With the proliferation of tools on the Internet, there are also a lot of people who download some tools (we will examine some of these in this chapter) and perform some cyber attack, without really understanding it. These people are termed *script kiddies* (also sometimes spelled kiddy's). Another important term is *phreaking*. This refers to hacking into phone systems. Hacking of phone systems actually predates hacking computer systems.

The Reconnaissance Phase

Any intelligent/experienced hacker is going to first attempt to find out information about a target before actually attempting an attack. Just as a bank robber would want to know about a bank's alarm systems, number of guards, police response time, etc., a black hat hacker will want to know about your systems security. What may surprise you is how much information can be found easily on the Internet, without even attaching to the target system.

Passive Scanning Techniques

One of the easiest things one can do is check the target organization's websites. It is common for businesses to put information up that can be very useful to an attacker. For example, let's assume company XYZ lists John Doe as their IT manager. An enterprising hacker scans bulletin boards and discussion groups for references to John Doe at XYZ. That attacker might find information useful in spear phishing attacks (phishing targeted at a specific individual or group of individuals), or the attacker might find information useful in social engineering. For example, a number of former employees complain that John Doe is demanding and quick to fire people. Then, an enterprising hacker could call someone at XYZ claiming to be working for John Doe. The hacker claims he is trying to log on remotely to that person's computer to update that person's system. After a few moments, the hacker tells the person he forgot the password John Doe gave him and is very concerned he will get fired if he doesn't complete this assignment; then he asks that person for his or her password. The information the attacker gleaned from the Web gave him enough information to make this social engineering attack plausible.

It is also possible for an attacker to scan bulletin boards, chat rooms, discussion groups, etc. looking for questions from IT staff at the target organization. For example, if an administrator posts in a discussion group asking about a particular server problem, this can give the attacker valuable information about that target network.

Another way attackers can use the Web to find out information about a target is through job ads. For example if a company routinely advertises for ASP.Net developers, and never for PHP, Pearl, etc., then it is likely that their web applications are developed with ASP.Net running on a Windows web server (Internet Information Services). This can allow the attacker to focus only on a small group of possible attacks (those against ASP.Net/Windows). Other information can be garnered from job ads. For example, if a small company, less than 200 employees, has an advertisement for a network administrator twice a year, it is more likely that the last administrator is no longer with them. A small company would not need multiple administrators. Knowing the current administrator is new means he or she is not as familiar with their own systems. Also if this trend of advertising for new administrators extends over a couple of years, it means the company has high turnover and there is some problem the attacker may be able to exploit.

There are also specific websites that provide information that an attacker may find useful. The first such website is netcraft.com, shown in Figure 6.1. This website provides information about websites. For example, you can find out what kind of server a site is running, and in some cases how long it has been since it was last rebooted.

FIGURE 6.1   www.Netcraft.com.

Another site that can be useful for attackers is www.archive.org. This site, shown in Figure 6.2, archives older versions of websites. The server scours the web archiving sites. The frequency with which a site is archived depends on its popularity.

Active Scanning Techniques

The previously mentioned techniques are all considered passive, as they do not require the attacker to connect to the target system. Since the attacker is not actually connecting to the target system, it is impossible for an intrusion-detection system (IDS) to detect the scan. Active scans are far more reliable, but may be detected by the target system. There are a few types of active scans.

FIGURE 6.2   www.archive.org.

Port Scanning

Port scanning is the process of attempting to contact each network port on the target system and see which ones are open. There are 1,024 well-known ports that are usually associated with specific services. For example port 161 is associated with simple network management protocol. If an attacker detects port 161 open on the target system, he or she might decide to try SNMP-related attacks. Even more information can be derived from a port scan. For example, ports 137, 138, and 139 are all associated with NetBIOS, a very old Windows method of network communication, not used in Windows anymore. However NetBIOS is often used for systems where Windows machines need to communicate with Linux machines. So discovering those ports open reveals something about the target network.

A simple Google search for "port scanner" will reveal a host of well-known, widely used, and often free port scanners. However, the most popular port scanner in the hacking and security community is the free tool Nmap (http://nmap.org/). There is a Windows version of it, shown in Figure 6.3.

Nmap allows you to customize your scan making it more or less stealthy, and targeting certain systems. The most common types of scans are listed here:

- **Ping scan:** This scan simply sends a ping to the target port. Many network administrators block incoming ICMP packets for the purpose of stopping ping scans.

- **Connect scan:** This is the most reliable scan, but also the most likely to be detected. With this type of scan a complete connection is made with the target system.

- **SYN scan:** This scan is very stealthy. Most systems accept SYN (Synchronize) requests. This scan is similar to the SYN flood DoS attack described in Chapter 4, "Denial of Service Attacks." In this scan you send a SYN packet, but never respond when the system sends a SYN/ACK. However, unlike the DoS SYN flood, you only send one packet per port. This is also called the half-open scan.

- **FIN scan:** This scan has the FIN flag, or connection finished flag set. This is also not an unusual packet for systems to receive, so is considered stealthy.

FIGURE 6.3 Nmap GUI

Each of these scans provokes a different response on the target machine and thus provides different information to the port scanner:

- With a FIN Scan or an XMAS scan if the target port is closed the system sends back an RST flag packet (RST means reset). If it is open there is no response.

- With a SYN scan, if the port is closed, the response is an RST; if it is open, the response is a SYN/ACK.

- ACK scans and NULL scans only work on UNIX systems.

Nmap also lets you set a number of flags (either with the command-line version of Nmap or the Windows version). These customize your scan. The allowed flags are listed here:

-O	Detects operating system
-sP	Is a ping scan
-sT	TCP connect scan
-sS	SYN scan
-sF	FIN scan
-sX	Xmas tree scan
-sN	NULL scan
-sU	UDP scan
-sO	Protocol scan
-sA	ACK scan
-sW	Windows scan
-sR	RPC scan
-sL	List/DNS scan
-sI	Idle scan
-Po	Don't ping
-PT	TCP ping
-PS	SYN ping
-PI	ICMP ping
-PB	TCP and ICMP ping
-PM	ICMP netmask
-oN	Normal output
-oX	XML output
-oG	Greppable output
-oA	All output
-T	Timing

	-T0	paranoid
	-T 1	Sneaking
	-T 2	Polite
	-T 3	Normal
	-T 4	Aggressive
	-T 5	Insane

As you can see there are a number of options available to an attacker using Nmap. One can spend a lot of time just learning Nmap. There are, of course, a number of other port scanning tools. We have focused on Nmap because it is free and it is so widely used. It also is prominently figured on the EC Council Certified Ethical Hacker certification.

Vulnerability Assessment

Vulnerability assessment is checking a system to see if it is vulnerable to specific attacks. These tools can be used by attackers to assess your system; however, they are designed to allow you to assess your system. These tools are not particularly stealthy and thus will probably be detected by an intrusion-detection system. In fact, vulnerability assessment tools are commonly used by network administrators to test their own networks. These tools will be covered in Chapter 11, "Network Scanning and Vulnerability Scanning."

Enumeration

Another technique that is popular before the actual attack is enumeration. Enumeration is simply the process of finding out what is on the target system. If the target is an entire network, then the attacker is trying to find out what servers, computers, and printers are on that network. If the target is a specific computer, then the attacker is trying to find out what users and shared folders exist on that system.

A simple Google search will help you find a number of enumeration tools. One of the easiest to use is Cain and Abel, shown in Figure 6.4.

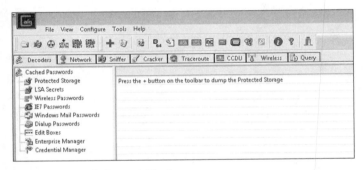

FIGURE 6.4   Cain and Abel.

Cain and Abel can do a lot more than just enumeration, but for our purposes that is what we are focusing on here. For enumeration, simply click on the Network tab and you will find all machines connected to the network you are on. This obviously requires some level of access before you can enumerate the target network.

A few other enumeration tools that are popular with hackers and can easily be found on the Internet are

- Sid2User
- Cheops (Linux only)
- UserInfo
- UserDump
- DumpSec
- Netcat
- NBTDump

This is not an exhaustive list, but it includes some of the most widely used enumeration tools.

To defend against scanning you should use the following techniques:

- Be careful how much information you put on the Internet about your organization and its network.

- Make it a company policy that technical personnel who use bulletin boards, chat rooms, etc. for technical data must not use their real name or reveal the company's name.

- Use an IDS that detects many scans.

- Block incoming Internet Control Message Protocol (ICMP) packets.

These won't make scanning and reconnaissance impossible on your system, but they will make certain the attacker gathers significantly less information.

Actual Attacks

Now that we have discussed how attackers scan a target system, let's look at a few attacks that are commonly used. Obviously this won't be an exhaustive list, but it will provide you some insight into the attack methodologies used. In Chapter 4 we discussed denial of service attacks and some tools used to cause these attacks. In this section we will look at other sorts of attacks and the techniques and tools used to make them happen.

SQL Script Injection

This may be the most popular attack on websites. In recent years, more websites have taken steps to ameliorate the dangers of this attack, but my informal surveys still find about one-third of websites susceptible. This attack is based on passing structured query language commands to a web application and getting the website to execute them.

The way the most basic SQL injection works is this. Many websites/applications have a page where users enter their username and password. That username and password will have to be checked against some database to see if they are valid. Regardless of the type of database (Oracle, SQL Server, MySQL, etc.), all databases speak Structured Query Language (SQL). SQL looks and functions a great deal like English. For example, to check a username and password you might want to query the database and see if there is any entry in the users table that matches that username and password that was entered. If there is, then you have a match. The SQL statement might look something like this:

```
'SELECT * FROM tblUsers WHERE USERNAME = 'jdoe' AND PASSWORD = 'letmein'
```

The problem with this, while it is valid SQL, is that we have hard coded the username and password. For a real website we would have to take whatever the user entered into the username field and password field and check that. This can be easily done (regardless of what programming or scripting language the website is programmed in). It would look something like this:

```
'SELECT * FROM tblUsers WHERE USERNAME = '" + txtUsername.Text +' AND PASSWORD = '"
+ txtPassword.Text +"'" .
```

If you enter username `'jdoe'` and password `'letmein'`, this code produces the following SQL command:

```
SELECT * FROM tblUsers WHERE USERNAME = 'jdoe' AND PASSWORD = 'letmein'
```

Now if there is a username jdoe in tblUsers, and the password for it is letmein, then this user will be logged on. If not, then an error will occur.

SQL injection works by putting in some SQL into the username and password block that is always true. For example, suppose you enter `'OR X=X'` into the username and password boxes. This will cause the program to create this query:

```
SELECT * FROM tblUsers WHERE USERNAME = ''OR X=X' AND PASSWORD = ''OR X=X'
```

Notice we start with a single quotation mark (`'`) before the `OR X=X`. This is to close the open quote the attacker knows must be in the code. And if you see `''`, that essentially is a blank or null. So what we are telling the database is to log us in if the username is blank, or if X=X, and if the password is blank, or if X=X. If you think about this for a second, you will see that X always equals x, so this will always be true.

There is no significance to `'OR X=X'`; it is simply a statement that will always be true. Attackers try other similar statements, such as the following:

```
' or 'a' ='a
' or '1' ='1
' or (1=1)
```

This is only one example of SQL injection; there are other methods, but this is the most common. The defense against this attack is to filter all user input before processing it. This is often referred to as input validation. This prevents an attacker from entering SQL commands rather than a username and password. Unfortunately, many sites do not filter user input and are still vulnerable to this attack.

Cross-Site Scripting

With cross-site scripting, an attacker injects client-side script into web pages viewed by other users. The key is that the attacker enters scripts into an area that other users interact with. So that when they go to that part of the site the attacker's script is executed, rather than the intended website functionality. For example, assume a shopping site allows users to review products. Rather than typing in a review, the attacker types in JavaScript that redirects the user to a phishing website. When another user views that "review," the script will execute and take them to the new site. Again, this can be prevented by simply filtering all user input. As of this writing, all the major online shopping portals, such as Amazon.com, do filter input and are not susceptible to this attack. However, many smaller sites are still susceptible.

This attack, as well as SQL injection, illustrate why it is critical that all IT personnel be familiar with security, not just security administrators. If more web developers were more familiar with security, these two attacks would not be widespread.

Password Cracking

Doing password cracking is easiest when one can actually get physical access to a machine. This is not as difficult as it sounds. Many organizations (such as universities) have kiosk machines were one can use the system with minimal/guest privileges. A skilled hacker can use this access to gain further access.

OphCrack

A very popular tool for cracking Windows passwords is OphCrack. OphCrack can be downloaded from http://ophcrack.sourceforge.net. It is based on an understanding of how Windows passwords work. Windows passwords are stored in a hash file in one of the system directories, usually C:\WINDOWS\system32\config\ in a SAM file. SAM is an acronym for Security Accounts Manager. The passwords are stored as a hash. (Hashes will be discussed in detail in Chapter 8, "Encryption.") What Windows does is hash the password you type in and compare it to the hash found in the SAM file. If there is a match, then you are logged in. Now to prevent someone from copying the SAM file and taking it off to try to brute force it, as soon as Windows begins the boot process, the SAM file is locked by the operating system. What OphCrack does is to boot to Linux and then get the SAM file and look up the hashed passwords in a large table of hashed values it has, looking for a match. If it finds one, then the matching text in that table of hashed values is the password. You can see OphCrack in Figure 6.5.

FIGURE 6.5   OphCrack.

This tool is remarkably easy to use. Just put the OphCrack CD into the machine, reboot. During the boot process you can press F12 for a boot menu and tell the system to boot from CD. You will then start OphCrack. It should be noted that longer passwords (as of this writing longer than 10 characters) are usually not crackable by OphCrack.

Now assuming OphCrack is successful (it isn't always), what can the attacker do with this? At best he or she simply got the local machine admin account, and not a domain account. Well, this can be used to then gain domain access. One simple technique is to create a script that will in turn create a domain admin account. The script is simple:

```
net user /domain /add localaccountname password
net group /domain "Domain Admins" /add localaccount
```

Now obviously if the attacker executes this script it will not work. One must be a domain admin for it to work. So the attacker saves this script to the all users startup folder. The next time a domain admin logs on to this system, the script will successfully execute. But the attacker may not want to wait until that happens. So in order to speed up the process, the attacker causes some minor problem in the system (changes settings, alters configuration, etc.). In many organizations, the tech support personnel are in the domain admins group. When a tech support person logs on to the system to correct the problem, the script will successfully run.

Summary

In this chapter we have examined just a few techniques hackers utilize. But these techniques and tools have illustrated the need for a variety of security measures. The scanning techniques illustrate the need for blocking certain traffic at the firewall and for running an IDS. The SQL injection attack demonstrates why security must be a part of application development. And the OphCrack tool illustrates why physical security is important and why the principle of least privileges is important. Putting tech support staff into the domain admins group violates the concept of least privileges and makes the privilege escalation script possible.

Test Your Skills

MULTIPLE CHOICE QUESTIONS

1. SQL injection is based on what?

   A. Having database admin privileges

   B. Creating an SQL statement that is always true

   C. Creating an SQL statement that will force access

   D. Understanding web programming

2. Which of the following is a vulnerability scanner specifically for Windows systems?

   A. Nmap

   B. OphCrack

   C. Nessus

   D. MBSA

3. How can you prevent cross-site scripting?

   A. Filter user input.

   B. Use an IDS.

   C. Use a firewall.

   D. It cannot be prevented.

4. What is an advantage of using Nessus?

   A. It is free for businesses.

   B. It has a wide range of vulnerabilities it can check for.

   C. It is designed for Windows systems.

   D. It includes an IDS.

5. OphCrack depends on the attacker doing what?

   A. Getting physical access to the machine

   B. Getting domain admin privileges

   C. Using social engineering

   D. Using a scanning tool

6. If you wish to view items that have been removed from a website, what is the best way to do that?

   A. Use Nessus.

   B. Use Nmap.

   C. Use www.netcraft.com.

   D. Use www.archive.org.

7. Which of the following is a popular port scanner?

   A. Nessus

   B. OphCrack

   C. MBSA

   D. Nmap

8. Blocking incoming ICMP packets will prevent what type of scan?

   A. SYN

   B. Ping

   C. FIN

   D. Stealth

9. A person who uses hacking techniques for illegal activities is referred to as what?

   A. A hacker

   B. A gray hat hacker

   C. A phreaker

   D. A cracker

10. A person who hacks into phone systems is referred to as what?

    A. A hacker

    B. A gray hat hacker

    C. A phreaker

    D. A cracker

11. A person who uses tools to hack without understanding the underlying technology is called what?

    A. A script kiddy

    B. A gray hat hacker

    C. A novice

    D. A white hat hacker

12. Trying to list all the servers on a network is referred to as what?

    A. Port scanning

    B. Enumeration

    C. Vulnerability scanning

    D. Scouting

13. Which of the following is a popular enumeration tool?

    A. Nessus

    B. Nmap

    C. MBSA

    D. Cheops

14. Which of the following is considered the most stealthy port scan?

    A. SYN

    B. Connect

    C. Ping

    D. NMAP

15. What is the most stealthy way to find out what type of server a website is running?

    A. Use Nmap.

    B. Use Cain and Abel.

    C. Use www.netcraft.com.

    D. Use www.archive.org.

EXERCISES

EXERCISE 6.1: Using www.Archive.Org

This exercise gives you practice in using www.archive.org. Go to www.archive.org and pull up at least two previous versions of your college/university's website. What information can you find that is no longer on the website?

EXERCISE 6.2: **Using Nmap**

This exercise introduces you to the Nmap tool. You should download and install Nmap. Then run at least three different scans on either your own computer or on a designated lab computer.

NOTE: While it is not illegal to scan a computer, it may violate some security policies for some colleges and universities. Make certain you only scan a designated lab computer.

EXERCISE 6.3: **Using OphCrack**

Download OphCrack to a CD. Then reboot your own machine to OphCrack and attempt to crack your own local passwords.

NOTE: It is critical that you only use this on your own machine or a designated lab machine. Using it on other machines will probably violate security policies at your college/university/company.

EXERCISE 6.4: **Using Netcraft.com**

Visit www.netcraft.com and do a search on at least three different websites of your choosing. Note what information you are able to gather about the website.

PROJECTS

PROJECT 6.1: **Passive Reconnaissance**

Select a local organization, and conduct a passive reconnaissance. This should include searching job boards, the organization's own website, user groups/bulletin boards, social networking sites, www.archive.org, etc. Gather as much information about the target network as you can.

PROJECT 6.2: **Port Scanners**

Use your favorite search engine to locate at least two other port scanners. Download and install them, then try them on your own machine or a designated lab computer. Compare and contrast these tools to Nmap. Are they easier to use? More informative?

PROJECT 6.3: **MBSA**

Download and install MBSA and run a vulnerability scan on your own computer or on a designated lab computer. What problems did you find? Was the tool easy to use?

Case Study

Jane is a hacker intent on breaking into the XYZ Corporation. She uses a variety of passive reconnaissance techniques and gathers extensive information about the company. Jane finds out what model routers are being used from network administrator questions/comments in user groups. She finds a complete list of the IT staff and their phone numbers from a personnel directory on the company website. She also was able to find out what services are running by using a port scan.

From this scenario, consider the following questions:

1. What reasonable steps could the company have taken to prevent Jane from finding out about company hardware, like router models?

2. What steps should the company take to prevent or at least reduce the efficacy of port scans?

## Chapter 7

Industrial Espionage in Cyberspace

Chapter Objectives

After reading this chapter and completing the exercises, you will be able to do the following:

- ■ Know what is meant by industrial espionage
- ■ Understand the low-technology methods used to attempt industrial espionage
- ■ Be aware of how spyware is used in espionage
- ■ Know how to protect a system from espionage

Introduction

When you hear the word espionage, perhaps you conjure up a number of exciting and glamorous images. Perhaps you have visions of a well-dressed man who drinks martinis, shaken but not stirred, traveling to glamorous locations with equally glamorous travel companions. Or perhaps you envision some exciting covert operation with high-speed car chases and guns blazing in faraway exotic lands. Contrary to popular media portrayals, espionage is often much less exciting than those visions. The ultimate goal of espionage is to obtain information that would not otherwise be made available. Generally, espionage is best done with as little fanfare as possible. Blazing gun battles and glamorous locations tend to be the antithesis of intelligence gathering. Rather, information is the goal. If possible, it is best to obtain that information without the target organization even realizing that its information has been compromised.

Many people assume that such spying is only engaged in by governments, intelligence agencies, and nefarious international organizations, such as Al Qaida. While those entities do indeed engage in espionage, they are certainly not the only organizations that do so. The aforementioned organizations desire to acquire information for political and military goals. However, economic goals are also dependent on accurate and often sensitive data. With billions of dollars at stake, private companies can become engaged in industrial espionage as either a target or a perpetrator. What company would not like to know exactly what its competitor is doing? In fact, corporate or economic espionage is on the rise.

Corporate or economic espionage is a growing problem, but it can be difficult to accurately assess just how great a problem it is. Companies that perpetrate corporate espionage do not share the fact that they do it, for obvious reasons. Companies that are victims of such espionage often do not wish to reveal that fact, either. Revealing that their security was compromised could have a negative impact on their stock value. It is also possible, in certain cases, that such a breach of security might open the company to liability claims from customers whose data may have been compromised. For these reasons, companies often are hesitant to disclose any industrial espionage activities. Because you will want to protect yourself and your company, it is important that you learn about espionage methods and protections. In the exercises at the end of this chapter, you will run antispyware, key loggers, and screen-capture software so that you are aware of how they work and, hence, will be cognizant of the risks they pose. While we did cover those in previous chapters, we will expand on that in this chapter's exercises.

What Is Industrial Espionage?

Industrial espionage is simply the use of spying techniques to find out key information that is of economic value. Such data might include details on a competitor's new project, a list of a competitor's clients, research data, or any information that might give the spying organization an economic advantage. While the rationale for corporate espionage is different from military espionage, corporate techniques are often the same as those methods employed by intelligence agencies and can include electronic monitoring, photocopying files, or compromising a member of the target organization. Not only does economic espionage use the same techniques as intelligence agencies, but it often also uses the same people. There have been a number of incidents in which former intelligence agents were found working in corporate espionage. When such individuals bring their skills and training to the world of corporate espionage, the situation becomes much more difficult for computer security experts.

In Practice

Leaving with Sensitive Data

While various computer experts and government agencies attempt to estimate the impact and spread of corporate espionage, its very nature makes accurate estimates impossible. Not only do the perpetrators not wish to disclose their crimes, but often the victims will not disclose the event, either. However, anecdotal evidence would suggest that the most common form of espionage is simply an employee who quits, takes a job with another firm, and leaves with sensitive data. In many cases, these employees choose data that is readily available within the company and, as such, the data is considered a "gray area" as to its confidentiality. For example, a salesperson may leave with a printout of contacts and customers so that he can solicit them on behalf of the next employer. It is critical that you have a very well-worded nondisclosure and noncompete agreement with all employees. It is best to solicit the services of an employment attorney to draw up this agreement. Additionally, you might consider limiting an employee's access to data prior to terminating his or her employment. You should also conduct exit interviews and consider confiscating items such as company phonebooks, which may at first seem insignificant but which could contain data useful to another company. It is also the case that thumb drives, smart phones, and other technologies provide a method for taking data out of a company. Some companies restrict the use of these devices.

Information as an Asset

Many people are used to viewing tangible objects as assets but have difficulty appreciating how mere information can be a real asset. Companies spend billions of dollars every year on research and development. The discovered information is worth at least the amount of resources taken to derive the information plus the economic gain produced by the information. For example, if a company spends $200,000 researching a process that will in turn generate $1 million in revenue, then that data is worth at least $1.2 million. You can think of this economic gain as a simple equation:

```
VI (value of information) = C (cost to produce) + VG (value gained)
```

While some people are not yet fully cognizant of the concept, data does indeed represent a valuable asset. When we speak of the "information age" or our "information-based economy," it is important to realize that these terms are not just buzzwords. Information is a real commodity. It is as much an economic asset as any other item in the company's possession. In fact, it is most often the case that the data residing on a company's computer is worth far more than the hardware and software of the computer system itself. It is certainly the case that the data is much more difficult to replace than the computer hardware and software.

To help you truly appreciate the concept of information as a commodity, consider the process of earning a college degree. You spend four years sitting in various classrooms. You pay a significant amount of money for the privilege of sitting in a room and listening to someone speak at length on some topic. At the end of the four years, the only tangible product you receive is a single piece of paper. Surely you can get a piece of paper for far less cost and with much less effort. What you actually paid for was the information you received. The same is true of the value of many professions. Doctors, attorneys, engineers, consultants, managers, and so forth all are consulted for their expert information. Information itself is the valuable commodity.

The data stored in computer systems has a high value for two reasons. First, there is a great deal of time and effort that goes into creating and analyzing the data. If you spend six months with a team of five people gathering and analyzing information, then that information is worth at least an amount equal to the salaries and benefits of those people for that length of time. Second, data often has intrinsic value, apart from the time and effort spent acquiring those facts. If the facts are about a proprietary process, invention, or algorithm, its value is obvious. However, any data that might provide a competitive edge is inherently valuable. For example, insurance companies frequently employ teams of statisticians and actuaries who use the latest technology to try to predict the risks associated with any given group of potential insureds. The resulting statistical information might be quite valuable to a competing insurance company. Even a customer contact list has a certain inherent value.

Thus, as you work in the computer security field, always keep in mind that any data that might have economic value is an asset to your organization and that such data provides an attractive target for any competitors who may not have ethical inhibitions against using espionage. If your company management thinks that this threat is not real, then they are very much mistaken. Any company is a potential victim of corporate espionage. You should take steps to protect your valuable information—and the first critical step in this process is asset identification.

Asset identification is the process of listing the assets that you believe support your organization. This list should include things that impact direct day-to-day operations as well as those that are tied to your company's services or products. The CERT website (www.cert.org/archive/pdf/tutorial-workbook.pdf) offers a very useful worksheet that you can use to itemize the assets in your organization. This workbook also offers a number of other useful worksheets for assuring information security within your organization. As the table of contents in Figure 7.1 shows, this workbook is also a tutorial that steps you through all the information security considerations.

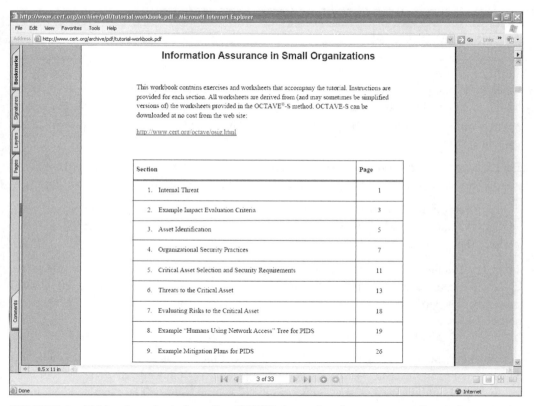

FIGURE 7.1   Table of contents from the CERT Information Assurance on Small Organizations workbook.

Table 7.1 is a variation on the worksheet provided by CERT. Armed with this table and based on your knowledge and experience with the company, you can complete your asset identification following the steps outlined below.

TABLE 7.1   Asset Identification Worksheet

Information	Systems	Services and Applications	Other Assets

1. In the first column of the table, list the information assets. You should list the types of information used by people in your company—the information people need to do their jobs. Examples are product designs, software programs, system designs, documentation, customer orders, and personnel data.

2. For each entry in the *Information* column, fill in the names of the systems on which the information resides. In each case, ask yourself which systems people need to perform their jobs.

3. For each entry in the Information column, fill in the names of the related applications and services. In each case, ask yourself what applications or services are needed for individuals to perform their jobs.

4. In the last column, list any other assets that may or may not be directly related to the other three columns. Examples are databases with customer information, systems used in production, word processors used to produce documentation, compilers used by programmers, and human resources systems.

Once you complete the proceeding steps and fill out the Asset Identification worksheet, you will have a good understanding of the critical assets for your organization. With this information, you will know how best to devote your defensive efforts. Some specific protective steps will be examined later in this chapter.

Real-World Examples of Industrial Espionage

Now that you have been introduced to the concept of corporate espionage, let's look at five actual cases. These case studies are of real-world espionage found in various news sources. This section should give you an idea of what types of espionage activities actually occur. Note that while some of these cases are a bit old, they do illustrate the way industrial espionage is done. And it is frequently the case that details of an industrial espionage incident do not emerge until many years later, if at all.

Example 1: VIA Technology

VIA Technology actually provides two examples of industrial espionage. In the first instance, the chief executive officer (CEO) of the firm, which was based in Taipei, was indicted for copyright infringement for allegedly stealing technology from one of his own customers, a networking company called D-Link (Network World Fusion, 2003).

According to the allegations, VIA engineer Jeremy Chang left VIA to work for D-Link. For several months while at D-Link, Chang continued to receive a paycheck from VIA. Then he promptly resigned from D-Link and returned to VIA. Once Chang rejoined VIA, a D-Link document that detailed one of their simulation programs for testing integrated circuits was posted to an FTP server owned by VIA.

The prosecutors allege that Chang continued to receive a check from VIA because he had never really resigned. They allege that Chang was in fact a "plant" sent to D-Link to acquire D-Link's technology for VIA. VIA maintains that his continuation to receive a check was simply an oversight, and Chang denies that he posted the document in question. Whatever the truth of the case, it should make any employer think twice about hiring decisions and nondisclosure agreements.

To make matters worse for VIA, another company accused VIA of stealing code for its optical readers. In both cases, the story of the possible theft of technology alone has had a negative impact on the stock value of both companies.

Example 2: General Motors

In 1993, General Motors (GM) and one if its partners began to investigate a former executive, Inaki Lopez. GM alleged that Lopez and seven other former GM employees had transferred GM proprietary information to Volkswagen (VW) in Germany via GM's own network (Brinks et al., 2003). The information allegedly stolen included component price data, proprietary construction plans, internal cost calculations, and a purchasing list.

In 1996, GM followed up the ongoing criminal investigation with civil litigation against Lopez, VW, and the other employees. In November 1996, GM expanded its legal battle by invoking the various Racketeer Influenced and Corrupt Organizations Act (RICO) statutes, originally intended to be used against organized crime conspiracies (*Economist*, 1996). By May 2000, a federal grand jury indicted Lopez on six counts related to fraud and racketeering. As of this writing, the case is not resolved (*USA Today*, 2000). At the time Lopez was indicted, he was residing in Spain and the U.S. Justice Department was negotiating for his extradition. Thus, you can see that corporate espionage is neither new nor restricted to technology companies.

Example 3: Interactive Television Technologies, Inc.

On August 13, 1998, someone broke into the computer systems of Interactive Television Technologies, Inc. and stole the data for a project the company was working on (Secure Telecom, 1998). That project involved four years of intense research and a substantial financial investment. The product was to be a way whereby anyone with a television could have Internet access via the Web. This product, code named "Butler," would have been worth a substantial amount to its inventors. However, with all the research material stolen, it was only a matter of time before several other companies came out with competing products, thus preventing Interactive Television Technologies from pursuing a patent.

To date, no arrests have been made and no leads are available in this case. This situation was a case of very skillful hackers breaking into a computer system and taking exactly what they needed. One can only speculate about their motives. They may well have sold the research data to competitors of Inter-active Television Technologies, or they may have simply put the data out in the open via the Internet. Whatever the motives or profits for the perpetrators, the outcome for the victim company was catastrophic.

Example 4: Bloomberg, Inc.

According to the *American Bar Association Journal* (2003), in August 2003, Oleg Zezev, a 29-year-old PC technician from Kazakhstan, broke into the Bloomberg Inc. computer system and used the alias Alex to obtain information and then blackmail the firm.

Zezev entered Bloomberg's computer system and accessed various accounts, including Michael Bloomberg's (CEO and founder of Bloomberg L.P.) personal account as well as accounts for other Bloomberg employees and customers. Zezev copied information from these accounts, including email inbox screens, Michael Bloomberg's credit card numbers, and screens relating to the internal functions of Bloomberg. He also copied internal information that was only accessible by Bloomberg employees.

Zezev then threatened to expose the data he had stolen to the public and, in essence, tell everyone exactly how he had broken into Bloomberg's network unless he received $200,000.

After deliberating for less than six hours, the jury in the U.S. District Court in Manhattan found the perpetrator guilty of all four charges: conspiracy, attempted extortion, sending threatening electronic messages, and computer intrusion. Although this is not industrial espionage in the classic sense, it does illustrate the compromising situations in which a company and its employees can be placed when security is breached.

Example 5: Avant Software

In 1997, executives at Avant Software in Santa Clara County, California, were charged with attempting to steal secrets from their rival, Cadence Design. The case focused on a former consultant for Avant, Mitsuru "Mitch" Igusa. After Igusa had taken a job at Cadence, he began emailing files to his home; it is alleged that he later turned those files over to Avant.

Industrial Espionage and You

These five cases notwithstanding, most companies will deny any involvement in anything that even hints at espionage. However, not all companies are quite so shy about the issue. Larry Ellison, CEO of Oracle Corporation, has openly defended his decision to hire private investigators to sift through

Microsoft garbage in an attempt to garner information (CNET News, 2001). Clearly, espionage is no longer a problem just for governments and defense contractors. It is a very real concern in the modern business world. The savvy computer security professional will be aware of this concern and will take the appropriate proactive steps.

How Does Espionage Occur?

There are two ways that espionage can occur. An easy, low-technology avenue would be for current or former employees to simply take the data or for someone to use social engineering methods (discussed in Chapter 3, "Cyber Stalking, Fraud, and Abuse") to extract data from unsuspecting company employees. The second, more technology-oriented method is for the individuals to use spyware, which includes the use of cookies and key loggers. There are other technological methods we will discuss.

Low-Tech Industrial Espionage

Corporate espionage can occur without the benefit of computers or the Internet. Disgruntled former (or current) employees can copy sensitive documents, divulge corporate strategies and plans, or perhaps reveal sensitive information. In fact, whether the method used is technological or not, disgruntled employees are the single greatest security risk to any organization. A corporate spy need not hack into a system in order to obtain sensitive and confidential information if an employee is willing to simply hand over the information. Just as with military and political espionage, the motives for the employee to divulge the information vary. Some engage in such acts for obvious financial gains. Others may elect to reveal company secrets merely because they are angry over some injustice (real or imagined). Whatever the motive, any organization has to be cognizant of the fact that it has any number of employees who may be unhappy with some situation and have the potential to divulge confidential information.

Certainly, one can obtain information without the benefit of modern technology; however, computer technology (and various computer-related tactics) can certainly assist in corporate espionage, even if only in a peripheral manner. Some incidents of industrial espionage are conducted with technology that requires little skill on the part of the perpetrator, as illustrated in Figures 7.2 and 7.3. This technology can include using universal serial bus (USB) flash drives, compact discs (CDs), or other portable media to take information out of the organization. Even disgruntled employees who wish to undermine the company or make a profit for themselves will find it easier to burn a wealth of data onto a CD and carry that out in their coat pocket rather than attempt to photocopy thousands of documents and smuggle them out. And the new USB flash drives, smaller than your average key chain, are a dream come true for corporate spies. These drives can plug into any USB port and store a tremendous amount of data. As of this writing, one can easily purchase small portable devices capable of holding 2 terabytes or more of data.

FIGURE 7.2   Low-tech espionage is easy.

FIGURE 7.3   Low-tech espionage is portable.

While information can be taken from your company without overt hacking of the system, you should keep in mind that if your system is unsecure, it is entirely possible that an outside party would compromise your system and obtain that information without an employee as an accomplice. In addition to these methods, there are other low-tech, or virtually "no-tech," methods used to extract information. Social engineering, which was discussed at great length in Chapter 3, is the process of talking a person into giving up information she otherwise would not divulge. This technique can be applied to industrial espionage in a number of ways.

The first and most obvious use of social engineering in industrial espionage is in direct conversation in which the perpetrator attempts to get the targeted employee to reveal sensitive data. As illustrated in Figure 7.4, employees will often inadvertently divulge information to a supplier, vendor or salesperson without thinking the information is important or that it could be given to anyone. This involves simply trying to get the target to talk more than they should. In 2009, there was a widely publicized case of a Russian spy ring working in the United States. One of their tactics was simply to befriend key employees in target organizations and, through ongoing conversations, slowly elicit key data.

Another interesting way of using social engineering would be via email. In very large organizations, one cannot know every member. This loophole allows the clever industrial spy to send an email message claiming to come from some other department and perhaps simply asking for sensitive data. A corporate spy might, for example, forge an email to appear to be coming from the legal office of the target company requesting an executive summary of some research project.

FIGURE 7.4   Social engineering used as low-tech espionage.

Computer security expert Andrew Briney (Information Security, 2003) places people as the number one issue in computer security.

Spyware Used in Industrial Espionage

Clearly, any software that can monitor activities on a computer can be used in industrial espionage. *Security IT World,* an online e-zine, featured an article in their October 2003 issue that dealt with the fact that monitoring a computer is an easy thing to do in the twenty-first century. The problem still persists to this day, with many security experts stating that spyware is at least as widespread as viruses. One method to accomplish monitoring is via spyware, which we discussed in detail in Chapter 5, "Malware." Clearly, software or hardware that logs key strokes or takes screenshots would be most advantageous to the industrial spy.

The application of this type of software to espionage is obvious. A spy could get screenshots of sensitive documents, capture logon information for databases, or in fact capture a sensitive document as it is being typed. Any of these methods would give a spy unfettered access to all data that is processed on a machine that contains spyware.

Steganography Used in Industrial Espionage

Steganography is a different way of keeping messages secret. Rather than hide them through encryption, it protects communication via obscuring them. Messages are hidden within images. And in some cases other images are hidden within images. The word steganography comes from the Greek *steganos*, meaning covered or secret, and *graphy*, meaning writing or drawing. There are several technical means to accomplish this, but the most common is to conceal the data in the least significant bits of an image file. However, data can be concealed in any sort of digital file.

It should also be noted that historically there have been nontechnical means of hiding messages. A few notable examples include the following:

- The ancient Chinese wrapped notes in wax and swallowed them for transport.

- In ancient Greece a messenger's head might be shaved, a message written on his head, then his hair was allowed to grow back.

- In 1518, Johannes Trithmeus wrote a book on cryptography and described a technique where a message was hidden by having each letter taken as a word from a specific column

You might think that steganography requires a great deal of technical knowledge to accomplish; however, there are many software packages available that will perform the steganography for you. Quick Stego and Invisible Secrets are two very easy-to-use software tools that will do steganography for you. MP3Stego is a free tool that hides data inside MP4 files. These are just a few of the tools that one can find on the Internet. The widespread availability of cheap or free tools that are easy to use makes steganography a greater threat to any organization.

Phone Taps and Bugs

Of course, there is always the possibility of using phone taps. A phone tap is simply the process of tying into the phone line at some point and intercepting calls. This is often done at some utility location inside the building one wishes to tap. Obviously, this sort of attack requires the attacker to at least enter on or near the premises, compromise phone equipment, and to have the skill to tap into the phone line.

Protecting against Industrial Espionage

By now, you are aware that there are many ways that your organization's valuable information assets can be compromised. The question thus becomes this: What steps can you take to alleviate the danger? Note that I said "alleviate" the danger. There is nothing you can do to make any system, any infor-mation, or any person, totally secure. Totally unbreakable security is simply a myth. The best you can do is work to achieve a level of security that makes the effort required to get information more costly than the value of the information.

One obvious protection is to employ antispyware software. As was mentioned earlier in this book, many antivirus programs also have antispyware capabilities. This software, coupled with other security measures such as firewalls and intrusion-detection software (both examined in Chapter 9, "Computer Security Software"), should drastically reduce the chance that an outside party will compromise your organization's data. Furthermore, implementing organizational policies (also discussed in Chapter 9) that help guide employees on safely using computer and Internet resources will make your system rela-tively secure. If you add to your protection arsenal the strategy of encrypting all transmissions, your system will be as secure as you can reasonably make it. (Chapter 8, "Encryption, is devoted to encryption.) However, all of these techniques (firewalls, company policies, antispyware, encryption, and so forth) will only help in cases in which the employee is not the spy. What do you do to ameliorate the danger of employees intentionally stealing or compromising information? Actually, there are several courses of action any organization can take to lesson risks due to internal espionage. Here are 12 steps you can use:

1. Always use all reasonable network security: firewalls, intrusion-detection software, antispy-ware, patching and updating the operating system, and proper usage policies.

2. Give the personnel of the company access to only the data that they absolutely need to perform their jobs. This concept is referred to as *least privileges*. The employees are given the minimum privileges necessary to perform their job tasks. Use a "need-to-know" approach. One does not want to stifle discussion or exchange of ideas, but sensitive data must be treated with great care.

3. If possible, set up a system for those employees with access to the most sensitive data in which there is a rotation or a separation of duties. In this way, no one employee has access and control over all critical data at one time.

4. Limit the number of portable storage media in the organization (such as CD burners, zip disks, and flash drives) and control access to these media. Log every use of such media and what was stored. Some organizations have even prohibited cell phones because many phones allow the user to photograph items and send the pictures electronically.

5. Do not allow employees to take documents/media home. Bringing materials home may indicate a very dedicated employee working on her own time or a corporate spy copying important documents and information.

6. Shred documents and melt old disks/tape backups/CDs. A resourceful spy can often find a great deal of information in the garbage. If any storage media is disposed of, it should be completely wiped. Degaussing is a good technique for hard drives and USB drives.

7. Do employee background checks. You must be able to trust your employees, and you can only do this with a thorough background check. Do not rely on "gut feelings." Give particular attention to information technology (IT) personnel who will, by the nature of their jobs, have a greater access to a wider variety of data. This scrutiny is most important with positions such as database administrators, network administrators, and network security specialists.

8. When any employee leaves the company, scan the employee's PC carefully. Look for signs that inappropriate data was kept on that machine. If you have any reason to suspect any inappropriate usage, then store the machine for evidence in any subsequent legal proceedings.

9. Keep all tape backups, sensitive documents, and other media under lock and key, with limited access to them.

10. If portable computers are used, then encrypt the hard drives. Encryption prevents a thief from extracting useable data from a stolen laptop. There are a number of products on the market that accomplish this encryption, including the following:

    ■ Trucrypt (see Figure 7.5) is one of my favorite tools for encrypting drives, folders or partitions. The tool is free, and remarkably easy to use. It can be found at www.truecrypt.org/.

    ■ Microsoft Windows includes two types of encryption. Windows 7 Enterprise or Ultimate edition includes BitLocker, for encrypting entire hard drives. And all versions of Windows since Windows 2000 have included Encrypted File System for encrypting specific files or folders.

    ■ This list is not exhaustive; therefore, it is highly recommended that you carefully review a variety of encryption products before making a selection.

11. Have all employees with access to any sensitive information sign nondisclosure agreements. Such agreements give you, the employer, a recourse should an ex-employee divulge sensitive data. It is amazing how many employers do not bother with this rather simple protection.

FIGURE 7.5   Trucrypt.

FIGURE 7.6   Windows EFS.

12. Security awareness sessions: Clearly, employee education is one of the most important things you can do. An organization should have some method for routinely advising employees about security issues. An excellent way to do that is to have an intranet site that has security bulletins posted to it. It is also a good idea to have periodic training sessions for employees. These need not be lengthy or in depth. Most nontechnical employees only need an introduction to security concepts.

Unfortunately, following these simple rules will not make you totally immune to corporate espionage. However, using these strategies will make any such attempts much more difficult for any perpetrator and, thus, you will improve your organization's data security.

Industrial Espionage Act

The Industrial Espionage Act of 1996 was the first U.S. law to criminalize theft of commercial trade secrets. This law provides for significant penalties for violators. Quoting from the actual law:

(a) Whoever, with intent to convert a trade secret, that is related to or included in a product that is produced for or placed in interstate or foreign commerce, to the economic benefit of anyone other than the owner thereof, and intending or knowing that the offense will injure any owner of that trade secret, knowingly —

(1) steals, or without authorization appropriates, takes, carries away, or conceals, or by fraud, artifice, or deception obtains such information;

(2) without authorization copies, duplicates, sketches, draws, photographs, downloads, uploads, alters, destroys, photocopies, replicates, transmits, delivers, sends, mails, communicates, or conveys such information;

(3) receives, buys, or possesses such information, knowing the same to have been stolen or appropriated, obtained, or converted without authorization;

(4) attempts to commit any offense described in paragraphs (1) through (3); or

(5) conspires with one or more other persons to commit any offense described in paragraphs (1) through (3), and one or more of such persons do any act to effect the object of the conspiracy, shall, except as provided in subsection (b), be fined under this title or imprisoned not more than 10 years, or both.

Spear Phishing

Phishing, as you know, is a process of attempting to get personal information from a target in order to steal the target's identity or compromise the target's system. A common technique is to send out a mass email that is designed to entice recipients into clicking on a link that purports to be some financial institutions website but is actually a phishing website.

Spear phishing is using the same technology in a targeted manner. For example, if an attacker wanted to get into the servers at a defense contractor, he might craft email and phishing websites specifically to target software and network engineers at that company. The emails might be made to appear of interest to that specific subgroup of people. Or the attacker might even take the time to learn personal details of a few of these individuals and target them specifically. This technique has been used against executives at various companies. In 2010 and 2011, this problem began to grow significantly.

Summary

A number of conclusions can be drawn from the examination of industrial espionage. The first conclusion: It does indeed occur. The case studies clearly demonstrate that industrial espionage is not some exotic fantasy dreamed up by paranoid security experts. It is an unfortunate, but quite real, aspect of modern business. If your firm's management chooses to ignore these dangers, then they do so at their own peril.

The second thing that can be concluded from this brief study of industrial espionage is that there are a variety of methods by which espionage can take place. An employee revealing confidential information is perhaps the most common. However, compromising information systems is another increasingly popular means of obtaining confidential and potentially valuable data. You will want to know the best way to protect your company and yourself. In the upcoming exercises at the end of this chapter, you will run screen-capture software, key loggers, and antispyware.

Test Your Skills

Multiple Choice Questions

1. What is the ultimate goal of espionage?

    A. To subvert a rival government

    B. To obtain information that has value

    C. To subvert a rival business

    D. To obtain information not otherwise available

2. What is the best outcome for a spy attempting an espionage activity?

    A. To obtain information without the target even realizing he did so

    B. To obtain information with or without the target realizing he did so

    C. To obtain information and discredit the target

    D. To obtain information and cause harm to the target

3. What is the usual motivating factor for corporate/industrial espionage?

    A. Ideological

    B. Political

    C. Economic

    D. Revenge

4. Which of the following types of information would be a likely target for industrial espionage?

   A. A new algorithm that the company's IT department has generated

   B. A new marketing plan that the company has formulated

   C. A list of all the company's customers

   D. All of the above are correct.

5. Which of the following is a likely reason that an organization might be reluctant to admit it has been a victim of corporate espionage?

   A. It would embarrass the IT department.

   B. It would embarrass the CEO.

   C. It might cause stock value to decline.

   D. It might lead to involvement in a criminal prosecution.

6. What is the difference between *corporate* and *industrial* espionage?

   A. None; they are interchangeable terms.

   B. Industrial espionage only refers to heavy industry, such as factories.

   C. Corporate espionage only refers to executive activities.

   D. Corporate espionage only refers to publicly traded companies.

7. You can calculate the value of information by what formula?

   A. Resources needed to produce the information, plus resources gained from the information

   B. Resources needed to produce the information, multiplied by resources gained from the information

   C. Time taken to derive the information, plus money needed to derive the information

   D. Time taken to derive the information, multiplied by money needed to derive the information

8. If a company purchases a high-end UNIX server to use for its research and development department, what is probably the most valuable part of the system?

   A. The high-end UNIX server

   B. The information on the server

   C. The devices used to protect the server

   D. The room to store the server

9. Information is an asset to your company if it

    A. Cost any sum of money to produce

    B. Cost a significant sum of money to produce

    C. Might have economic value

    D. Might cost significant money to reproduce

10. What is the greatest security risk to any company?

    A. Disgruntled employees

    B. Hackers

    C. Industrial spies

    D. Faulty network security

11. Which of the following is the best definition for *spyware*?

    A. Software that assists in corporate espionage

    B. Software that monitors activity on a computer

    C. Software that logs computer keystrokes

    D. Software that steals data

12. What is the highest level of security you can expect to obtain?

    A. A level of security that makes the effort required to get information more than the value of the information

    B. A level of security comparable with government security agencies, such as the Central Intelligence Agency

    C. A level of security that has a 92.5% success rate in stopping intrusion

    D. A level of security that has a 98.5% success rate in stopping intrusion

13. In the context of preventing industrial espionage, why might you wish to limit the number of company CD burners and control access to them in your organization?

    A. An employee could use such media to take sensitive data out.

    B. An employee could use such media to copy software from the company.

    C. CDs could be a vehicle for spyware to get on your system.

    D. CDs could be a vehicle for a virus to get on your system.

14. Why would you want to scan an employee's computer when he leaves the organization?

    A. To check the work flow prior to leaving

    B. To check for signs of corporate espionage

    C. To check for illegal software

    D. To check for pornography

15. What is the reason for encrypting hard drives on laptop computers?

   A. To prevent a hacker from reading that data while you are online

   B. To ensure that data transmissions are secure

   C. To ensure that another user on that machine will not see sensitive data

   D. To prevent a thief from getting data off of a stolen laptop

EXERCISES

EXERCISE 7.1: Learning about Industrial Espionage

1. Using the Web, library, journals, or other resources, look up a case of industrial or corporate espionage not already mentioned in this chapter. The following websites might be of some help to you in finding a case:

   http://citeseer.ist.psu.edu/320204.html

   www.newhaven.edu/california/CJ625/p6.html

   www.fidex.com/hackinglaws.htm

2. Write a brief essay describing the facts in the case. The parties in the case and the criminal proceeding are of interest, but most of your discussion should focus on the technical aspects of the case. Be sure to explain how the espionage was conducted.

EXERCISE 7.2: Using Antispyware

Note that this exercise may be repeated with different antispyware products. It is a good idea for any person interested in computer security to be familiar with multiple antispyware products.

1. Go to the website of one of the antispyware utilities. (See Chapter 5 if you need more direction.)

2. Find instructions on the vendor's website.

3. Download the trial version of that software.

4. Install it on your machine.

5. After installation, run the utility. What did it find? Record your results.

6. Let the utility remove or quarantine anything it found.

EXERCISE 7.3: Learning about Key Loggers

Note that this exercise may only be completed on machines where you have explicit permission to do so (no public computers).

1. Using any website, find and download a key logger. The following websites might help you locate a key logger:

   www.kmint21.com/familykeylogger/

   www.blazingtools.com/bpk.html

2. Install the key logger on your PC.

3. Examine how it behaves on your machine and if you notice anything that might indicate the presence of illicit software.

4. Run the antispyware software you downloaded in Exercise 2. Does the antispyware software detect the key logger?

EXERCISE 7.4: Screen-Capture Spyware

1. Using the Web, find and download a screen-capturing spyware application. The following websites might be helpful to you in selecting an appropriate product. Warning: Since you are downloading spyware, it is likely that your systems antivirus/antispyware will give you a warning on some of these sites:

   www.win-spy.com/doorway/index80.htm

   http://marketwatch-cnet.com.com/3000-2384-10188787.html?tag=lst-0-2

2. Install and configure the application on your computer.

3. Run the application and note what it finds.

4. Run the antispyware from Exercise 2 and see whether it detects your spyware program.

EXERCISE 7.5: Learning about Hardware-Based Key Loggers

In this chapter, as well as in Chapter 5, we discussed software-based key loggers. However, there are also hardware-based key loggers.

1. Use the Internet to learn more about hardware-based key loggers. (You may wish to search for "Keykatcher" as a starting point.)

2. Write an essay outlining the way in which these key loggers work and how they could be implemented for either security or industrial espionage.

PROJECTS

PROJECT 7.1: Preventing Corporate Espionage

Using one of the websites listed in this book (you can also choose from the preferred resources in Chapter 1) or other resources, find a set of guidelines on general computer security. Write a brief essay comparing and contrasting those guidelines against the ones given in this chapter. Keep in mind that the guidelines in this chapter relate specifically to corporate espionage and not to general computer security.

PROJECT 7.2: Handling Employees

Write a brief essay describing steps regarding the handling of employees. These steps should include all steps that you believe any organization should take to prevent corporate espionage. It is important that you support your opinions with sources and reasons.

If possible, visit a company and talk with someone in either the IT or personnel departments to determine how that company handles issues such as employee termination, rotation of duties, control of access to data, and so forth. Compare and contrast your steps to those used by the company you visited.

PROJECT 7.3: Asset Identification in Your Organization

Using the Asset Identification table found in this chapter or a similar table of your own design, identify the most valuable data in your organization (school or business) and what parties would most likely wish to access that data. Then write a brief guideline on how you might go about securing that data. In this project, you should tailor your security recommendations to the specific type of data you are trying to protect and against the most likely perpetrators of industrial espionage.

Case Study

David Doe is a network administrator for the ABC Company. David is passed over for promotion three times. He is quite vocal in his dissatisfaction with this situation. In fact, he begins to express negative opinions about the organization in general. Eventually, David quits and begins his own consulting business. Six months after David's departure, it is discovered that a good deal of the ABC Company's research has suddenly been duplicated by a competitor. Executives at ABC suspect that David Doe has done some consulting work for this competitor and may have passed on sensitive data. However, in the interim since David left, his computer has been formatted and reassigned to another person. ABC has no evidence that David Doe did anything wrong.

What steps might have been taken to detect David's alleged industrial espionage? What steps might have been taken to prevent his perpetrating such an offense?

Chapter | **8**

Encryption

Chapter Objectives

After reading this chapter and completing the exercises, you will be able to do the following:

- Explain the basics of encryption
- Discuss modern cryptography methods
- Select appropriate cryptography for your organization
- Understand the function and protocols of UPNs

Introduction

There are many aspects of computer and information security. *Encryption*, the process of scrambling a message or other information so that it cannot be easily read, is one of the most critical parts to the security puzzle. If you have the best firewall, very tight security policies, hardened operating systems, virus scanners, intrusion-detection software, antispyware, and every other computer security angle covered but send your data in raw, plain text, then you simply are not secure.

In this chapter, you will obtain what can be termed a "manager's understanding" of *cryptography*—the art of writing in or deciphering secret code. It is important to understand that this chapter will not make you a cryptographer. In fact, reading several volumes on encryption would not accomplish that lofty goal. Rather, this chapter is designed to give you a basic overview of what encryption is, some idea of how it works, and enough information so that you can make intelligent decisions about what sorts of encryption to incorporate in your organization. You will learn the basic history of encryption, the fundamental concepts, and after you have completed the exercises at the end of the chapter you'll have enough knowledge to at least be able to ask the right questions. Now this does not mean we won't cover some technical details, because we will. But the focus of this chapter is to give you a broad understanding of the relevant concepts.

We will go into the actual process of some of the cryptography algorithms presented. For example, we will show you the process of DES and RSA. It is beyond the scope of this book to go in depth into every cryptographic algorithm available, but it is useful for you to see a few of them described in detail.

Cryptography Basics

The aim of cryptography is not to hide the existence of a message, but rather to hide its meaning—the process known as encryption. To make a message unintelligible, it is scrambled according to a particular algorithm, which is agreed upon beforehand between the sender and the intended recipient. Thus, the recipient can reverse the scrambling protocol and make the message comprehensible (Singh, 2001a). This reversal of the scrambling is referred to as *decryption*. The advantage of using encryption/decryption is that, without knowing the scrambling protocol, the message is difficult to re-create.

There are two basic types of cryptography: *symmetric and asymmetric*. Symmetric means the same key is used to encrypt the message and to decrypt the message. With asymmetric cryptography, a different key is used to encrypt the message than is used to decrypt the message. That may sound a bit odd, and some readers may be pondering how that is possible. Later in this chapter, we will explore exactly how that works. For now the important point is to understand the basic concept of symmetric and asymmetric cryptography. But first, let's take a brief look at the history of encryption.

History of Encryption

The idea of encryption is probably as old as written communication. The basic concept is actually fairly simple. Messages must be changed in such a way that the message cannot be easily read by an enemy, but they can be easily decoded by the intended recipient. In this section, you will examine a few historical methods of encryption. It should be noted that these are very old methods, and they cannot be used for secure communication today. The methods discussed in this section would be easily cracked, even by an amateur. However, they are wonderful for conveying the concept of encryption without having to incorporate a great deal of math, which is required of the more complex encryption methods.

FYI: Cryptographers

Encryption is a very broad and complex subject area. Even amateur cryptographers typically have some mathematical training and have studied cryptographic methods for several years.

If you are interested in learning more about the history of cryptography than what we touch upon here, you may wish to read one of the many books written on the subject. Or, you might consult the following websites which are shown in Figure 8.1 and Figure 8.2.

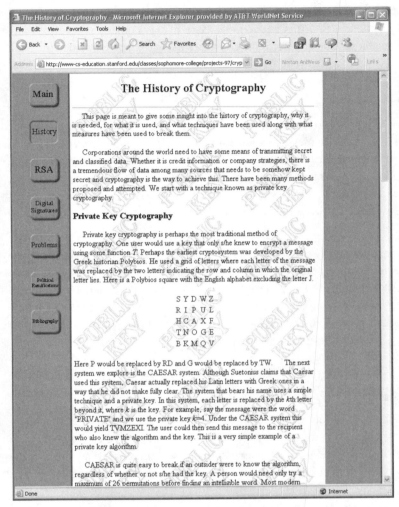

FIGURE 8.1   Stanford's cryptography history website.

- The Stanford University History of Cryptography website: www-cs-education.stanford.edu/classes/sophomore-college/projects-97/cryptography/history.html

- Cryptography.org: http://cryptography.org/

Understanding the simple methods described here and other methods listed on the aforementioned websites should give you a sense of how cryptography works as well as what is involved in encrypting a message. Regardless of whether you go on to study modern, sophisticated encryption methods, it is important for you to have some basic idea of how encryption works at a conceptual level. Having a basic grasp of how encryption works, in principle, will make you better able to understand the concepts of any encryption method you encounter in the real world.

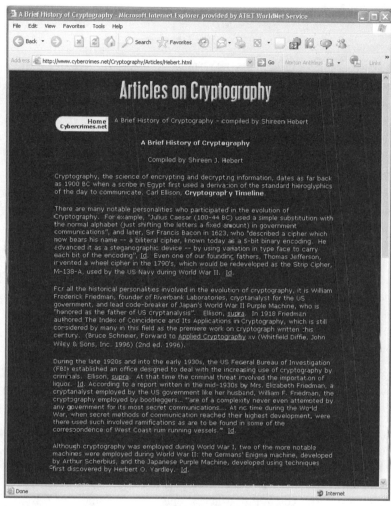

FIGURE 8.2   Hebert's cryptography history website.

The Caesar Cipher

One of the oldest encryption methods is the *Caesar cipher*. This method is purported to have been used by the ancient roman Caesars—thus the name. It is actually quite simple to do. You choose some number by which to shift each letter of a text. For example, if the text is

```
A cat
```

And you choose to shift by two letters, then the message becomes

```
C ecv
```

Or, if you choose to shift by three letters, it becomes

```
D fdw
```

Julius Caesar was reputed to have used a shift of three to the right. However, you can choose any shifting pattern you wish. You can shift either to the right or left by any number of spaces you like. Because this is a very simple method to understand, it makes a good place to start our study of encryption. It is, however, extremely easy to crack. You see, any language has a certain letter and word frequency, meaning that some letters are used more frequently than others (*Letter Frequency Distributions in the English Alphabet*, 2003). In the English language, the most common single-letter word is *A*. The most common three-letter word is *the*. Those two rules alone could help you decrypt a Caesar cipher. For example, if you saw a string of seemingly nonsense letters and noticed that a three-letter word was frequently repeated in the message, you might easily surmise that this word was *the*—and the odds are highly in favor of this being correct. Furthermore, if you frequently noticed a single-letter word in the text, it is most likely the letter *A*. You now have found the substitution scheme for *A, T, H,* and *E.* You can now either translate all of those letters in the message and attempt to surmise the rest or simply analyze the substitute letters used for *A, T, H,* and *E* and derive the substitution cipher that was used for this message. Decrypting a message of this type does not even require a computer. It could be done in less than ten minutes using pen and paper by someone with no background in cryptography. There are other rules that will help make cracking this code even easier. For example, in the English language the two most common two letter combinations are *ee* and *oo*. That gives you even more to work on.

The substitution scheme you choose (e.g., +2, +1) is referred to as a *substitution alphabet* (i.e., *B* substitutes for *A*, *U* substitutes for *T*). Thus, the Caesar cipher is also referred to as a *mono-alphabet substitution* method, meaning that it uses a single substitution for the encryption.

The Caesar cipher, however, is not useless. Since most programming languages have some function to convert a character or number to its ASCII code, a programmer can write a simple function that loops through text converting each character to its ASCII code, then either adding or subtracting the appropriate number. Again, it must be stressed that this is not a secure method of encrypting messages, but it is an interesting exercise to begin introducing you to the basic concepts of encryption. This is a good place for students to start getting a grasp of the concept of cryptography.

In Practice

Converting to ASCII Code

ASCII (American Standard Code for Information Interchange) is a standard code for every letter (upper- and lowercase), number, and key on your keyboard. It was proposed by ANSI (www.ansi.org) in 1963, and finalized in 1968. ASCII's purpose was to establish compatibility between the various types of data processing equipment. All keystrokes can be converted to a numeric ASCII code.

ASCII, pronounced "ask-key," is the common code for microcomputer equipment. The standard ASCII character set consists of 128 decimal numbers ranging from 0 through 127 assigned to letters, numbers, punctuation marks, and the most common special characters. The Extended ASCII Character Set also consists of 128 decimal numbers and ranges from 128 through 255, representing additional special, mathematical, graphic, and foreign characters. For example, the capital letter *A* is ASCII code 65, and the Return key is ASCII code 13.

TABLE 8.1 ASCII Decimal Values

Decimal	Value	Decimal	Value
000	NUL (Null char.)	033	! (exclamation mark)
001	SOH (Start of Header)	034	" (double quote)
002	STX (Start of Text)	035	# (number sign)
003	ETX (End of Text)	036	$ (dollar sign)
004	EOT (End of Transmission)	037	% (percent)
005	ENQ (Enquiry)	038	& (ampersand)
006	ACK (Acknowledgment)	039	' (single quote)
007	BEL (Bell)	040	((left/opening parenthesis)
008	BS (Backspace)	041	) (right/closing parenthesis)
009	HT (Horizontal Tab)	042	* (asterisk)
010	LF (Line Feed)	043	+ (plus)
011	VT (Vertical Tab)	044	, (comma)
012	FF (Form Feed)	045	- (minus or dash)
013	CR (Carriage Return)	046	. (dot)
014	SO (Shift Out)	047	/ (forward slash)
015	SI (Shift In)	048	0
016	DLE (Data Link Escape)	049	1
017	DC1 (XON) (Device Control 1)	050	2
018	DC2 (Device Control 2)	051	3
019	DC3 (XOFF) (Device Control 3)	052	4
020	DC4 (Device Control 4)	053	5
021	NAK (Negative Acknowledgment)	054	6
022	SYN (Synchronous Idle)	055	7
023	ETB (End of Trans. Block)	056	8
024	CAN (Cancel)	057	9
025	EM (End of Medium)	058	: (colon)
026	SUB (Substitute)	059	; (semicolon)
027	ESC (Escape)	060	< (less than)
028	FS (File Separator)	061	= (equal sign)
029	GS (Group Separator)	062	> (greater than)
030	RS (Request to Send)(Record Separator)	063	? (question mark)
031	US (Unit Separator)	064	@ (AT symbol)
032	SP (Space)	065	A

Decimal	Value	Decimal	Value
066	B	097	a
067	C	098	b
068	D	099	c
069	E	100	d
070	F	101	e
071	G	102	f
072	H	103	g
073	I	104	h
074	J	105	i
075	K	106	j
076	L	107	k
077	M	108	l
078	N	109	m
079	O	110	n
080	P	111	o
081	Q	112	p
082	R	113	q
083	S	114	r
084	T	115	s
085	U	116	t
086	V	117	u
087	W	118	v
088	X	119	w
089	Y	120	x
090	Z	121	y
091	[(left/opening bracket)	122	z
092	\ (back slash)	123	{ (left/opening brace)
093	] (right/closing bracket)	124	| (vertical bar)
094	^ (caret/circumflex)	125	} (right/closing brace)
095	_ (underscore)	126	~ (tilde)
096	`	127	DEL (delete)

As we discussed in Chapter 2, "Networks and the Internet," decimal numbers can be converted to binary numbers. So, as you can probably guess, there are binary equivalents (as well as hexadecimal equivalents) to each of these decimal values. Like the ASCII decimal values, there are tables available for determining either the binary or hexadecimal values. Table 8.2 is an example of a table for determining hexadecimal values.

TABLE 8.2 ASCII Hexadecimal Values

*	0	1	2	3	4	5	6	7	8	9	A	B	C	D	E	F
0	NUL	SOH	STX	ETX	EOT	ENQ	ACK	BEL	BS	TAB	LF	VT	FF	CR	SO	SI
1	DLE	DC1	DC2	DC3	DC4	NAK	SYN	ETB	CAN	EM	SUB	ESC	FS	GS	RS	US
2		!	"	#	$	%	&	'	(	)	*	+	,	-	.	/
3	0	1	2	3	4	5	6	7	8	9	:	;	<	=	>	?
4	@	A	B	C	D	E	F	G	H	I	J	K	L	M	N	O
5	P	Q	R	S	T	U	V	W	X	Y	Z	[	\	]	^	_
6	`	a	b	c	d	e	F	g	h	i	j	k	l	m	n	o
7	p	q	r	s	t	u	V	w	x	y	z	{			}	~

Like the conversion to binary numbers that we discussed in Chapter 2, there are many readily available converters that can make determining the ASCII equivalencies much easier than searching through tables. A simple search of the Internet will turn up many such converters. Figure 8.3 is an example of a converter found at www.cplusplus.com/doc/papers/ascii.html. This particular converter, given any one value, will generate the other three. In this illustration, the uppercase A was entered and the decimal, hexadecimal, and binary (oct.) numbers were all generated.

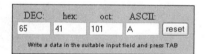

FIGURE 8.3 ASCII converter.

Multi-Alphabet Substitution

Eventually, a slight improvement on the Caesar cipher was developed, called *multi–alphabet substitution*. In this scheme, you select multiple numbers by which to shift letters (i.e., multiple substitution alphabets). For example, if you select three substitution alphabets (12, 22, 13), then

A CAT

becomes

C ADV

Notice that the fourth letter starts over with another +2, and you can see that the first *A* was transformed to *C* and the second *A* was transformed to *D*. This makes it more difficult to decipher the underlying text. While this is harder to decrypt than a Caesar cipher, it is not overly difficult. It can be done with simple pen and paper and a bit of effort. It can be cracked very quickly with a computer. In fact, no one would use such a method today to send any truly secure message, for this type of encryption is considered very weak.

At one time multi-alphabet substitution was considered quite secure. In fact a special version of this, called a Vigenère cipher was used in the 1800s and early 1900s. The Vigenère cipher was invented in 1553 by Giovan Battista Bellaso. It is a method of encrypting alphabetic text by using a series of different Caesar ciphers based on the letters of a keyword. Figure 8.4 shows the Vigenère cipher.

```
  |A B C D E F G H I J K L M N O P Q R S T U V W X Y Z
A|A B C D E F G H I J K L M N O P Q R S T U V W X Y Z
B|B C D E F G H I J K L M N O P Q R S T U V W X Y Z A
C|C D E F G H I J K L M N O P Q R S T U V W X Y Z A B
D|D E F G H I J K L M N O P Q R S T U V W X Y Z A B C
E|E F G H I J K L M N O P Q R S T U V W X Y Z A B C D
F|F G H I J K L M N O P Q R S T U V W X Y Z A B C D E
G|G H I J K L M N O P Q R S T U V W X Y Z A B C D E F
H|H I J K L M N O P Q R S T U V W X Y Z A B C D E F G
I|I J K L M N O P Q R S T U V W X Y Z A B C D E F G H
J|J K L M N O P Q R S T U V W X Y Z A B C D E F G H I
K|K L M N O P Q R S T U V W X Y Z A B C D E F G H I J
L|L M N O P Q R S T U V W X Y Z A B C D E F G H I J K
M|M N O P Q R S T U V W X Y Z A B C D E F G H I J K L
N|N O P Q R S T U V W X Y Z A B C D E F G H I J K L M
O|O P Q R S T U V W X Y Z A B C D E F G H I J K L M N
P|P Q R S T U V W X Y Z A B C D E F G H I J K L M N O
Q|Q R S T U V W X Y Z A B C D E F G H I J K L M N O P
R|R S T U V W X Y Z A B C D E F G H I J K L M N O P Q
S|S T U V W X Y Z A B C D E F G H I J K L M N O P Q R
T|T U V W X Y Z A B C D E F G H I J K L M N O P Q R S
U|U V W X Y Z A B C D E F G H I J K L M N O P Q R S T
V|V W X Y Z A B C D E F G H I J K L M N O P Q R S T U
W|W X Y Z A B C D E F G H I J K L M N O P Q R S T U V
X|X Y Z A B C D E F G H I J K L M N O P Q R S T U V W
Y|Y Z A B C D E F G H I J K L M N O P Q R S T U V W X
Z|Z A B C D E F G H I J K L M N O P Q R S T U V W X Y
```

FIGURE 8.4   Vigenère

Match the letter of your keyword on the top with the letter of your plain text on the left to find the cipher text. For example, using the chart shown in Figure 8.4, if you are encrypting the word *cat* and your key is *horse*, then the cipher text is *jok*.

Binary Operations

Various operations on *binary numbers* (numbers made of only 0s and 1s) are well known to programmers and programming students. But for those readers not familiar with them, a brief explanation follows. When working with binary numbers, there are three operations not found in normal math: AND, OR, and XOR operations. Each is illustrated below.

AND

To perform the AND operation, you take two binary numbers and compare them one place at a time. If both numbers have a one in both places, then the resultant number is a 1. If not, then the resultant number is a 0, as you see here:

```
1 1 0 1
1 0 0 1
------_____
1 0 0 1
```

OR

The OR operation checks to see whether there is a 1 in either or both numbers in a given place. If so, then the resultant number is 1. If not, the resultant number is 0, as you see here:

```
1 1 0 1
1 0 0 1
------_____
1 1 0 1
```

XOR

The XOR operation impacts your study of encryption the most. It checks to see whether there is a 1 in a number in a given place, but *not* in both numbers at that place. If it is in one number but not the other, then the resultant number is 1. If not, the resultant number is 0, as you see here:

```
1 1 0 1
1 0 0 1
------_____
0 1 0 0
```

XORing has a very interesting property in that it is reversible. If you XOR the resultant number with the second number, you get back the first number. And, if you XOR the resultant number with the first number, you get the second number:

```
0 1 0 0
1 0 0 1
------_____
1 1 0 1
```

Binary encryption using the XOR operation opens the door for some rather simple encryption. Take any message and convert it to binary numbers and then XOR that with some key. The key is some string of digits (1s and 0s) that should be random (or at least as random as possible). Converting a message to a binary number is really a simple two-step process. First, convert a message to its ASCII code, then convert those codes to binary numbers. Each letter/number will generate an 8-bit binary number. Then you can use a random string of binary numbers of any given length as the key. Simply XOR your message with the key to get the encrypted text, then XOR it with the key again to retrieve the original message. This method is easy to use and great for computer science students; however, it does not work well for truly secure communications because the underlying letter and word frequency remains. This exposes valuable clues that even an amateur cryptographer can use to decrypt the message. Yet, it does provide a valuable introduction to the concept of *single-key encryption*, which will be discussed in more detail in the next section. While simply XORing the text is not the method typically employed, single-key encryption methods are widely used today. And binary operations are often a part of the process.

Symmetric key cryptography often uses two processes: substitution and transposition. The substitution portion is accomplished by XORing the plain text message with the key. The transposition is done by swapping blocks of the text.

Modern Methods

Modern cryptography methods, as well as computers, make decryption a rather advanced science. Therefore, encryption must be equally sophisticated in order to have a chance of success.

What you have seen so far regarding encryption is simply for educational purposes. As has been noted several times, you would not have a truly secure system if you implemented any of the previously mentioned encryption schemes. You may feel that this has been overstated in this text. However, it is critical that you have an accurate view of what encryption methods do and do not work. It is now time to discuss a few methods that are actually in use today.

Before we delve too deeply into this topic, let's start with some basic definitions you will need:

- **Key:** The bits that are combined with the plain text to encrypt it. In some cases this is random numbers, in other cases it is the result of some mathematical operation.
- **Plain text:** The unencrypted text.
- **Cipher text:** The encrypted text.
- **Algorithm:** A mathematical process for doing something.

Single-Key (Symmetric) Encryption

Basically, single-key encryption means that the same key is used to both encrypt and decrypt a message. This is also referred to as symmetric key encryption. There are two types of symmetric algorithms: stream and block. A block cipher divides the data into blocks (often 64-bit blocks, but newer algorithms sometimes use 128-bit blocks) and encrypts the data one block at a time. Stream ciphers encrypt the data as a stream of bits, one bit at a time.

Data Encryption Standard   *Data Encryption Standard*, or *DES* as it is often called, was developed by IBM in the early 1970s. DES is a block cipher. The DES uses short keys and relies on complex procedures to protect its information. The actual DES algorithm is quite complex and beyond the scope of this text. The basic concept, however, is as follows (Federal Information Processing Standards, 2004):

> ## FYI: Block Ciphers and Stream Ciphers
>
> When applying a key to plain text to encrypt it and produce the cipher text, you must also choose how to apply the key and the algorithm. In a block cipher, the key is applied to blocks (often 64 bits in size) at a time. This differs from a stream cipher that encrypts 1 bit at a time.

1. Data is divided into 64-bit blocks, and those blocks are then transposed.

2. Transposed data is then manipulated by 16 separate steps of encryption involving substitutions, bit-shifting, and logical operations using a 56-bit key.

3. Data is then further scrambled using a swapping algorithm.

4. Data is finally transposed one last time.

One advantage that DES offers is efficiency. Some implementations of DES offer data throughput rates on the order of hundreds of megabytes per second. In plain English, what this means is that it can encrypt a great deal of data very quickly. You might assume that 16 steps would cause encryption to be quite slow; however, that is not the case using modern computer equipment. The problem with DES is the same problem that all symmetric key algorithms have: How do you transmit the key without risking it becoming compromised? This issue led to the development of public key encryption. And another problem is that over time it has become no longer viable for modern encryption. The 56-bit key is simply not long enough.

3DES or Triple DES, was created as a replacement for DES. At the time, the cryptography community was searching for a viable alternative. While that was still being worked on, a stop-gap measure was created. It essentially applies DES three times with three different keys, thus the name 3DES.

AES, or Advanced Encryption Standard, was the algorithm eventually chosen to replace DES. It is a block cipher that works on 128 bit blocks. It can have one of three key sizes of 128, 192, or 256 bits. This was selected by the United States Government to be the replacement for DES and is now the most widely used symmetric key algorithm.

Blowfish   Blowfish is a symmetric block cipher. It uses a variable-length key ranging from 32 to 448 bits (McCrypto.net, 2004). This flexibility in key size allows you to use it in various situations. Blowfish was designed in 1993 by Bruce Schneier. It has been analyzed extensively by the cryptography community and has gained wide acceptance. It is also a non-commercial (i.e., free of charge) product, thus making it attractive to budget-conscious organizations. It should also be pointed out that Blowfish was also a finalist for the U.S. Department of Defense, when they were seeking a replacement for DES.

RC4   The other symmetric algorithms we have discussed have all been block ciphers. RC4 is a stream cipher developed by Ron Rivest. The RC is an acronym for Ron's Cipher. There are other RC versions such as RC5 and RC6.

Public Key (Asymmetric) Encryption

Public key encryption is essentially the opposite of single-key encryption. With any public key encryption algorithm, one key is used to encrypt a message (called the public key) and another is used to decrypt the message (called the private key). You can freely distribute your public key so that anyone can encrypt a message to send to you, but only you have the private key and only you can decrypt the message. The actual mathematics behind the creation and application of the keys will vary between different asymmetric algorithms. We will look at the math for RSA later in this section. It should be pointed out, however, that many public key algorithms are dependent, to some extent, on large prime numbers, factoring, and number theory.

Many commonly used algorithms, such as PGP, use public key encryption. It is very easy to implement since the public key can be freely distributed to anyone and sometimes even put on a website for download.

Caution

Encryption Strength

Federal law prohibits the exportation of encryption beyond a certain strength. Currently, that exact limit is being contested in various court cases. It is recommended that you consult current federal guidelines before implementing encryption in your organization.

Public key encryption is fast becoming the most widely used type of encryption because there are no issues to deal with concerning distribution of the keys. With symmetric key encryption, you must get a copy of the key to every person to whom you wish to send your encrypted messages. If that key were lost or copied, someone else might be able to decrypt all of your messages. With public key encryption, you can freely distribute your public key to the entire world, yet only you can decrypt messages encrypted with that public key.

PGP   *PGP*, a public key system, stands for *Pretty Good Privacy*. It is a widely used system that is considered very secure by most experts (International PGP Website, 2004). There are several software implementations available as freeware for most desktop operating systems. There are PGP plug-ins for MSN Messenger and many other popular communications software packages (McCune, 2004). A simple Yahoo! or Google search for *PGP* will help you find many of these software products.

FYI: "Old" Encryption

PGP is more than ten years old. Some readers might wonder whether it is old and outdated. Cryptography is unlike other technological endeavors in this regard: Older is better. It is usually unwise to use the "latest thing" in encryption for the simple reason that it is unproven. An older encryption method, provided it has not yet been broken, is usually a better choice because it has been subjected to years of examination by experts and to cracking attempts by both experts and less honorably motivated individuals. This is sometimes hard for computer professionals to understand since the newest technology is often preferred in the computer business.

PGP was invented by Phil Zimmerman (Zimmerman, 2004). Before creating PGP, Mr. Zimmerman had been a software engineer for 20 years and had experience with existing forms of cryptography. A great deal of controversy surrounded the birth of PGP because it was created without an easy means for government intrusion and its encryption was considered too strong for export. This caused Mr. Zimmerman to be the target of a three-year government investigation. However, those legal matters are now resolved and PGP is one of the most widely used encryption methods available.

The important things to know about PGP are that it is

- A public key encryption
- Considered quite secure
- Available free of charge

These facts make it well worth your time to investigate PGP as a possible solution for your organization's encryption needs.

RSA   The *RSA* method is a very widely used encryption algorithm. You cannot discuss cryptography without at least some discussion of RSA. This is a public key method developed in 1977 by three mathematicians, Ron Rivest, Adi Shamir, and Len Adlema. The name RSA is derived from the first letter of each mathematician's last name (Burnett and Paine, 2001). Let us take a look at the math involved in RSA. It should be pointed out that knowing the math behind this, or any other algorithm, is not critical for most security professionals. But some readers will have an interest in going deeper into cryptography and this will be a good place to start.

First to create the key you start by generating two large random primes, p and q, of approximately equal size. Now you need to pick two numbers so that when multiplied together the product will be the size you want (i.e., 128 bits, 256 bits, etc.).

Now multiply p and q to get n.

Let $n = pq$

The next step is to multiple something called the Euler's totient for each of these primes. Basically, the Euler's totient is the total number of co-prime numbers. Two numbers are considered co-prime if they have no common factors. For example if the original number is 7, then 5 and 7 would be co-prime. It just so happens that for prime numbers, this is always the number minus 1. For example 7 has 6 numbers that are co-prime to it. (If you think about this a bit you will see that 1,2,3,4,5,6 are all co-prime with 7.)

Let $m = (p - 1)(q - 1)$

Now we are going to select another number, we will call this number e. We want to pick e so that it is co-prime to m.

Choose a small number e, co-prime to m.

We are almost done generating a key. Now we just find a number *d* that when multiplied by *e* and modulo *m* would yield a 1. (Note: *Modulo* means to divide two numbers and return the remainder. For example 8 modulo 3 would be 2.)

Find *d*, such that *de* % *m* = 1

Now you will publish *e* and *n* as the public key. Keep *d* and *n* as the secret key. To encrypt, you simply take your message raised to the *e* power and modulo *n*.

= m^e % *n*

To decrypt you take the cipher text and raise it to the *d* power modulo *n*.

P = C^d % *n*

If all this seems a bit complex to you, first you must realize that many people work in network security without being familiar with the actual algorithm for RSA (or any other cryptography for that matter). However, if you wish to go deeper into cryptography then this is a very good start. It involves some fundamental number theory, particularly regarding prime numbers. There are other asymmetric algorithms that work in a different manner. For example, elliptic curve cryptography is one such example.

Legitimate Versus Fraudulent Encryption Methods

The encryption methods discussed above are just a few of the more widely used modern encryption methods. Dozens of other methods are released to the public for free or are patented and sold for profit every year. However, it is important to realize that this particular area of the computer industry is replete with frauds and charlatans. One need only scan any search engine searching for *encryption* to find a plethora of advertisements for the latest and greatest "unbreakable" encryption. If you are not knowledgeable about encryption, how do you separate legitimate encryption methods from frauds?

There are many fraudulent cryptographic claims out there. You do not have to be a cryptography expert to be able to avoid many of those fraudulent claims. Here are some warning signs:

- **Unbreakable:** Anyone with experience in cryptography knows that there is no such thing as an unbreakable code. There are codes that have not yet been broken. There are codes that are very hard to break. But when someone claims that their method is "completely unbreakable," you should be suspicious.

- **Certified:** Guess what? There is no recognized certification process for encryption methods. Therefore, any "certification" the company has is totally worthless.

- **Inexperienced people:** A company is marketing a new encryption method. What is the experience of the people working with it? Does the cryptographer have a background in math, encryption, or algorithms? If not, has he submitted their method to experts in peer-reviewed journals? Or, is he at least willing to disclose how their method works so that it can be fairly judged? Recall that PGP's inventor had decades of software engineering and encryption experience.

Some experts claim that you should only use widely known methods, such as Blowfish and PGP, although it is certainly possible to use less well-known, or even new, encryption methods and have a very secure system. Consider the fact that today's widely used methods were once new and untested. However, if you are using a less well-known method, you need to take extra precautions to ensure that you are not being misled.

Digital Signatures

A digital signature is not used to ensure the confidentiality of a message, but rather to guarantee who sent the message. This is referred to as nonrepudiation. Essentially, it proves who the sender is. Digital signatures are actually rather simple, but clever. They simply reverse the asymmetric encryption process. Recall that in asymmetric encryption, the public key (which anyone can have access to) is used to encrypt a message to the recipient, and the private key (which is kept secure, and private) can decrypt it. With a digital signature, the sender encrypts something with his or her private key. If the recipient is able to decrypt that with the sender's public key, then it must have been sent by the person purported to have sent the message.

Hashing

A hashing is a type of cryptographic algorithm that has some specific characteristics. First and foremost it is one-way. That means you cannot "unhash" something. The second characteristic is that you get a fixed-length output no matter what input is given. This is exactly how Windows stores passwords. For example, if your password is *password*, then Windows will first hash it producing something like this:

```
0BD181063899C9239016320B50D3E896693A96DF
```

Windows will then store that in the SAM (Security Accounts Manager) file in the Windows System directory. When you log on, Windows cannot unhash your password (remember it is one-way). So, what Windows does is take whatever password you type in, hash it, and then compare the result with what is in the SAM file. If they match (exactly), then you can log in.

Storing Windows passwords is just one application of hashing. There are others. For example, in computer forensics it is common to hash a drive before you begin forensic examination. Then later you can always hash it again to see if anything was changed (accidently or intentionally). If the second hash matches the first, then nothing has been changed.

There are various hashing algorithms. The two most common are MD5 and SHA (it was SHA-1 but since then later versions like SHA-256 are becoming more common).

Authentication

When one logs on to a system, the system needs to authenticate the user (and sometimes the user needs to authenticate the system!). There are many authentication protocols. A few of the more common are briefly described here:

- **PAP:** Password Authentication Protocol is the simplest form of authentication and the least secure. Usernames and passwords are sent unencrypted, in plain text.

- **SPAP:** Shiva Password Authentication Protocol is an extension to PAP that does encrypt the username and password that is sent over the Internet.

- **CHAP:** Challenge Handshake Authentication Protocol calculates a hash after the user has logged in. Then it shares that hash with the client system. Periodically the server will ask the client to provide that hash (this is the challenge part). If the client cannot, then it is clear that the communications have been compromised .MS-CHAP is a Microsoft-specific extension to CHAP.

- **Kerberos:** Kerberos is used widely, particularly with Microsoft operating systems. It was invented at MIT and derives its name from the mythical three-headed dog that was reputed to guard the gates of Hades. The system is a bit complex but the basic process is as follows:

  When a user logs in, the authentication server verifies the user's identity and then contacts the ticket granting server (these are often on the same machine). The ticket granting server sends an encrypted "ticket" to the user's machine. That ticket identifies the user as being logged in. Later when the user needs to access some resource on the network, the user's machine uses that ticket granting ticket to get access to the target machine. There is a great deal of verification for the tickets, and these tickets expire in a relatively short time.

Encryptions Used in Internet

What sort of encryption is used on bank websites and e-commerce? In general, symmetric algorithms are faster, and require a shorter key length to be as secure as asymmetric algorithms. However, there is the problem of how to securely exchange keys. So most e-commerce solutions use an asymmetric algorithm to exchange symmetric keys and then use the symmetric keys to encrypt the actual data.

When visiting websites that have an HTTPS at the beginning, rather than HTTP, the *S* denotes *secure*. That means traffic between your browser and the web server is encrypted. This is usually done with either SSL (Secure Sockets Layer) or TLS (Transport Layer Security). SSL, the older of the two technologies, was developed by Netscape. SSL and TLS are both asymmetric systems.

Virtual Private Networks

A *VPN* is a *virtual private network*. This is essentially a way to use the Internet to create a virtual connection between a remote user or site and a central location. The packets sent back and forth over this connection are encrypted, thus making it private. The VPN must emulate a direct network connection.

There are three different protocols that are used to create VPNs:

- Point-to-Point Tunneling Protocol (PPTP)
- Layer 2 Tunneling Protocol (L2TP)
- Internet Protocol Security (IPsec)

These are each discussed in more depth in the following sections.

PPTP

Point-to-Point Tunneling Protocol (PPTP) is the oldest of the three protocols used in VPNs. It was originally designed as a secure extension to Point-to-Point Protocol (PPP). PPTP was originally proposed as a standard in 1996 by the PPTP Forum—a group of companies that included Ascend Communications, ECI Telematics, Microsoft, 3Com, and U.S. Robotics. It adds the features of encrypting packets and authenticating users to the older PPP protocol. PPTP works at the data link layer of the OSI model (discussed in Chapter 2).

PPTP offers two different methods of authenticating the user: Extensible Authentication Protocol (EAP) and Challenge Handshake Authentication Protocol (CHAP). EAP was actually designed specifically for PPTP and is not proprietary. CHAP is a three-way process whereby the client sends a code to the server, the server authenticates it, and then the server responds to the client. CHAP also periodically re-authenticates a remote client, even after the connection is established.

PPTP uses Microsoft Point-to-Point Encryption (MPPE) to encrypt packets. MPPE is actually a version of DES. DES is still useful for many situations; however, newer versions of DES, such as DES 3, are preferred.

L2TP

Layer 2 Tunneling Protocol (L2TP) was explicitly designed as an enhancement to PPTP. Like PPTP, it works at the data link layer of the OSI model. It has several improvements to PPTP. First, it offers more and varied methods for authentication—PPTP offers two, whereas L2TP offers five. In addition to CHAP and EAP, L2TP offers PAP, SPAP, and MS-CHAP.

In addition to more authentication protocols available for use, L2TP offers other enhancements. PPTP will only work over standard IP networks, whereas L2TP will work over X.25 networks (a common protocol in phone systems) and ATM (asynchronous transfer mode, a high-speed networking technology) systems. L2TP also uses IPsec for its encryption.

IPsec

IPsec is short for *Internet Protocol Security*. It is the latest of the three VPN protocols. One of the differences between IPsec and the other two methods is that it encrypts not only the packet data (recall the discussion of packets in Chapter 2), but also the header information. It also has protection against unauthorized retransmission of packets. This is important because one trick that a hacker can use is to simply grab the first packet from a transmission and use it to get their own transmissions to go through. Essentially, the first packet (or packets) has to contain the login data. If you simply resend that packet (even if you cannot crack its encryption), you will be sending a valid logon and password that can then be followed with additional packets. Preventing unauthorized retransmission of packets prevents this from happening.

Summary

A basic element of computer security is encryption. Sending sensitive data that is not encrypted is simply foolish. This chapter provided the basic information on how cryptography works. The most important thing to remember is that, ultimately, it is not your computer or your network that will be compromised but rather your data. Encrypting the data when transmitting it is an integral part of any security plan.

In the exercises at the end of this chapter, you will practice using different cipher methods and learn more about a number of encryption methods.

Test Your Skills

MULTIPLE CHOICE QUESTIONS

1. Which of the following most accurately defines encryption?

   A. Changing a message so it can only be easily read by the intended recipient

   B. Using complex mathematics to conceal a message

   C. Changing a message using complex mathematics

   D. Applying keys to a message to conceal it

2. Which of the following is the oldest encryption method discussed in this text?

   A. PGP

   B. Multi-alphabet encryption

   C. Caesar cipher

   D. Cryptic cipher

3. What is the main problem with simple substitution?

   A. It does not use complex mathematics.

   B. It is easily broken with modern computers.

   C. It is too simple.

   D. It maintains letter and word frequency.

4. Which of the following is an encryption method using two or more different shifts?

   A. Caesar cipher

   B. Multi-alphabet encryption

   C. DES

   D. PGP

5. Which binary mathematical operation can be used for a simple encryption method?

   A. Bit shift

   B. OR

   C. XOR

   D. Bit swap

6. Why is binary mathematical encryption not secure?

   A. It does not change letter or word frequency.

   B. It leaves the message intact.

   C. It is too simple.

   D. The mathematics of it is flawed.

7. Which of the following is most true regarding binary operations and encryption?

   A. They are completely useless.

   B. They can form a part of viable encryption methods.

   C. They are only useful as a teaching method.

   D. They can provide secure encryption.

8. What is PGP?

   A. Pretty Good Privacy, a public key encryption method

   B. Pretty Good Protection, a public key encryption method

   C. Pretty Good Privacy, a symmetric key encryption method

   D. Pretty Good Protection, a symmetric key encryption method

9. Which of the following methods is available as an add-in for most email clients?

   A. DES

   B. RSA

   C. Caesar cipher

   D. PGP

10. Which of the following is a symmetric key system using 64-bit blocks?

   A. RSA

   B. DES

   C. PGP

   D. Blowfish

11. What advantage does a symmetric key system using 64-bit blocks have?

    A. It is fast.

    B. It is unbreakable.

    C. It uses asymmetric keys.

    D. It is complex.

12. What size key does a DES system use?

    A. 64 bit

    B. 128 bit

    C. 56 bit

    D. 256 bit

13. What type of encryption uses different keys to encrypt and decrypt the message?

    A. Private key

    B. Public key

    C. Symmetric

    D. Secure

14. Which of the following methods uses a variable-length symmetric key?

    A. Blowfish

    B. Caesar

    C. DES

    D. RSA

15. What should you be most careful of when looking for an encryption method to use?

    A. Complexity of the algorithm

    B. Veracity of the vendor's claims

    C. Speed of the algorithm

    D. How long the algorithm has been around

16. Which of the following is most likely to be true of an encryption method that is advertised as unbreakable?

    A. It is probably suitable for military use.

    B. It may be too expensive for your organization.

    C. It is likely to be exaggerated.

    D. It is probably one you want to use.

17. Which of the following is most true regarding certified encryption methods?

    A. These are the only methods you should use.

    B. It depends on the level of certification.

    C. It depends on the source of the certification.

    D. There is no such thing as certified encryption.

18. Which of the following is most true regarding new encryption methods?

    A. Never use them until they have been proven.

    B. You can use them, but you must be cautious.

    C. Only use them if they are certified.

    D. Only use them if they are rated unbreakable.

19. Which of the following is the oldest protocol used by VPN?

    A. PPTP

    B. L2TP

    C. IPsec

    D. SPAP

20. Which of the following is used by PPTP to encrypt packets?

    A. Microsoft Point-to-Point Encryption

    B. Layer 2 Tunneling Protocol

    C. Extensible Authentication Protocol

    D. Challenge Handshake Authentication Protocol

EXERCISES

EXERCISE 8.1: Using the Caesar Cipher

Note: This exercise is well suited for group or classroom exercises.

1. Write a sentence in normal text.

2. Use a Caesar cipher of your own design to encrypt it.

3. Pass it to another person in your group or class.

4. Time how long it takes that person to break the encryption.

5. (Optional) Compute the mean time for the class to break Caesar ciphers.

EXERCISE 8.2: **Using Multi-Alphabet Ciphers**

Note: This exercises also works well for group settings and is best used in conjunction with the preceding exercise.

1. Write a sentence in normal text.

2. Use a multi-alphabet cipher of your own design to encrypt it.

3. Pass it to another person in your group or class.

4. Time how long it takes that person to break the encryption.

5. (Optional) Compute the mean time for the class to break these and compare that to the mean time required to break the Caesar ciphers.

EXERCISE 8.3: **Using PGP**

1. Download a PGP attachment for your favorite email client. Doing a web search for PGP and your email client (i.e., PGP and Outlook or PGP and Eudora) should locate both modules and instructions.

2. Install and configure the PGP module.

3. Send encrypted messages to and from a classmate.

EXERCISE 8.4: **Finding Good Encryption Solutions**

1. Scan the Web for various commercial encryption algorithms.

2. Find one that you feel may be "snake oil."

3. Write a brief paper explaining your opinion.

EXERCISE 8.5: **Learn More about VPN**

1. Using the Web, journals, books, or other resources, find out more about VPN.

2. Write a brief essay describing how VPN could increase the security of your transmissions.

PROJECTS

PROJECT 8.1: RSA Encryption

Using the Web or other resources, write a brief paper about RSA, its history, methodology, and where it is used. Students with a sufficient math background may choose to delve more deeply into the RSA algorithm's mathematical basis.

PROJECT 8.2: Programming Caesar Cipher

Note: This project is for those students with some programming background.

Write a simple program in any language you prefer (or your instructor dictates) that can perform a Caesar cipher. In this chapter, you not only saw how this cipher works, but were also given some ideas on how to use ASCII codes to make this work in any standard programming language.

PROJECT 8.3: Other Encryption Methods

Write a brief essay describing any encryption method not already mentioned in this chapter. In this paper, describe the history and origin of that algorithm. You should also provide some comparisons with other well-known algorithms.

Case Study

Jane Doe is responsible for selecting an encryption method that is suitable for her company, which sells insurance. The data they send is sensitive but is not military or classified in nature. Jane is looking at a variety of methods. She ultimately selects a commercial implementation of RSA. Was this the best choice? Why or why not?

Chapter | **9**

Computer Security Software

Chapter Objectives

After reading this chapter and completing the exercises, you will be able to do the following:

- Evaluate the effectiveness of a scanner based on how it works
- Choose the best type of firewall for a given organization
- Understand antispyware methods
- Employ intrusion-detection systems to detect problems on your system
- Understand honey pots

Introduction

Throughout this book, various aspects of computer crime and computer security have been discussed. At this point in your studies, you should have a good idea of what the real dangers are and what adequate security policies include, as well as a basic understanding of the various forms of computer crime. However, if you are striving to secure your network, you will need more technical details on the various security devices and software you might choose to employ. This chapter reviews these items with enough detail to allow you to make intelligent decisions on which types of products you will see.

Most of these devices have been mentioned and briefly described in the preceding chapters. The intent of this chapter is to delve more deeply into details of how these devices work. This information is of particular value to those readers who intend to eventually enter the computer security profession. Simply having a theoretical knowledge of computer security is inadequate. You must have some practical skills. This chapter will be a good starting point for gaining those skills, and the exercises at the end of the chapter will give you a chance to practice setting up and evaluating various types of firewalls, IDSs, and antivirus applications.

Virus Scanners

A virus scanner is essentially software that tries to prevent a virus from infecting your system. This fact is probably abundantly obvious to most readers. Knowing how a virus scanner works, however, is another matter. This topic was discussed briefly in our previous discussions on viruses, but will be elaborated on in this chapter.

In general, virus scanners work in two ways. The first method is that they contain a list of all known virus definitions. The virus definitions are simply files that list known viruses, their file size, properties, and behavior. Generally, one of the services that vendors of virus scanners provide is a periodic update of this file. This list is typically in a small file, often called a *.dat* file (short for data). When you update your virus definitions, what actually occurs is that your current file is replaced by the more recent one on the vendor's website.

The antivirus program can then scan your PC, network, and incoming email for known virus files. Any file on your PC or attached to an email is compared to the virus definition file to see whether there are any matches. With emails, this can be done by looking for specific subject lines and content. Known virus files often have specific phrases in the subject line and the body of the messages they are attached to. Yet viruses and worms can have a multitude of headers, some of which are very common, such as *re:hello* or *re:thanks.* Scanning against a list of known viruses alone would result in many false positives. Therefore, the virus scanner also looks at attachments to see whether they are of a certain size and creation date that matches a known virus or whether it contains known viral code. The file size, creation date, and location are the telltale signs of a virus.

How Does a Virus Scanner Work?

An article in the July 2004 issue of *Scientific American,* titled "How Does a Virus Scanner Work," stated that a virus scanner is essentially software that searches for the signature or pattern of known virus. Keep in mind that the scanner only works if you keep it updated. And, of course, it only works with known viruses.

The second way a virus scanner works is to watch for certain types of behaviors that are typical of a virus. This might include any program that attempts to write to your hard drive's boot sector, change system files, automate your email software, or self-multiply. Programs that attempt to modify the system Registry (for Windows systems) or alter any system settings may also be indicative of a virus.

Another feature that virus scanners search for is a file that will stay in memory after it executes. This is called a *Terminate and Stay Resident (TSR)* program. Some legitimate programs do this, but it is often a sign of a virus. Additionally, some virus scanners use more sophisticated methods, such as scanning your system files and monitoring any program that attempts to modify those files.

It is also important to differentiate between on-demand virus scanning and ongoing scanners. An *ongoing virus scanner* runs in the background and is constantly checking your PC for any sign of a virus. *On-demand virus scanners* run only when you launch them. Many modern antivirus scanners offer both options.

Virus-Scanning Techniques

In general, there are five ways a virus scanner might scan for virus infections. Some of these were mentioned in the previous section, but they are outlined and defined below:

- **Email and attachment scanning:** Since the primary propagation method for a virus is email, email and attachment scanning is the most important function of any virus scanner. Some virus scanners actually examine your email on the email server before downloading it to your machine. Other virus scanners work by scanning your emails and attachments on your computer before passing it to your email program. In either case, the email and its attachments should be scanned prior to you having any chance to open it and release the virus on your system.

- **Download scanning:** Anytime you download anything from the Internet, either via a Web link or through some FTP program, there is a chance you might download an infected file. Download scanning works much like email and attachment scanning, but does so on files you select for downloading.

- **File scanning:** This is the type of scanning in which files on your system are checked to see whether they match any known virus. This sort of scanning is generally done on an on-demand basis instead of an ongoing basis. It is a good idea to schedule your virus scanner to do a complete scan of the system periodically. I personally recommend a weekly scan, preferably at a time when no one is likely to be using the computer.

- **Heuristic Scanning:** This is perhaps the most advanced form of virus scanning. This sort of scanning uses rules to determine whether a file or program is behaving like a virus and is one of the best ways to find a virus that is not a known virus. A new virus will not be on any virus definition list, so you must examine its behavior to determine whether it is a virus. However, this process is not foolproof. Some actual virus infections will be missed, and some nonvirus files might be suspected of being a virus.

- **Sandbox:** Another approach is the sandbox approach. This basically means that you have a separate area, isolated from the operating system, in which a download or attachment is run. Then if it is infected, it won't infect the operating system.

  One way to accomplish this is for the operating system to set aside a protected area of memory to open the suspected file and to monitor its behavior. This is not 100% effective, but it is far safer than simply opening files on your system and hoping there is no infection.

  A related concept is called a "sheep dip" machine. This is useful in corporate networks. You set up a system that is identical in configuration to your standard workstations. However, this sheep dip machine is not networked. Suspect files are opened first on this system. Then the system is monitored for a period of time for signs of infection. Once the file has cleared this check, it can then be opened on normal workstations.

  A simple way to do this in a home or small office is to set up a virtual machine on your computer and to open suspected attachments or downloads in the virtual machine first. If they are okay, then open them on your main system.

FYI: How Most Commercial Scanners Work

Most commercial virus scanners use multiple methods, including most, if not all, of the methods listed here. Any virus scanner that uses only one scanning modality would be virtually worthless from a practical virus defense perspective. These modalities are how a scanner works regardless of whether it is using a heuristic scan, download scan, email scan, and so on.

- **Active code scanning:** Modern websites frequently embed active codes, such as Java applets and ActiveX. These technologies can provide some stunning visual effects to any website. However, they can also be a vehicle for malicious code. Scanning such objects before they are downloaded to your computer is an essential feature in any quality virus scanner.

- **False positives and false negatives:** Regardless of the type of virus scanner, any antivirus software will occasionally have an error. There are two types of errors that you should be concerned with. It is possible that your antivirus software will mistake a legitimate program for a virus. For example, you might have a program that is supposed to make some adjustment to the Windows Registry or to scan your email address book. Mistaking a legitimate program for a virus is referred to as a false positive. It is also possible that your antivirus will fail to recognize a virus. This is referred to as a false negative. The best way to minimize false negatives is to keep your antivirus software updated. For false positives, it is recommended that you simply quarantine suspected viruses and not automatically delete them.

Commercial Antivirus Software

There are three brands of antivirus software that virtually dominate the antivirus market today and a number of companies that offer a commercial scanner also offer a free version that does not provide as many features as the commercial product. For example, AVG AntiVirus, available from www.grisoft.com, is a commercial product, but the company also offers the AVG AntiVirus Free Edition. McAfee, Norton, and Kapersky are three very well-known antivirus vendors. All three products are good choices, and also come with additional options, such as spam filters and personal firewalls. Any of these three products can be purchased for a home machine for about $30 to $60 (depending on options you add). This purchase price includes a one-year subscription to update the virus files so that your antivirus software will recognize all known virus attacks. Organizational licenses are also available to cover an entire network.

Of course, there are other antivirus solutions available. Several free virus scanners can easily be found on the Internet. McAfee, Norton, and Kapersky are mentioned here because they are so commonly used, and it is likely that you will encounter them frequently. But that is not to indicate that I am discouraging you using other systems. However, I strongly recommend that you stick with widely used, well-supported antivirus products.

Firewalls

A firewall is, in essence, a barrier between your network and the outside world. At a minimum, it will filter incoming packets based on certain parameters such as packet size, source IP address, protocol, and destination port. Linux and Windows (beginning with Windows XP and in all subsequent Windows versions) ship with a simple firewall. For Windows, the firewall in Windows 7 was expanded to handle filtering both inbound and outbound traffic.

In an organizational setting, you will want a dedicated firewall between your network and the outside world. This might be a router that also has built-in firewall capabilities. (Cisco Systems is one company that is well known for high-quality routers and firewalls.) Or, it might be a server that is dedicated solely to running firewall software. Selecting a firewall, however, is an important decision. If you lack the expertise to make that decision, then you should arrange for a consultant to assist you in this respect.

Benefits and Limitation of Firewalls

A firewall, no matter what type you get (types are described in the next section), is basically a tool to block certain traffic. A set of rules determine what traffic to allow in, and what traffic to block. Obviously, a firewall is a critical piece of your security strategy. I cannot even conceive of any reason to run any system without one. However, it is not a panacea for security. It cannot block every attack. For example, a firewall won't stop you from downloading a Trojan horse. It also cannot stop internal attacks. But a firewall can be an excellent way to stop a denial of service attack or to prevent a hacker from scanning the internal details of your network.

Firewall Types and Components

Up to this point, most discussion of firewalls has focused on packet-filtering firewalls. However, there are several other types of firewalls or components to firewalls that are listed below.

- Screening firewall
- Application gateway
- Circuit-level gateway

The following sections will discuss each of these and assess the advantages and disadvantages of each.

Screening Firewall

Screening firewalls, the most basic type of firewall, are simply another name for packet-filtering firewalls. This type of firewall works in the network layer of the OSI model (see Chapter 2, "Networks and the Internet"). It simply examines incoming packets and either allows or denies them entrance based on a set of rules that were put into its configuration. They can filter packets based on packet size, protocol type used, destination IP address, source IP address, destination port, source port, and so forth. For example, a packet filter might deny all traffic on ports 1024 and up, or it might block all incoming traffic using the TFTP protocol. You can use incoming and outgoing filters to dictate what information passes into or out of your local network.

Many routers offer this type of firewall option. These firewalls are usually very easy to configure and quite inexpensive. As mentioned, some operating systems include built-in packet-filtering capabilities.

There are a few disadvantages to the screening/packet-filtering firewall solution. One disadvantage is that they do not actually examine the packet or compare it to previous packets; therefore, they are quite susceptible to either a ping flood or SYN flood. They also do not offer any user authentication. Additionally, in many cases, a packet-filtering firewall will be used as a bastion host. A *bastion host* is a single point of contact between the Internet and a private network. It usually will only run a limited number of services (those that are absolutely essential to the private network) and no others.

Application Gateway

An *application gateway* (also known as *application proxy* or *application-level proxy*) is a program that runs on a firewall. When a client program, such as a Web browser, establishes a connection to a destination service, such as a web server, it connects to an application gateway, or proxy. The client then negotiates with the proxy server in order to gain access to the destination service. In effect, the proxy establishes the connection with the destination behind the firewall and acts on behalf of the client, hiding and protecting individual computers on the network behind the firewall. This process actually creates two connections. There is one connection between the client and the proxy server and another connection between the proxy server and the destination.

Once a connection is established, the application gateway makes all decisions about which packets to forward. Since all communication is conducted through the proxy server, computers behind the firewall are protected.

With an application gateway, each supported client program requires a unique program to accept client application data. This sort of firewall allows for individual user authentication, which makes them quite effective at blocking unwanted traffic. However, a disadvantage is that these firewalls use a lot of system resources and are susceptible to SYN floods and ping floods.

Circuit-Level Gateway

A *circuit-level gateway* is similar to an application gateway but is more secure and generally implemented on high-end equipment. A circuit-level gateway relays a TCP connection but does no additional processing or filtering of the protocol (Wack, 1995). In this system, your username is checked and granted access before the connection to the router is established. This means that you as an individual, either by username or IP address, must be verified before any further communication can take place. Once this verification takes place and the connection between the source and destination is established, the firewall simply passes bytes between the systems. A virtual "circuit" exists between the internal client and the proxy server. Internet requests go through this circuit to the proxy server, and the proxy server delivers those requests to the Internet after changing the IP address. External users only see the IP address of the proxy server. Responses are then received by the proxy server and sent back through the circuit to the client. While traffic is allowed through, external systems never see the internal systems.

While highly secure, this approach may not be appropriate for some public situations, such as e-commerce sites. This type of firewall does not allow features, such as URL filtering. They also frequently offer only limited auditing capabilities.

How Firewalls Examine Packets

In addition to how the firewall operates, you can further differentiate firewalls based on how they examine incoming packets. There are two main approaches to this task, and each is briefly examined below.

Stateful Packet Inspection

The *stateful packet inspection (SPI)* firewall will examine each packet, denying or permitting access based not only on the examination of the current packet, but also on data derived from previous packets in the conversation. This means that the firewall is aware of the context in which a specific packet was sent. This makes these firewalls far less susceptible to ping floods and SYN floods, as well as being less susceptible to spoofing. For example, if the firewall detects that the current packet is an ICMP packet and a stream of several thousand packets have been continuously coming from the same source IP, it is clearly a denial of service attack and the packets will be blocked.

The SPI firewall can also look at the actual contents of the packet. This allows for some very advanced filtering capabilities. Most high-end firewalls use the stateful packet inspection method; when possible, this is the recommended type of firewall.

Stateless Packet Inspection

Stateless packet inspection does not involve actually examining the contents of each packet, which is a significant weakness in using such an inspection technology. Also, the stateless packet inspection does not examine a packet within the context of an ongoing TCP conversation. It does not know what the preceding or subsequent packets are doing, thus making it vulnerable to ping floods and other denial of service attacks.

Firewall Configurations

In addition to the various types of firewalls, there are also various configuration options. The type of firewall tells you how it will evaluate traffic and hence decide what to allow and not to allow. The configuration gives you an idea of how that firewall is set up in relation to the network it is protecting. Some of the major configurations/implementations for firewalls include the following:

- Network host-based

- Dual-homed host

- Router-based firewall

- Screened host

Each of these is discussed in the following sections.

Network Host-Based

A *network host-based firewall* is a software solution installed on an existing machine with an existing operating system. The most significant concern in using this type of firewall is that no matter how good the firewall solution is, it is contingent upon the underlying operating system. In such a situation, it is absolutely critical that the machine hosting the firewall have a hardened operating system.

Dual-Homed Host

A *dual-homed host* is a firewall running on a server with at least two network interfaces. The server acts as a router between the network and the interfaces to which it is attached. To make this work, the automatic routing function is disabled, meaning that an IP packet from the Internet is not routed directly to the network. You can choose what packets to route and how to route them. Systems inside and outside the firewall can communicate with the dual-homed host but cannot communicate directly with each other.

Router-Based Firewall

As was previously mentioned, you can implement firewall protection on a router. In larger networks with multiple layers of protection, this is commonly the first layer of protection. Although one can implement various types of firewalls on a router, the most common type used is packet filtering. If you use a broadband connection in your home or small office, you can get a packet-filtering firewall router to replace the basic router provided to you by the broadband company. In recent years, router-based firewalls have become increasingly common and are in fact the most common firewall used today.

Screened Host

A *screened host* is really a combination of firewalls. In this configuration, you use a combination of a bastion host and a screening router. The screening router adds security by allowing you to deny or permit certain traffic from the bastion host. It is the first stop for traffic, which can continue only if the screening router lets it through.

Commercial and Free Firewall Products

There is a variety of commercial firewall products from which you can choose. If all you want is a basic packet-filtering solution, many software vendors offer this. Major antivirus software vendors (including those mentioned previously in this chapter) often offer the firewall software as a bundled option with their antivirus software. Other companies, such as Zone Labs, sell firewall and intrusion-detection software. Zone Labs, for example, offers the ZoneAlarm Security Suite, which provides all the tools for complete Internet security. Major manufacturers of routers and hubs, such as Cisco Systems, also offer firewall products. How much security you need is a difficult question to answer. A bare minimum recommendation is to have a packet-filtering firewall/proxy server between your network and the Internet—but that is a bare minimum. There are also many free firewall applications available. Zone Labs, mentioned above for their commercial product, also offers a free download of the ZoneAlarm firewall protection.

Outpost Firewall, available from www.agnitum.com/products/outpost/, is a product designed for the home or small office user. Like the Zone Labs product, it has both a free version and an enhanced commercial version. Information on this product is shown in Figure 9.1. Note that the free version is an older version of the software and does not include many of the enhancements of the commercial version. But it may be sufficient for your needs.

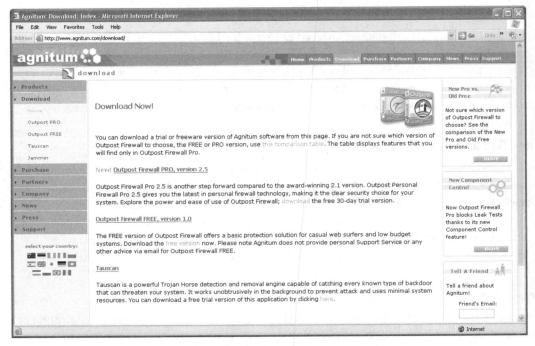

FIGURE 9.1   Firewall protection from Agnitum.

Listed and shown below are a number of other sources for information on free firewall protection. Each of these websites offers links to a number of sources for free firewall protection as well as to other useful security tools. You may want to explore these sites as well as add them to your list of resource sites:

- www.free-firewall.org/

- www.homenethelp.com/web/howto/free-firewall.asp

- www.firewallguide.com/freeware.htm

Firewall Logs

Firewalls are also excellent tools when attempting to ascertain what has happened after an incident occurs. Almost all firewalls, regardless of type or implementation, will log activity. These logs can provide valuable information that can assist in determining the source of an attack, methods used to attack, and other data that might help either locate the perpetrator of an attack or at least prevent a future attack using the same techniques. Any security-conscious network administrator should make it a routine habit to check the firewall logs.

Antispyware

Antispyware, as discussed earlier in this book, scans your computer to see whether there is spyware running on your machine. This is an important element of computer security software that was at one time largely ignored. Even today, not enough people take spyware seriously or guard against it. Most antispyware works by checking your system for known spyware files. Each application must simply be checked against a list of known spyware. This means that you must maintain some sort of subscription service so that you can obtain routine updates to your spyware definition list. Most antivirus solutions now also check for antispyware.

In today's Internet climate, running antispyware is as essential as running antivirus software. Failing to do so can lead to serious consequences. Personal data, and perhaps sensitive business data, could easily be leaking out of your organization without your knowledge. And, as was pointed out earlier in this book, it is entirely possible for spyware to be the vehicle for purposeful industrial espionage.

Barring the use of antispyware, or even in conjunction with such software, you can also protect yourself via your browser's security settings as was discussed in a previous chapter. Additionally, several times throughout this book, you have been warned to be cautious about attachments and Internet downloads. You would also be well advised to avoid downloading various Internet "enhancements," such as "skins" and "toolbars." If you are in an organization, prohibiting such downloads should be a matter of company policy. Unfortunately, many websites today require some sort of add-in such as Flash in order to function properly. The best advice for this situation is to only allow add-ins on trusted, well-known sites.

Intrusion-Detection Software

Intrusion-detection software (IDS) has become much more widely used in the last few years. Essentially, an IDS will inspect all inbound and outbound port activity on your machine/firewall/system and look for patterns that might indicate an attempted break-in. For example, if the IDS finds that a series of ICMP packets were sent to each port in sequence, this probably indicates that your system is being scanned by network-scanning software, such as Cerberus. Since this is often a prelude to an attempt to breach your system security, it can be very important to know that someone is performing preparatory steps to infiltrate your system.

Entire volumes have been written on how IDS systems work. This chapter cannot hope to cover that much information. However, it is important that you have a basic idea of how these systems work.

The sections below will first examine the broad categories in which IDS systems tend to be viewed and then will also look at some specific approaches to IDS. While this information is not all inclusive, it does address the more common terminology used.

IDS Categorization

There are a number of ways in which IDS systems can be categorized. The most common IDS categorizations are as follows:

- Misuse detection versus anomaly detection

- Passive systems versus reactive systems

- Network-based systems versus host-based systems

Misuse Detection vs. Anomaly Detection

An IDS that uses *misuse detection* analyzes the information it gathers and compares it to large databases of attack signatures (*IDS signatures*) (Webopedia, 2004). Much like a virus-detection system, this form of IDS looks for specific attacks that have already been documented. However, similar to virus scanners, this form of IDS is only as good as the IDS signatures against which it compares the packets.

On the other hand, *anomaly detection* involves actual software that works to detect intrusion attempts and notify the administrator. This is what many people think of when they talk about intrusion-detection systems. The general process is simple: The system looks for any anomalous behavior. Any activity that does not match the pattern of normal user access is noted and logged. The software compares observed activity against expected normal usage profiles. Profiles are usually developed for specific users, groups of users, or applications. Any activity that does not match the definition of normal behavior is considered an anomaly and is logged.

Passive Systems Versus Reactive Systems

In a *passive system,* the IDS detects a potential security breach, logs the information, and signals an alert. In a *reactive system,* the IDS responds to the suspicious activity by logging off a user or reprogramming the firewall to block network traffic from the suspected malicious source (Webopedia, 2011).

Network-Based System Versus Host-Based System

In a network-based system (NIDS), the individual packets flowing through a network are analyzed. This system can detect malicious packets that are designed to be overlooked by a firewall's simplistic filtering rules (Webopedia, 2004). In a host-based system (HIDS), the activity of each individual computer or host is examined.

> **FYI: Normal Activity Patterns**
>
> With anomaly-based IDS, it can take some time to create what is considered "normal" activity patterns. While these activity patterns are being established, you may experience a high rate of false alarms.
>
> You should also note that, if the network already contains malicious code, then the activity of this code would be considered normal.

IDS Approaches

There are many approaches to detection and prevention. Some of these methods are implemented in various software packages, while others are simply strategies that an organization can employ to decrease the likelihood of a successful intrusion.

Preemptive Blocking

This approach, sometimes called banishment vigilance, seeks to prevent intrusions before they occur. This is done by noting any danger signs of impending threats and then blocking the user or IP address from which these signs originate. Examples of this technique include attempting to detect the early foot printing stages of an impending intrusion, then blocking the IP or user that is the source of the foot printing activity. If you find that a particular IP address is the source of frequent port scans and other scans of your system, then you would block that IP address at the firewall.

This sort of intrusion detection and avoidance can be complicated. Usually, a software system will simply alert the administrator that suspicious activity has taken place. A human administrator will then make the decision whether or not to block the person. If the software automatically blocks any addresses it deems suspicious, you run the risk of blocking out legitimate users. It should also be noted that nothing prevents the offending user from moving to a different machine to continue their attack. This sort of approach should only be one part of an overall intrusion-detection strategy and not the entire strategy.

Snort

There are a number of vendors who supply IDS systems, each with its own strengths and weaknesses. Which system is best for your environment is contingent on many factors including the network environment, security level required, budget constraints, and the skill level of the person who will be working directly with the IDS. One popular open-source IDS is Snort, which can be downloaded for free from www.snort.org/.

We will examine Snort briefly in this section. While it is not the only IDS available, it is free, and that makes it an attractive option for many people. We will walk through the basic configuration of Snort for Windows.

First you must visit www.snort.org and register. It is free. Then download the Snort installation program and the latest rules. Make certain you download the installer that has a .exe extension. The .rpm extensions are for Linux. Also, I have found that certain versions of Microsoft Internet Explorer do not work well with the Snort website, so it is recommended that you use an alternative browser such as Mozilla Firefox.

Once you have downloaded both the rules and the installation, start the installation. Most of it is quite simple. There is a screen that asks you if you wish to support database connectivity. For most live situations you would want to dump your Snort records to some database. However, for demonstration purposes choose "I do not plan to log to a database," as shown in Figure 9.2.

FIGURE 9.2   Snort database selection.

Other than this, simply use all default settings. At the end of the install, it will also attempt to install WinPCAP. If for some reason this fails, you will need to download and install it separately. WinPCAP is an open source tool for capturing packets. All intrusion-detection systems depend on packet capturing.

Now copy rules you downloaded from wherever you saved them to c:\snort\rules. Then you need to copy the configuration file from c:\snort\rules\etc\snort.conf to C:\snort\etc. Now open that configuration file using WordPad, not Notepad. Notepad does not support word wrap, and it will be difficult to read the configuration file in Notepad.

The first step is to change the HOME_NET *any* to your machines IP address, as shown in Figure 9.3. In a live situation, we would also set the other IP addresses (web server, SQL server, DNS server, etc.)

```
###################################################
# Step #1: Set the network variables.  For more information, see
README.variables
###################################################

# Setup the network addresses you are protecting
var HOME_NET any

# Set up the external network addresses.  A good start may be
"any"
var EXTERNAL_NET any

# List of DNS servers on your network
var DNS_SERVERS $HOME_NET

# List of SMTP servers on your network
var SMTP_SERVERS $HOME_NET

# List of web servers on your network
var HTTP_SERVERS $HOME_NET

# List of sql servers on your network
var SQL_SERVERS $HOME_NET
```

FIGURE 9.3   HOME_NET address.

Now you need to find and change the rules paths. They will have Linux style paths, as shown in Figure 9.4.

```
# Path to your rules files (this can be a relative path)
# Note for Windows users:  You are advised to make this an
absolute path,
# such as:  c:\snort\rules
var RULE_PATH ../rules
var SO_RULE_PATH ../so_rules
var PREPROC_RULE_PATH ../preproc_rules
```

FIGURE 9.4   Linux-style paths.

You will need to change them to Windows style paths, as shown in Figure 9.5.

```
var RULE_PATH c:\snort\rules
var SO_RULE_PATH c:\snort\rules\so_rules
var PREPROC_RULE_PATH c:\snort\rules\preproc_rules
```

FIGURE 9.5   Windows-style paths.

You will now need to find and change the library paths. This is a bit harder because the names of the paths and the files are a bit different in Windows. The Linux style library paths will appear as the ones shown in Figure 9.6.

```
# path to dynamic preprocessor libraries
dynamicpreprocessor directory
/usr/local/lib/snort_dynamicpreprocessor/

# path to base preprocessor engine
dynamicengine /usr/local/lib/snort_dynamicengine/libsf_engine.so

# path to dynamic rules libraries
# dynamicdetection directory /usr/local/lib/snort_dynamicrules
```

FIGURE 9.6   Linux-style library paths.

You can find your Windows pathnames and filenames by looking in the folder shown in Figure 9.7.

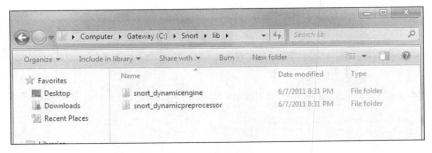

FIGURE 9.7   Windows-style library paths.

Note: If you find that you do not have a particular file or path in your system, just make sure it is commented out in the configuration file.

Now you must find the reference data and change it from Linux paths to Windows style paths as shown in Figure 9.8.

```
# metadata reference data.  do not modify these lines
include C:\Snort\etc\classification.config
include C:\Snort\etc\reference.config
```

FIGURE 9.8   Reference paths.

You are almost done. Now search for

```
#output log_tcp dump
```

and after that put this line

```
output alert_fast: alert.ids
```

Note: the pound sign (#) indicates a comment.

Now you will need to use the command line to start Snort. Simply navigate to c:\snort\bin. There are several different ways to start Snort. Many of the common ones are shown here in Table 9.1. I recommend you try the simplest first.

TABLE 9.1   Snort Commands

Command	Purpose
snort -v	Start Snort as just a packet sniffer
snort -vd	Start Snort as a packet sniffer, but have it sniff packet data rather than just the headers
snort -dev -l ./log	Start Snort in logging mode so it logs packets
snort -dev -l ./log -h *192.168.1.1/24* -c snort.conf (Put your IP address where you see italics.)	Start Snort in IDS mode

Snort is free and open source, but many people have a great deal of difficulty working with it the first time. The slightest error in your configuration file or the command-line startup will cause it to not run correctly. The purpose of this section is just to introduce you to Snort. For more information on Snort, try the following:

- **Snort Manual:** www.snort.org/assets/82/snort_manual.pdf

- **Writing your own Snort rules:** packetstormsecurity.nl/papers/IDS/snort_rules.htm

- **Snort Manual:** www.cs.uiuc.edu/class/fa05/cs591han/papers/snort_manual.pdf

Honey Pots

A honey pot is an interesting technology. Essentially, it assumes that an attacker is able to breach your network security. And it would be best to distract that attacker away from your valuable data. Therefore, one creates a server that has fake data. Perhaps an SQL server or Oracle server loaded with fake data, and just a little less secure than your real servers. Then, since none of your actual users ever access this server, monitoring software is installed to alert you when someone does access this server.

A honey pot achieves two goals. First, it will take the attacker's attention away from the data you wish to protect. Second, it will provide what appears to be interesting and valuable data, thus leading the attacker to stay connected to the fake server, giving you time to try and track them. There are commercial solutions, like Specter (www.specter.com/default50.htm). These solutions are usually quite easy to set up and include monitoring/tracking software. You may also find it useful to check out www.honeypots.org for more information on honey pots in general, and on specific implementations.

Other Preemptive Techniques

Besides IDS, antivirus, firewalls, and honey pots, there are a variety of preemptive techniques an administrator can use to attempt to reduce the chances of a successful attack being executed against his or her network.

Intrusion Deflection

This method is becoming increasingly popular among the more security-conscious administrators. The essence of it is quite simple. An attempt is made to attract the intruder to a subsystem set up for the purpose of observing him. This is done by tricking the intruder into believing that he has succeeded in accessing system resources when, in fact, he has been directed to a specially designed environment. Being able to observe the intruder while he practices his art will yield valuable clues and can lead to his arrest.

This is often done by using what is commonly referred to as a *honey pot*. Essentially, you set up a fake system, possibly a server that appears to be an entire subnet. You make that system look very attractive by perhaps making it appear to have sensitive data, such as personnel files, or valuable data, such as account numbers or research. The actual data stored in this system is fake. The real purpose of the system is to carefully monitor the activities of any person who accesses the system. Since no legitimate user ever accesses this system, it is a given that anyone accessing it is an intruder.

Infiltration

This method refers to efforts on the part of the administrator or security specialist to acquire information from various illicit sources. Many administrators rely solely on various security bulletins from vendors. With infiltration, the administrator proactively seeks out intelligence on potential threats/groups. In other words, it is not a software or hardware implementation, but rather a process of infiltrating hacker/cracker online groups in order to keep tabs on what sort of vulnerabilities are currently being exploited by these groups and what target systems are considered attractive targets. This form of intrusion detection is not widely used for two reasons. The first reason is that it is quite time-consuming. The second reason is that it requires spying skills, which many administrators may not possess.

Intrusion Deterrence

This method involves simply trying to make the system seem like a less-palatable target. In short, an attempt is made to make any potential reward from a successful intrusion attempt appear more difficult than it is worth. This approach includes tactics such as attempting to reduce the apparent value of the current system's worth through camouflage. This essentially means working to hide the most valuable aspects of the system. The other tactic in this methodology involves raising the perceived risk of a potential intruder being caught. This can be done in a variety of ways, including conspicuously displaying warnings and warning of active monitoring. The perception of the security of a system can be drastically improved, even when the actual system security has not been improved.

Summary

It is absolutely critical that any network have a firewall and proxy server between the network and the outside world. It is critical that all machines in the network (servers and workstations alike) have updated virus protection. It is also a good idea to consider intrusion-detection software and anti-spyware, as well. In the upcoming exercises, you will have an opportunity to practice setting up various types of firewalls and IDS systems.

Test Your Skills

MULTIPLE CHOICE QUESTIONS

1. Which of the following is the most common way for a virus scanner to recognize a virus?

    A. To compare a file to known virus attributes

    B. To use complex rules to look for virus-like behavior

    C. To only look for TSR programs

    D. To look for TSR programs or programs that alter the Registry

2. What is one way of checking emails for virus infections?

    A. Block all emails with attachments

    B. Block all active attachments (e.g., ActiveX, scripting)

    C. Look for subject lines that are from known virus attacks

    D. Look for emails from known virus sources

3. What is a TSR program?

    A. Terminal Signal Registry programs that alter the system Registry

    B. Terminate and System Remove that erase themselves when complete

    C. Terminate and Scan Remote that scan remote systems prior to terminating

    D. Terminate and Stay Resident that actually stay in memory after you shut them down

4. What is the name for scanning that depends on complex rules to define what is and is not a virus?

    A. Rules-based scanning (RBS)

    B. Heuristic scanning

    C. TSR scanning

    D. Logic-based scanning (LBS)

5. Which of the following is not one of the basic types of firewalls?

    A. Screening firewall

    B. Application gateway

    C. Heuristic firewall

    D. Circuit-level gateway

6. Which of the following is the most basic type of firewall?

    A. Screening firewall

    B. Application gateway

    C. Heuristic firewall

    D. Circuit-level gateway

7. Which of the following is a disadvantage to using an application gateway firewall?

    A. It is not very secure.

    B. It uses a great deal of resources.

    C. It can be difficult to configure.

    D. It can only work on router-based firewalls.

8. What is SPI?

    A. Stateful packet inspection

    B. System packet inspection

    C. Stateful packet interception

    D. System packet interception

9. What is the term for a firewall that is simply software installed on an existing server?

    A. Network host based

    B. Dual-homed

    C. Router based

    D. Screened host

10. What is a major weakness with a network host-based firewall?

    A. Its security is dependent on the underlying operating system.

    B. It is difficult to configure.

    C. It can be easily hacked.

    D. It is very expensive.

11. What is the term for blocking an IP address that has been the source of suspicious activity?

    A. Preemptive blocking

    B. Intrusion deflection

    C. Proactive deflection

    D. Intrusion blocking

12. What is the term for a fake system designed to lure intruders?

    A. Honey pot

    B. Faux system

    C. Deflection system

    D. Entrapment

13. Which of the following is the correct term for simply making your system less attractive to intruders?

    A. Intrusion deterrence

    B. Intrusion deflection

    C. Intrusion camouflage

    D. Intrusion avoidance

14. What method do most IDS software implementations use?

    A. Anomaly detection

    B. Preemptive blocking

    C. Intrusion deterrence

    D. Infiltration

15. How do most antispyware packages work?

    A. By using heuristic methods

    B. By looking for known spyware

    C. The same way antivirus scanners work

    D. By seeking out TSR cookies

EXERCISES

EXERCISE 9.1: **Setting Up a Firewall**

Microsoft Windows XP and Linux both offer built-in packet-filtering firewalls of some sort.

1. Using the documentation for whichever operating system you have, decide what packets you wish to block.

2. Set your firewall to filter those packets.

Note: Ideally, if you have access to both operating systems, the best exercise is to experiment setting up firewalls for both.

EXERCISE 9.2: **Router-Based Firewalls**

Note: This exercise is for those labs with access to a lab router-based firewall.

1. Consult your router documentation for instructions on how to configure the firewall.

2. Configure your router-based firewall to block the same items you chose to block in Exercise 1.

EXERCISE 9.3: **Evaluating Firewalls**

Write a brief essay explaining whether you think the router-based solution or the built-in operating system solution is best. Explain your reasons.

EXERCISE 9.4: **Active Code**

Using the Web or other resources, find out why blocking active code (e.g., ActiveX, Scripts) might or might not be a good idea for some situations. Write a brief essay explaining your position.

EXERCISE 9.5: **Hardware Used by a Company**

Visit the IT department of a company and ascertain what hardware they use in their computer system's defense. Do they use a hardware firewall in addition to a software firewall? What form of intrusion-detection software do they use? Do they use antivirus and antispyware on the workstations within the company? Write a brief report summarizing your findings.

PROJECTS

PROJECT 9.1: **How Does the Microsoft Firewall Work?**

Using Microsoft documentation, the Web, and other resources, find out what methodologies the Microsoft Windows XP firewall uses. Write a brief essay explaining the strengths and weaknesses of that approach. Also discuss situations in which you feel that approach is adequate and those in which it might be inadequate.

PROJECT 9.2: **How Does Antivirus Software Work?**

Using documentation from the vendor, the Web, or other resources, find out what methodology Norton AntiVirus uses, as well as the methods that McAfee uses. Armed with this information, write a brief essay comparing and contrasting any differences. Also discuss situations in which one might be recommended over the other.

PROJECT 9.3: **Using Snort**

Note: This is a longer project and appropriate for groups.

Go to the Snort.org website (www.snort.org/) and download Snort. Using the vendor documentation or other resources, configure Snort. Then use port scanners on the machine that has Snort configured and note whether Snort detects the scan.

Case Study

Jane Smith is responsible for security at the ABC Company. She has a moderate budget with which to purchase security solutions. To date, she has installed a router-based firewall between the network and the outside world. She also has a commercial virus scanner on every machine on the network. What other actions might you recommend to her? Would you recommend a different firewall? Why or why not?

Chapter | **10**

Security Policies

Chapter Objectives

After reading this chapter and completing the exercises, you will be able to do the following:

- Recognize the importance of security policies.
- Understand the various policies and the rationale for them.
- Know what elements go into good policies.
- Create policies for network administration.
- Evaluate and improve existing policies.

Introduction

So far in this book we have explored various threats to networks. And in Chapter 9, "Computer Security Software," we examined a variety of technical defenses against such attacks. However, the fact is that technology by itself cannot solve all network security problems. There are some issues that technology cannot stop. Examples of this include the following:

- Virus software won't prevent a user from manually opening an attachment and releasing a virus.
- A technologically secured network is still very vulnerable if former employees (perhaps some unhappy with the company) still have working passwords. Or if passwords are simply put on Post-it notes on computer monitors.
- A server is not secure if it is in a room that nearly everyone in the company has access to.
- Your network is not secure if end users are vulnerable to social engineering.

Another reason that technology alone is not the answer is that technology must be appropriately applied. Policies are used to guide you in how to implement and manage security, including security technology. In this chapter, we will examine computer security policies, including the elements that go into creating good security policies as well as examples of how to establish a network security policy.

What Is a Policy

A security policy is a document that defines how an organization will deal with some aspect of security. There can be policies regarding end-user behavior, IT response to incidents, or policies for specific issues and incidents.

Security policies can also be created to deal with regulatory requirements. These types of policies direct members of the organization as to how to comply with certain regulations. A good example would be a policy informing healthcare workers how to comply with HIPAA when using electronic medical records software.

Or policies can simply be advisory, advising employees how they should handle certain items, but not requiring compliance. For example a policy might advise users that emailing from a smart phone using a WiFi hotspot can be unsecure, but not forbid it.

Defining User Policies

When discussing user policies, there is one rule you must keep in mind: You should have a policy for every foreseeable situation. Failure to have policies that address a given problem will usually result in that problem being exacerbated. Something may seem like common sense to you, but may not be to someone with no training or experience in computer networks or network security.

The misuse of systems is a major problem for many organizations. A large part of the problem comes from the difficulty in defining exactly what is misuse. Some things might be obvious misuse, such as using company time and computers to search for another job or to view illicit websites. However, other areas are not so clear, such as an employee using her lunchtime to look up information about a car she is thinking of buying. Generally, good user policies will outline specifically how people are to use the system and how they should not. For a policy to be effective, it needs to be very clear and quite specific. Vague statements such as "computers and Internet access are only for business use" are simply inadequate. I would recommend something more clear and perhaps more enforceable, perhaps something like "computers and Internet access are only for business purposes during business hours. However, employees may use the computer/Internet access for personal use during nonwork time such as breaks, lunch, and before work. However, such use must be in compliance with Internet usage policies." That is clear, direct, and also enforceable.

Other areas for potential misuse are also covered by user policies, including password sharing, copying data, leaving accounts logged on while employees go to lunch, etc. All of these issues ultimately have a significant impact on your network's security and must be clearly spelled out in your user policies. We will now examine several areas that effective user policies must cover:

- Passwords

- Internet use

- Email attachments

- Installing/uninstalling software

- Instant messaging

- Desktop configuration

Passwords

Keeping passwords secure is critical. In Chapter 8, "Encryption," appropriate passwords were discussed as part of operating system hardening. A good password is at least eight characters long, uses numbers and special characters, and has no obvious relevance to the end user. For example, a Dallas Cowboys fan would be ill advised to use a password like *cowboys* or *godallas*, but might be well advised to use a password such as *%trEe987* or *123DoG$$*, since those don't reflect the person's personal interests and therefore would not be easily guessed. Issues such as minimum password length, password history, and password complexity come under administrative policies, not user policies. User policies dictate how the end user should behave. For reliable security, I recommend a passphrase that has been altered to include numbers and special characters. This can be something easy to remember but altered so that it will not be vulnerable to guessing or brute-force attacks. An example would be taking the phrase "I like double cheese burgers" and altering it to be IliK3double3ch33$eburg3r$. Notice the e's were changed to 3's, the s's to $'s and two random letters were capitalized. You now have a 25-character password that is also complex. It is easy to remember and very difficult to break.

However, no password is secure, no matter how long or how complex, if it is listed on a sticky note stuck to the user's computer monitor. This may seem obvious, but it is not at all uncommon to go into an office and find a password either on the monitor or in the top drawer of the desk. Every janitor or anyone who simply passes by the office can get that password.

It is also not uncommon to find employees sharing passwords. For example, Bob is going to be out of town next week, so he gives Juan his password so that Juan can get into his system, check email, etc. The problem is that now two people have that password. And what happens if during the week Bob is gone, Juan gets ill and decides he will share the password with Shelly so that she can keep checking that system while Juan is out sick? It does not take long for a password to get to so many people that it is not longer useful at all from a security perspective.

Issues like minimum length of passwords, password age, and password history are issues of administrative policies. System administrators can force these requirements. However, none of that will be particularly helpful if the users don't manage their passwords in a secure fashion.

All of this means you need explicit policies regarding how users secure their passwords. Those policies should specify the following:

- Passwords are never to be kept written down in any accessible place. The preference is that they not be written down at all, but if they are, they should be in a secure area such as a lock box at your home (i.e., not in the office right next to your computer).

- Passwords must never be shared with any person for any reason.

- If an employee believes his password has been compromised, he should immediately contact the IT department so his password can be changed and so that logon attempts with the old password can be monitored and traced.

Internet Use

Most organizations provide their users with some sort of Internet access. There are several reasons for this. The most obvious reason is email. However, that is hardly the only reason to have Internet access in a business or academic setting. There is also the Web, and even chat rooms (believe it or not, they can, and in some cases are being used for business communications). All of which can be used for legitimate purposes within any organization, but can also be serious security problems. Appropriate polices must be in place to govern the use of these technologies.

The World Wide Web is a wonderful resource for a tremendous wealth of data. Throughout this book, we have frequently referenced websites where one can find valuable security data and useful utilities. The Internet is also replete with useful tutorials on various technologies. However, even non-technology-related business interests can be served via the Web. Here are a few examples of legitimate business uses of the Web:

- Sales staff checking competitor's websites to see what products or services they offer, in what areas, perhaps even getting prices

- Creditors checking businesses AM Best or Standard and Poor's rating to see how their business financial rating is doing

- Business travelers checking weather conditions, and getting prices for travel

- Online training with webinars

- Web meetings

- Online bill payment or in some cases even filing regulatory and government documents

Of course, there are other web activities that are clearly not appropriate on a company's network:

- Using the Web to search for a new job

- Any pornographic use

- Any use which violates local, state, or federal laws

- Use of the Web to conduct your own business (i.e., you have another enterprise you are involved in other than the company's business)

In addition, there are gray areas. Some activities might be acceptable to some organizations, but not to others. Such activities might include

- Online shopping during the employee's lunch or break time

- Reading news articles online during lunch or break time

- Viewing humorous websites

What one person might view as absurdly obvious might not be to another. It is critical that any organization have very clear policies detailing specifically what is and what is not acceptable use of the Web at work. Giving clear examples of what is acceptable use and what is not is also important. You should also remember that most proxy servers and many firewalls can block certain websites. This will help prevent employees from misusing the company's web connection.

Email Usage

Most business and even academic activity now occurs via email. As we have discussed in several previous chapters, email also happens to be the primary vehicle for virus distribution. This means that email security is a significant issue for any network administrator.

Clearly you cannot simply ban all email attachments. However, you can establish some guidelines for how to handle email attachments. Users should only open an attachment if it meets the following criteria:

- It was expected (i.e., they requested documents from some colleague or client).

- If it was not expected, did it come from a known source? If so first send that person an email (or phone them) and ask if they sent the attachment. If so open it.

- It appears to be a legitimate business document (i.e., a spreadsheet, a document, a presentation, etc.).

It should be noted that some people might find such criteria unrealistic. There is no question they are inconvenient. However, with the prevalence of viruses, often attached to email, these measures are prudent. Many people choose not to go to this level to try and avoid viruses, and that may be your choice as well. Just bear in mind that millions of computers are infected with some sort of virus every single year.

No one should ever open an attachment that meets any of the following criteria:

- It comes from an unknown source.

- It is some active code or executable.

- It is an animation/movie.

- The email itself does not appear legitimate. (It seems to entice you to open the attachment, rather than simply being a legitimate business communication that happens to have an attachment.)

If the end user has any doubt whatsoever, then she should not open the email. Rather, she should contact someone in the IT department who has been designated to handle security. That person can then either compare the email subject line to known viruses or can simply come check out the email personally. Then if it appears legitimate the user can open the attachment.

FYI: About Attachments

The author of this book frequently follows "better safe than sorry" axiom on this matter. This means that when forwarded some joke, image, flash animation, etc. circulating the Internet, I simply delete it. That may mean that I will miss many humorous images and stories, but it also means I will miss many viruses. You would do well to consider emulating this practice.

Installing/Uninstalling Software

This is one matter that does have an absolute answer. End users should not be allowed to install anything on their machine. This includes wallpapers, screensavers, utilities—anything. The best approach is to limit their login privileges so that they cannot install anything. However, this should be coupled with a strong policy statement prohibiting the installation of anything on their PC. If they wish to install something, it should first be scanned by the IT department and approved. This process might be cumbersome but it is necessary. Some organizations go so far as to remove or at least disable media drives (CD, floppy, USB, etc.) from end-user PCs, so installations can only occur from files that the IT department has put on some network drive. This is usually a more extreme measure than most organizations will require but it is an option you should be aware of. In fact, Windows allows the administrator to disable allowing new USB devices. So the admin can install some USB devices that are approved for corporate use, then disallow any additional devices being added.

Instant Messaging

Instant messaging is also widely used and abused by employees in companies and organizations. In some cases, instant messaging can be used for legitimate business purposes. However, it does pose a significant security risk. There have been viruses which specifically propagated via instant messaging. In one incident, the virus would copy everyone on the user's buddy list with the contents of all conversations. Thus a conversation you thought was private was being broadcast to everyone you knew and had messaged with.

Instant messaging is also a threat from a purely informational security perspective. Nothing stops an end user from instant messaging out trade secrets, or confidential information, without the traceability of email going through the corporate email server. It is recommended that instant messaging simply be banned from all computers within an organization. If you find you absolutely must have it, then you must establish very strict guidelines for its use, including the following:

- Instant messaging can only be used for business communications, no personal conversations. Now this might be a bit difficult to enforce. Rules like this often are. More common rules, such as prohibiting personal web browsing, are also quite difficult to enforce. However it is still a good idea to have those rules in place. Then if you find a person violating them, you do have a company policy that you can refer to that prohibits such actions. However, you should be aware that in all likelihood you won't catch most violations of this rule.

- No confidential or private business information should be sent via instant messaging.

Desktop Configuration

Many users like to reconfigure their desktop. This means changing the background, screensaver, font size, resolution, etc. Theoretically speaking, this is not a security hazard. Simply changing your computer's background image cannot compromise your computer's security. However, there are other issues involved.

The first issue is where the background image comes from. Frequently, end users will download images from the Internet. This means there is a chance of getting a virus or Trojan horse, particularly one using a hidden extension (i.e., it appears to be a mypic.jpg but is really mypic.jpg.exe). There are also human resources/harassment issues if an employee uses a backdrop or screensaver that is offensive to other employees. Some organizations simply decide to prohibit any changes to the system configuration for this reason.

The second problem is technical. In order to give a user access to change screensavers, background images, and resolution, you must give them rights which will also allow them to change other system settings you might not want changed. The graphical display options are not separated from all other configuration options. This means that allowing the user to change their screensaver might open the door for them to alter other settings (such as the network card configuration or the Windows Internet Connection Firewall) that would compromise security.

Final Thoughts on User Policies

This section has provided an overview of appropriate and effective user policies. It is critical that any organization implement solid user policies. However, these policies will not be effective unless you have clearly defined consequences for violating them. Many organizations find it helpful to spell out specific consequences that escalate with each incident, such as the following:

- The first incident of violating any of these policies will result in a verbal warning.

- A second incident will result in a written warning.

- The third incident will result in suspension or termination. (In the case of academic settings, this would be suspension or expulsion.)

You must clearly list the consequences, and all users should sign a copy of the user policies upon being hired. This prevents anyone claiming they where not aware of the policies.

CAUTION

Termination or Expulsion

Any policy which can lead to expulsion from a school or termination from a job (or even a demotion) should first be cleared by your legal advisor. There can be significant legal ramifications for wrongful termination or expulsion. The author of this book is not an attorney, nor an expert in legal matters, and cannot provide you with legal advice. It is imperative that you do consult an attorney about these matters.

It is also important to realize that there is another cost to misuse of corporate Internet access. That cost is lost productivity. How much time does the average employee spend reading personal email, doing nonbusiness web activities, or instant messaging? It is hard to say. However, for an informal view, go to www.yahoo.com on any given business day, during business hours, and click on one of the news stories. At the bottom of the story you will see a message board for this story. It lists date and time of posts. See how many posts are done during business hours. It is unlikely that all of those people are out of work, retired, or at home sick.

Let us be completely clear. The Internet is the single greatest communication tool in human history. And it can have a tremendous positive effect on any business. I personally conduct almost all of my business activities through the Web. However, many employees do abuse the Internet, and it does decrease productivity for those who cannot be self-disciplined. Here are just a few studies supporting this assertion:

- A 2008 study showed employees wasting an average of 5.3 hours a week on idle Internet surfing.

- Ohio State University researchers found regular Facebook users had a lower GPA than nonusers (http://redandblack.com/2009/04/29/social-networking-decreases-productivity/)

- A 2010 study showed allowing Facebook access on the business network lead to a 1.5% loss in overall productivity. Some employees admitted to spending as much as 2 hours per day on Facebook while at work (www.techjournalsouth.com/2010/08/social-networking-at-work-leads-to-productivity-loss/).

Defining System Administration Policies

In addition to determining policies for users, you must have some clearly defined policies for system administrators. There must be a procedure for adding users, removing users, dealing with security issues, changing any system, etc. There must also be standards for handling any deviation.

New Employees

When a new employee is hired, the system administration policy must define specific steps to safeguard company security. New employees must be given access to the resources and applications their job function requires. The granting of that access must be documented (possibly in a log). It is also critical that the new employee receive a copy of the company's computer security/acceptable use polices and sign a document acknowledging receipt of such.

Before a new employee starts to work, the IT department (specifically network administration) should receive a written request from the business unit that person will be working for. That request should specify exactly what resources this user will need, when she will start, and have the signature of someone in the business unit with authority to approve such a request. Then the person who is managing network administration or network security should approve and sign the request. After you have implemented the new user on the system with the appropriate rights, you can file a copy of the request.

Departing Employees

When an employee leaves, it is critical to make sure all of his logins are terminated and all access to all systems is discontinued immediately. Unfortunately, this is an area of security that all too many organizations do not give enough attention to. When an employee leaves, you cannot be certain which employee will bear the company ill will, and which won't. It is imperative to have all of the former employee's access shut down on his last day of work. This includes physical access to the building. If a former employee has keys and is disgruntled, nothing can stop him from returning to steal or vandalize computer equipment. When an employee leaves the company, you need to ensure that on his last day the following actions take place:

- All logon accounts to any server, VPN, network, or other resource are disabled.

- All keys to the facility are returned.

- All accounts for email, Internet access, wireless Internet, cell phones, etc. are shut off.

- Any accounts for mainframe resources are canceled.

- The employee's workstation hard drive is searched.

The last item might seem odd. But if an employee was gathering data to take with him (proprietary company data) or conducting any other improper activities, you need to find out right away. If you do see any evidence of any such activity, you need to secure that workstation and keep it for evidence in any civil or criminal proceedings.

All of this might seem a bit extreme to some readers. It is true that with the vast majority of exiting employees you will have no issues to be concerned about. However, if you do not make it a habit of securing an employee's access when they depart, you will eventually have an unfortunate situation that could have been easily avoided.

Change Requests

The nature of IT is change. Not only do end users come and go, but requirements change frequently. Business units request access to different resources, server administrators upgrade software and hardware, application developers install new software, web developers change the website, etc. Change is occurring all the time. Therefore, it is important to have a change control process. This process not only makes the change run smoothly, but allows the IT security personnel to examine the change for any potential security problems, before it is implemented. A change control request should go through the following steps:

- An appropriate manager within the business unit signs, signifying approval of the request.

- The appropriate IT unit (database administration, network admin, email admin, etc.) verifies that the request is one they can fulfill (from both a technological and a budgetary/business perspective).

- The IT security unit verifies that this change will not cause any security problems.

- The appropriate IT unit formulates a plan to implement the change and a plan to roll back the change in the event of some failure.

- The date and time for the change is scheduled, and all relevant parties are notified.

Your change control process might not be identical to this one; in fact, you might be much more specific. However the key to remember is that in order for your network to be secure, you simply cannot have changes happening without some process for examining the impact of those changes prior to implementing them.

In Practice

Extremes of Change Control

Anyone with even a few years of experience in the IT profession can tell you that when it comes to change control there are all sorts of different approaches. The real problem is those IT groups that implement unreasonable extremes. This author has personally seen both. Without using the real names of the companies involved, let's examine a real case of each extreme.

Software consultants company X was a small company that did custom financial applications for various companies. They had a staff of less than 20 developers, who frequently traveled to client locations around the country. They literally had

- No documentation for any of their applications, not even a few notes.

- There was no change control process at all. When someone did not like a setting on a server, or some part of the network configuration, they simply changed it.

- There was no process for handling former employee access. In one case, a person had been gone for six months and still had a valid logon account.

Now clearly this is alarming from several perspectives, not just from a security viewpoint. However, that is one extreme, one that makes for a very chaotic environment that is very unsecure. Security-minded network administrators tend to move toward the opposite extreme, one which can have a negative impact on productivity.

Company B had over 2,000 employees, with an IT staff of about 100 people. In this company, however, the bureaucracy had overwhelmed the IT department to the point that their productivity was severely impacted. In one case, a person was a web server administrator and the decision had been made that he also needed database administration rights on a single database server. The process, however, took three months with one face-to-face meeting between his manager and the CIO, as well as two phone conferences and a dozen emails between his manager and the manager of the database group.

The company's convoluted change control process had a severely negative impact on productivity. Some employees informally estimated that even the low-level IT supervisors spent 40% of their time in meetings/conferences, reporting on meetings/conferences, or preparing for meetings/conferences. And the further one went up the IT ladder, the more one's time became consumed in bureaucratic activities.

Both of these examples are meant to illustrate two extremes in change control management that you should try to avoid. Your goal in implementing change control management is simply to have an orderly and safe way of managing change, not to be an impediment to productivity.

Security Breaches

Unfortunately, the reality is that your network will probably, at some point, have a security breach of some kind. This could mean that you are the target of a denial of service attack, your system is infected with a virus, or perhaps a hacker gains entrance and destroys or copies sensitive data. You must have some sort of plan for how to respond should any such event occur. This book cannot tell you specifically how to deal with each and every event that might occur; however, we can discuss some general guidelines for what to do in certain, general, situations. We will look at each of the main types of security breaches and what actions you should take for each.

Virus Infection

- When a virus strikes your system, immediately quarantine the infected machine or machines. This means literally unplugging the machines from the network. If it is a subnet, then unplug its switch and/or disconnect wireless access. Isolate the infected machines (unless your entire network is infected, in which case simply shut down your router/ISP connection to close you off from the outside world and prevent spread beyond your network). After implementing the quarantine, you can safely take the following steps.

- Scan and clean each and every infected machine. Since they are now off the network, this will be a manual scan.

- Log the incident, the hours/resources taken to clean the systems, and the systems which where affected.

- When you are certain the systems are clean, bring them online in stages (a few at a time). With each stage, check all machines to see that they are patched, updated, and have properly configured/running antivirus.

- Notify the appropriate organization leaders of the event and the actions you have taken.

- After you have dealt with the virus and notified the appropriate people, you should then have a meeting with appropriate IT staff to discuss what can be learned from this breach, and how you might prevent it from occurring in the future.

Denial of Service Attacks

- If you have taken the steps outlined earlier in this book (such as properly configuring your router and your firewall to reduce the impact of any attempted DoS), then you will already be alleviating some of the damage from this type of attack. Use your firewall logs or IDS to find out which IP address (or addresses) originated the attacks. Note the IP addresses, then (if your firewall supports this feature, and most do) deny that IP address access to your network.

- Use online resources (interNIC.net, etc.) to find out who the address belongs to.

- Contact that organization and inform them of what is occurring.

- Log all of these activities and inform the appropriate organizational leaders.

- After you have dealt with the DoS and notified the appropriate people, you should then have a meeting with appropriate IT staff to discuss what can be learned from this attack, and how you might prevent it from occurring in the future.

Intrusion by a Hacker

- Immediately copy the logs of all affected systems (firewall, targeted servers, etc.) for use as evidence.

- Immediately scan all systems for Trojan horses, changes to firewall settings, changes to port filtering, new services running, etc. In essence, you are performing an emergency audit to see what damage has been done.

- Document everything. Of all of your documentation, this must be the most thorough. You must specify which IT personnel took what actions at what times. Some of this data may be part of later court proceedings, so absolute accuracy is necessary. It is probably a good idea to log all activities taken during this time and to have at least two people verify and sign the log.

- Change all affected passwords. Repair any damage done.

- Inform the appropriate business leaders of what has happened.

- After you have dealt with the breach and notified the appropriate people, you should then have a meeting with appropriate IT staff to discuss what can be learned from this breach and how you might prevent it from occurring in the future.

These are just general guidelines, and some organizations may have much more specific actions they want taken in the event of some security breach. You should also bear in mind that throughout this book when we have discussed various sorts of threats to network security we have mentioned particular steps and policies that should be taken. The policies in this chapter are meant to be in addition to any already outlined in this book. It is an unfortunate fact that some organizations have no plan for what to do in case of an emergency. It is important that you do have at least some generalized procedures you can implement.

Defining Access Control

An important area of security policies that usually generates some controversy in any organization is access control. There is always a conflict between users' desire for unfettered access to any data or resources on the network and the security administrator's desire to protect that data and resources. This means that extremes in policies are not practical. You cannot simply lock down every resource as completely as possible, since that would impede the user's access to those resources. Conversely, you cannot simply allow anyone and everyone complete access to everything. The core of access control is the concept introduced in Chapter 1: least privileges. Each person is given the minimum privileges necessary to do his or her job. No more and no less.

This is where the least privileges concept comes into play. The idea is simple. Each user, including IT personnel, gets the least access they can have and still effectively do their job. Rather than ask the question "why not give this person access to X?" you should ask "why give this person access to X?" And if you don't have a very good reason, then don't. This is one of the fundamentals of computer security. The more people that have access to any resource, the more likely some breach of security is to occur.

Along with, and related to, least privileges is the concept of implicit deny. Implicit deny means that all users are implicitly denied access to network resources until an administrator explicitly grants them.

Separation of duty, job rotation, and mandatory vacations are also important and related concepts. Separation of duty means that no one person can perform critical tasks; at least two individuals are needed. This prevents one person from accidently, or intentionally, causing some security breach via inappropriate use of critical functions. Job rotation and mandatory vacations are both used to make sure that, periodically, the person performing a given job changes. This makes it more difficult for one person to exploit his or her position to breach security.

Obviously, trade-offs must be made between access and security. Examples abound. One common example involves sales contact information. Clearly, a company's marketing department needs access to this data. However, what happens if ones competitors get all of your company's contact information?

That could allow them to begin targeting your current client list. This requires a trade-off between security and access. In this case, you would probably give salespeople access only to the contacts that are within their territory. No one other than the sales manager should have complete access to all the marketing data.

Developmental Policies

Many IT departments include programmers/web developers. Unfortunately, many security policies do not address secure programming. No matter how good your firewalls, proxy server, virus scanning, and policies are, if your developers create code that is flawed, you will have security breaches. Clearly the topic of secure programming requires a separate volume to explore thoroughly. Nonetheless, we can consider a brief checklist for defining secure development policies. If your company currently has no secure programming initiatives, this checklist is certainly better than developing in a vacuum. It can also serve as a starting point to get you thinking, and talking, about secure programming:

- All code, especially code done by outside parties (contractors, consultants, etc.) must be checked for back doors/Trojan horses.

- All buffers must have error handling which prevents buffer overruns.

- All communication (such as using TCP sockets to send messages) must adhere to your organization's secure communications guidelines.

- Any code that opens any port or performs any sort of communication is thoroughly documented and the IT security unit is apprised of the code, what it will do, and how it will be used.

- All input is filtered for items that might facilitate an attack such as an SQL injection attack.

- All vendors should supply you with a signed document verifying that there are no security flaws in their code.

Following these guidelines will not guarantee that no flawed code gets introduced into your system, but it will certainly lower the odds, significantly. And the unfortunate fact is that these simple steps alone are more than most organizations are taking. A very good place to look at security policies is the SANS Institute (www.sans.org/security-resources/policies/).

Standards, Guidelines, and Procedures

Related to policies are standards, guidelines, and procedures. All of these documents are related to security policies and in fact support those policies. A standard is a general statement of the desired level of operation. For example, requiring 99.5% network uptime would be a standard. A guideline is a general suggestion on how to achieve some standard. Guidelines are broad and are sometimes optional (i.e., not mandatory). Finally, we have procedures. Procedures are specific instructions on how to handle a specific issue.

Summary

In this chapter, you learned the technology is not enough to ensure a secure network. You must have clear and specific policies detailing procedures on your network. Those policies must cover employee computer resource use, new employees, outgoing employees, access rights, how to respond to an emergency, and even how secure code in applications and websites is.

User policies must cover all aspects of how the user is expected to use company technology. In some cases, such as instant messaging and web use, policies may be difficult to enforce, but that does not change the fact that they must still be in place. If your user policies fail to cover a particular area of technology use, then you will have difficulty taking any action against any employee who performs that particular misuse.

We also learned that it is not just the end user who will need policies. The IT staff needs clearly delineated policies covering how to handle various situations. Of particular concern will be policies dictating how to handle new users or exiting users. You also need a carefully considered change management policy.

Test Your Skills

MULTIPLE CHOICE QUESTIONS

1. Which of the following does not demonstrate the need for policies?

    A. Antivirus software cannot prevent a user from downloading infected files.

    B. The most secure password is not at all secure if posted on a note by the computer.

    C. End users are generally not particularly bright and must be told everything.

    D. Technological security measures are dependent upon the employees' implementation.

2. Which of the following is not an area the user policies need to cover?

    A. Minimum length of passwords

    B. What websites one can or cannot visit

    C. If and when to share passwords

    D. What to do if you believe your password has been compromised

3. Which of the following is not an example of a user password policy?

    A. Users may not keep copies of passwords in their office.

    B. Passwords must be eight characters long.

    C. Users may only share passwords with their assistant.

    D. Passwords may not be shared with any employee.

4. What should an employee do if she believes her password has been revealed to another party?

    A. If it is a trusted employee or friend, just ignore it.

    B. Change your own password immediately.

    C. Notify the IT department.

    D. Ignore it.

5. Which of the following should not be recommended as acceptable email attachments?

    A. Flash animations

    B. Excel spreadsheets from a colleague

    C. Attachments you where expecting

    D. Plain text attachments from known sources

6. Which of the following is the best reason users should be prohibited from installing software?

    A. They may not install it correctly which could cause security problems for the workstation.

    B. They may install software that circumvents security.

    C. Software installation is often complex and should be done by professionals.

    D. If a users account does not have privileges to install, then it is likely that a Trojan horse will not be inadvertently installed under their account.

7. Which of the following is not a significant security risks posed by instant messaging?

    A. Employees may send harassing messages.

    B. Employees might send out confidential information.

    C. A virus or worm might infect the workstation via instant messaging.

    D. An instant messaging program could actually be a Trojan horse.

8. What must all user policies have in order to be effective?

    A. They must be reviewed by an attorney.

    B. They must have consequences.

    C. They must be notarized.

    D. They must be properly filed and maintained.

9. Which of the following is the appropriate sequence of events for a new employee?

    A. IT is notified of the new employee and the requested resources > employee is granted access to those resources > employee is briefed on security/acceptable use > employee signs acknowledging receipt of a copy of security rules.

    B. IT is notified of the new employee and the requested rights > employee is given access to those resources> employee signs acknowledging a receipt of a copy of security rules.

C. IT is notified of the new employee and assigns default rights > employee is briefed on security/acceptable use > employee signs acknowledging receipt of a copy of security rules.

D. IT is notified of the new employee and assigns default rights> employee signs acknowledging receipt of company security rules.

10. Which of the following is the appropriate sequence of events for a departing employee?

A. IT is notified of the departure > all logon accounts are shut down > all access (physical and electronic) is disabled.

B. IT is notified of the departure > all logon accounts are shut down > all access (physical and electronic) is disabled > the employee's workstation is searched/scanned.

C. IT is notified of the departure > all physical access is shut down > all electronic access is shut down.

D. IT is notified of the departure > all electronic access is shut down > all physical access is shut down.

11. Which of the following is the appropriate sequence for a change request?

A. Business unit manager requests change > IT unit verifies request > request is implemented.

B. Business unit manager requests change >IT unit verifies request > security unit verifies request > request is scheduled with rollback plan > request is implemented.

C. Business unit manager requests change >IT unit verifies request >request is scheduled with rollback plan > request is implemented.

D. Business unit manager requests change > IT unit verifies request > security unit verifies request > request is implemented.

12. What is the first step when discovering a machine or machines has been infected with a virus?

A. Log the incident

B. Scan and clean infected machines

C. Notify appropriate management

D. Quarantine infected machines

13. What is the rule in access control?

A. The most access you can securely give

B. The least access job requirements allow

C. Standard access for all users

D. Strictly limited access for most users

14. After dealing, on a technical level, with any security breach, what is the last thing to be done for any security breach?

  A. Quarantine infected machines

  B. Study the breach to learn how to prevent a recurrence

  C. Notify management

  D. Log the incident

15. Which of the following is a list of items that should be implemented in all secure code?

  A. All code checked for back doors or Trojans, all buffers have error handling to prevent buffer overruns, all communication activity thoroughly documented.

  B. All code checked for back doors or Trojans, all buffers have error handling to prevent buffer overruns, all communications adheres to organizational guidelines, all communication activity thoroughly documented.

  C. All code checked for back doors or Trojans, all buffers have error handling to prevent buffer overruns, all communication adheres to organizational guidelines.

  D. All code checked for back doors or Trojans, all communication adheres to organizational guidelines, all communication activity thoroughly documented.

EXERCISES

Each of these exercises is intended to give the student experience writing limited portions of a policy. Taken together the exercises represent a complete policy for a college campus computer network.

EXERCISE 10.1: **User Policies**

Using the guidelines provided in this chapter (and other resources as needed), create a document that defines user policies. The policies should clearly define acceptable and unacceptable use for all personnel. You may require some separate policies for administration, faculty, and students.

EXERCISE 10.2: **New Student Policy**

Using the guidelines provided in this chapter (and other resources as needed), create a step-by-step IT security policy for implementing a new user account for a student.

The policy should define what resources the student has access to, what she does not have access to, and for how long access is granted.

EXERCISE 10.3: **Leaving Student Policy**

Using the guidelines provided in this chapter (and other resources as needed), create a step-by-step IT security policy for handling user accounts/rights for a student who is leaving prematurely (drops, is expelled, etc.).

You will need to consider specialized student scenarios, such as a student who works as an assistant to a faculty member or as a lab assistant in a computer lab and may have access to resources most students do not.

EXERCISE 10.4: New Faculty/Staff Policy

Using the guidelines provided in this chapter (and other resources as needed), create a step-by-step IT security policy for implementing a new user account for a faculty or staff member.

The policy should define what resources the faculty or staff member has access to, what she does not have access to, and any restrictions. (Hint: Unlike student policies, you won't need to define time length since it should be indefinite.)

EXERCISE 10.5: Leaving Faculty/Staff Policy

Write a policy for how to handle a faculty departure (quit, fired, retired, etc.). Use the guidelines in this chapter and any other resources you like to get you started.

Make certain you consider not only shutting down access but also the possibility of proprietary research material existing on the faculty/staff member's workstation.

EXERCISE 10.6: Student Lab Use Policy

Considering the material in this chapter, create a set of policies for acceptable use of computer lab computers.

Make sure to specify web use, email use, and any other acceptable uses.

Carefully spell out unacceptable usage (i.e., is game playing acceptable?).

PROJECTS

PROJECT 10.1: Examining Policies

1. Examine the following web resources that discuss security policies:

   - Level 3 acceptable use policy: www.level3.com/764.html

   - Earthlink acceptable use policy: www.earthlink.net/about/policies/use/

   - SANS Institute policies: www.sans.org/resources/policies/

   - Information Security Policy World:
     www.information-security-policies-and-standards.com/

2. Summarize the main theme of these policy recommendations. Pay particular attention to any area that these recommendations differ from or exceed the recommendations of this chapter.

3. Choose which policy recommendation you believe is the most secure and state the reasons for your choice.

PROJECT 10.2: **Real-World Security Policies**

Ask a local business, or your college, to let you see their security policies. Study the policies carefully.

1. Summarize the main theme of these policy recommendations. Pay particular attention to any area that these recommendations differ from or exceed the recommendations of this chapter.

2. Choose which policy recommendation you believe is the most secure and state the reasons for your choice.

PROJECT 10.3: **Creating Security Policies**

Note: This works well as a group project.

At this point in the book, you have studied security including policies. After this chapter and the proceeding exercises and projects, you have examined several polices from various web resources and the policies of some actual organizations.

Take the brief policies you created for the exercises in this chapter and expand them to create an entire working security policy for your college. You will need to add administrative policies, developmental policies, and more.

Case Study

Hector is a security administrator for a defense contractor. This business frequently works with highly sensitive, classified material. Hector has developed a policy for departing employees. This policy handles everything mentioned in this chapter:

- All logon accounts to any server, VPN, network, or other resource are disabled.
- All keys to the facility are returned.
- All accounts for email, Internet access, wireless Internet, cell phones, etc. are shut off.
- Any accounts for any mainframe resources are canceled.
- The employee's workstation hard drive is searched.

Given the highly sensitive nature of the work at this company, what other actions might you add to this policy?

## Chapter 11

Network Scanning and Vulnerability Scanning

Chapter Objectives

After reading this chapter and completing the exercises, you will be able to do the following:

- Understand how to secure a system
- Probe a system for vulnerabilities
- Use vulnerability scanning tools
- Evaluate potential security consultants

Introduction

At this point, it should be clear that it is necessary to assess any system periodically for vulnerabilities. The first part of this chapter will discuss the essential steps that you should follow in assessing a system for vulnerabilities. The purpose of this chapter is to get someone who is new to computer security to begin thinking about these issues. This chapter is not meant to be a comprehensive treatment of the subject, nor a substitute for getting an expert consultant. In fact, many of the topics, such as disaster recovery and policies, have had entire volumes written on them. However, it should give you a basic blueprint you can follow. Specific details will depend on your particular environment, budget, skills, and security needs. The second part of this chapter will discuss various tools you can use to scan your network for vulnerabilities.

In this book, you have thus far examined a number of threats to individual computers and networks. You have learned specific defenses against each of these dangers. However, you have not yet looked at a comprehensive approach to security. In the second part of this chapter, you will learn many of the security procedures that can be implemented to provide your environment with more secure computing. Note that this chapter is about overall procedures that you need to perform in securing a system rather than specific step-by-step techniques.

Basics of Assessing a System

Disaster recovery, access rights, and appropriate policies are topics that are often overlooked by those new to security. To keep it simple and easy to remember, the stages of assessing a system's security can be separated into the six P's:

- Patch
- Ports
- Protect
- Policies
- Probe
- Physical

Patch

The first rule of computer security is to check patches. This is true for networks, home computers, laptops, tablets, smart phones, literally any computer. This means that the operating system, database management systems, development tools, Internet browsers, and so forth are all checked for patches. In a Microsoft environment, this should be easy, as the Microsoft website has a utility that will scan your system for any required patches to the browser, operating system, or Office products. It is a very basic tenet of security to ensure that all patches are up to date. This should be one of the first tasks when assessing a system.

It is also important to consider the types of patches. The most important are labeled *important* or *critical*. (Microsoft labels them critical, but other vendors may use other designation.) These must be applied, and without them your system simply is not secure. Next are recommended patches. These should be applied unless you have some compelling reason not to. And finally, we have optional patches. Your system will not be vulnerable without these. These optional patches usually enhance or correct some minor functionality in the system, but are not necessary for security.

FYI: Patching and Applications

Whenever there is a patch to an operating system or application, there is also documentation (sometimes in a Read Me file, sometimes at the download site) that indicates what the patch is fixing. This documentation also lists any known adverse interactions with other applications. Therefore, you should always read this documentation before you install a patch. In most cases, the problems are minimal and often involve obscure situations. But it is always good to check first to make sure that a service or application upon which you are dependent is not adversely impacted.

FYI: Ports on Routers

One security flaw seen in many organizations that are otherwise security conscious is a failure to close ports on routers. This is particularly a problem for large organizations with wide area networks (WANs) spread over multiple locations. The router between each location should be filtered and too often is not.

Once you have ensured that all patches are up to date, the next step is to set up a system to ensure that they are kept up to date. One simple method is to initiate a periodic patch review where, at a scheduled time, all machines are checked for patches. There are also automated solutions that will patch all systems in your organization. It is imperative that all machines be patched, not just the servers.

The question becomes when to patch. For home users it is usually recommended that automatic patching is turned on so that their systems get patched as soon as the patch is available. However, this is not recommended for network administrators. It is entirely possible that a particular patch may not be compatible with some software on your network. A good example occurred in 2010 with McAfee AntiVirus Business Edition. In April 2010, an update to McAfee caused computers running Windows XP Service Pack 3 to shut down. This caused a great many problems for networks with Windows XP workstations. It is recommended that you install patches on a test machine that has an identical configuration to your networks workstations. Then after the patch has been tested, it can be pushed out to the network.

Ports

As you learned in Chapter 2, "Networks and the Internet," all communication takes place via some port. Any port you do not explicitly need should be shut down. This means that those unused services on servers and individual workstations should be shut down. Both Windows (XP, Vista, or 7) and Linux have built-in port-filtering capability. Windows 2000 Professional was the first Windows operating system to include port-filtering capability. Windows XP expanded this to a fully functional firewall. And more recently Windows 7 added a firewall that could block outgoing as well as incoming traffic. Shutting down a service in Windows and port filtering are both discussed in more detail below.

You should also shut down any unused router ports in your network. If your network is part of a larger WAN, then it is likely you have a router connecting you to that WAN. Every open port is a possible avenue of entry for a malware or intruder. Therefore, every port you can close is one less opportunity for such attacks to affect your system.

In Practice

Shutting Down a Service in Windows

For an individual machine that is not running firewall software, you do not directly close ports; instead, you shut down the service using that port. For example, if you do not use an FTP service but you see that port is on, chances are that you unknowingly have an FTP service running on that machine. In Windows 7 or in Windows Server 2008, if you have administrative privileges, the following three steps can be taken to shut down an unneeded service.

1. Go to the Control Panel. Double-click Administrative Tools (note in Windows 7 you first have to click on System and Security).

2. Double-click Services. You should see a window similar to the one shown in Figure 11.1.

FIGURE 11.1 Services.

The window in Figure 11.1 shows all services installed on your machine, whether they are running or not. Notice that the window also displays information about whether a service is running, whether it starts up automatically, and so forth. In Windows XP, more information can be seen by selecting an individual service. When you double-click on an individual service in any version of Windows (Windows XP, Vista, 7, Server 2003, or Server 2008), you see a dialog box similar to Figure 11.2 that describes the details about that service.

FIGURE 11.2   Disabled services.

In the example shown in Figure 11.1, you see a fax service on a machine that does not require it. To illustrate the procedure, this service is going to be disabled. Before you turn off any service, however, you need to check whether other services depend on the one you are about to shut off. If other services depend on the one you want to turn off and you proceed to turn it off, you will cause the other services to fail.

3. Click on the Dependencies tab. In our case, the fax service has no dependencies.

4. Click the General tab.

5. Change the Startup type to Disabled.

6. Click the Stop button in the Service status section, if necessary. Your dialog box should look similar to Figure 11.2. The fax service is now shut down.

7. Click OK to accept the edits made and close the Properties dialog box. Close the Services dialog box and the Administrative Tools dialog box.

Shutting down unneeded ports and services is an essential and very basic part of computer security. As mentioned above, every port open (and every service running) is a possible avenue for a hacker or virus to get to your machine. Therefore, the rule is: If you don't need it, shut it down and block it.

It is best for you to first make a list of all software that you are running. Then, look up the ports and protocols that you will need for that software and allow only those. It is important to keep in mind that these are ports for incoming traffic. If your machine is not used as a database server, web server, or other type of server and if your machine is a stand-alone one, you can (and should) close all ports. Workstations on networks may need some ports open for network utilities. We will examine some interesting utilities later in this chapter.

Protect

The next phase of assessing a system's security is to ensure that all reasonable protective software and devices are employed. This means, at a minimum, a firewall between your network and the outside world. Firewalls were discussed in Chapter 2. You should also consider using an intrusion-detection system (IDS) on that firewall and any web servers. Remember we discussed Snort IDS in a previous chapter. An IDS is considered nonessential by some security experts; you can certainly have a secure network without one. However, they are the only way to know of impending attacks, and there are free, open source IDSs available. For that reason, I highly recommend them. The firewall and IDS will provide basic security to your network's perimeter, but you also need virus scanning. Each and every machine, including servers, must have a virus scanner that is updated regularly. The point has already been made that a virus infection is the greatest threat to most networks. As also previously discussed, it is probably prudent to consider antispyware software on all of your systems. This will prevent users of your network from inadvertently running spyware on the network.

In Practice

Finding a Firewall

When selecting a firewall to use, you have a number of options. You can purchase a very inexpensive router-based firewall for your high-speed Internet connection. You can get a router that is separate from your DSL or cable router. Or you can get one that includes the functions of your cable or DSL router with the firewall. The websites listed below should be helpful to you in finding more information on these options and determining which will best suit your needs.

- **Linksys**: www.linksys.com/products/product.asp?prid=20&grid=5 (Note: Linksys was purchased by Cisco, and the link should now take you to the Cisco site.)

- **Home PC Firewall Guide**: www.firewallguide.com/

- **Broadband Guide**: www.firewallguide.com/broadband.htm

In addition to the information on the firewall options available, you can also find many free or very inexpensive firewall packages on the Internet. Following is a list of some of the more popular firewalls available via the Internet.

- **Firestarter**: This is a free packet-filtering application for Linux available at www.fs-security.com. This software is installed a Linux machine designed to be used as your network firewall.

- **Norton Personal Firewall**: This product is inexpensive and is available for multiple operating systems. A free trial download is available from www.symantec.com.

- **McAfee Personal Firewall**: This product is similar in price and basic function to Norton Personal Firewall. You can find out more about this product at http://us.mcafee.com.

- **Outpost Firewall**: This product is designed for the home or small office user. It has both a free version and an enhanced commercial version. You can find out more about this product at www.agnitum.com/products/outpost/.

For medium-sized or larger networks, with more flexible budgets, you might consider the options listed below:

- Citrix offers an application gateway specifically tailored for web servers. This solution is relatively inexpensive and can be ideal for companies whose primary function is to provide websites or web services. Information is available at www.citrix.com/English/ps2/products/subfeature.asp?contentID=2300448

- The Firebox, from Watchguard Technologies (www.watchguard.com/products/fireboxx.asp), is an application gateway firewall that is router based. It is relatively easy to set up and configure and is appropriate for medium-sized networks.

And finally, for Linux users, you have a built-in firewall called IP Tables; this is the successor to the earlier IP Chains. This is an excellent solution for any system using Linux.

Policies

While policies were discussed in detail in Chapter 10, "Security Policies," we briefly review some aspects of policies here. It is absolutely essential that any organization have clearly written policies on computer security—and that those policies be strongly enforced by management. Those policies should cover acceptable use of organizational computers, the Internet, email, and any other aspect of the system. Policies should prohibit the installation of any software on the systems. Only IT personnel should install software and only after they have verified its safety.

Policies should also advise users against opening unknown/unexpected attachments. Something that I recommend is for people within an organization or department to use a codeword. If that codeword does not appear in the body of the email (or in the subject line), then they do not open the attachment. Most virus attacks spread via email attachments. The subject line and body of such email messages are generated automatically by the virus itself. If all of your legitimate attachments have a codeword in the subject line, it is highly unlikely that this word would be in the subject line of an email sent by a virus. This alone could prevent your users from inadvertently opening a virus.

Polices should also be in place that clearly delineate who has access to what data, how backups are performed, and what to do to recover data in the case of a disaster (commonly called a disaster recovery plan). Data access must be limited to only those personnel with an actual need to access the data. For example, not everyone in the human resources department needs access to disciplinary files on all employees. Does your organization have a plan for what to do if a fire destroys your servers with all their data? Where do you get new machines? Who gets them? Is there an offsite copy of the data backup? All of these questions must be addressed in a disaster recovery plan.

There should be a policy regarding passwords: acceptable minimum length, lifetime of a password, password history, and passwords to be avoided, such as any word that has a direct connection to the user. For example, a user who is a big fan of the Dallas Cowboys should not use a password that has any relation to that sports team. Also, passwords that relate to personal data, such as spouse's birthday, children's names, or pet's names, are poor choices. A password policy could also include recommendations or restrictions on a password.

FYI: Good Passwords

A good password is at least 8 (preferably 15) characters long; contains letters, numbers, and characters; and combines upper- and lowercase. A good general practice is to select a word that has no personal meaning to you, a random sequence of numbers, and then various-case letters and characters to further disguise the password. For example, you might use something such as $TrEe785. That password would be nearly impossible for anyone to guess and difficult for password-cracking software to break. It would, however, also be difficult to remember. For this reason, many people in the information security field are recommending the use of *passphrases* instead of passwords. These create longer passwords that are even more difficult to break. An example would be: *My telephone # is 555-555-1234.* This is a 30-character password containing uppercase, lowercase, numbers, and special characters. It is also much easier to remember than $TrEe785.

Additionally, a password should not be kept for long periods of time. A 90- or 180-day password replacement schedule is good for most situations. This is referred to as *password age*. (This, of course, must be weighed against the user's access to sensitive information or data. A company financial officer might change her password weekly; a nuclear arms engineer might change his password daily; and a mail clerk might need to change her password on a much less frequent basis.) You can set many systems (including Windows) to force the user to get a new password after a certain period of time. You should also make sure the person does not merely reuse old passwords, referred to as *password history* and also referred to in some operating systems as uniqueness. A good rule of thumb is a history depth of five— meaning that the person cannot reuse any of their previous five passwords. Additionally, you may need to implement a minimum password age to prevent users from immediately changing their password five times to return to their current password. Generally, a minimum of one day is recommended.

FYI: How Extensive Should Policies Be?

This question frequently arises: How extensive should policies be? Should they be a few brief pages or a lengthy manual? Various computer security experts will have differing opinions. My opinion is that the policies should be lengthy enough to cover your organizational needs, but not so lengthy as to be unwieldy. In short, overly long policy manuals are likely to be left unread by employees and hence not be followed. If you absolutely must have a long policy manual, then create a few brief submanuals for specific employee groups so as to increase the chances of the policies being read and followed. It is probably a good idea to have new hires briefed on security polices by someone from the IT Security department.

> **FYI: Checklists and Policies**
>
> For your convenience and to assist in getting you started in securing your systems and establishing good policies, the SANS Institute website contains examples of checklists and policies (www.sans.org/security-resources/policies/). Each of these is also available electronically through the companion website for this text.

Finally, policies should include specific instructions on what to do in case of an employee termination. It is imperative that all of that person's login accounts be immediately disabled and any physical access they have to any part of the system be immediately discontinued. Unfortunately, many organizations fail to address this properly and give an opportunity to a disgruntled former employee to inflict retribution on his or her former employer.

Probe

An important step in assessing any network is to probe the network. We will look at several probes later in this chapter. The key is to periodically probe your own network for security flaws. This should be a regularly scheduled event—perhaps once a quarter. At a minimum, a complete audit of your security should be completed once per year. That would, of course, include probing your ports. However, a true security audit would also include a review of your security policies, your patching system, any security logs you maintain, personnel files of those in secure positions, and so forth.

Physical

Lastly, you cannot ignore physical security. The most robustly secure computer that is left sitting unattended in an unlocked room is not at all secure. You must have some policy or procedure governing the locking of rooms with computers as well as the handling of laptops, PDAs, and other mobile computer devices. Servers must be in a locked and secure room with as few people as is reasonably possible having access to them. Backup tapes should be stored in a fireproof safe. Documents and old backup tapes should be destroyed before disposal (e.g., by melting tapes, magnetizing hard disks, breaking CDs).

Physical access to routers and hubs should also be tightly controlled. Having the most hi-tech, professional information security on the planet but leaving your server in an unlocked room to which everyone has access is a recipe for disaster. One of the most common mistakes in the arena of physical security is co-locating a router or switch in a janitorial closet. This means that, in addition to your own security personnel and network administrators, the entire cleaning staff has access to your router or switch, and any one of them could leave the door unlocked for an extended period of time.

There are some basic rules you should follow regarding physical security:

- **Server rooms:** The room where servers are kept should be the most fire-resistant room in your building. It should have a strong door with a strong lock, such as a deadbolt. Only those personnel who actually have a need to go in the room should have a key. You might also consider a server room log wherein each person logs in when they enter or exit the room. There are actually electronic locks that record who enters a room, when they enter, and when they leave. You may also wish to consider using biometric locks on critical areas such as server rooms. Consult local security vendors in your area for more details on price and availability.

- **Workstations:** All workstations should have an engraved identifying mark. You should also routinely inventory them. It is usually physically impossible to secure them as well as you secure servers, but you can take a few steps to improve their security. Some companies choose to attach the workstations to the desks with cables. This can be effective and affordable.

- **Miscellaneous equipment:** Projectors, CD burners, laptops, and so forth should be kept under lock and key. Any employee that wishes to use one should be required to sign it out, and it should be checked to see that it is in proper working condition and that all parts are present when it is returned.

Securing Computer Systems

In this section, you will examine various security specifics for an individual workstation, a server, and a network. You should be aware, however, that you do not need to reinvent the wheel. A number of very reputable organizations have put together step-by-step guides, or security templates, that you can use in your network setting. These can be modified to fit your particular organization, or they can be used as a starting point for you in forming your own security strategy.

- The National Security Agency has a website with a number of specific network security guides: www.nsA.gov/snac/

- The Center for Internet Security offers a number of security guides and benchmarks: www.cisecurity.com/

- The SANS institute has a number of sample policies you can download and modify or use: www.sans.org/resources/policies/

There are also templates that can be applied to many operating systems and applications (such as Microsoft Windows and Microsoft Exchange) that will implement certain security precautions. These templates can be found for many products and then simply installed on the appropriate machine. Some security professionals prefer to handle the details of security themselves, but many administrators find these templates to be useful—and they can be invaluable for the beginner.

- Windows Security templates: http://support.microsoft.com/kb/816585

- MS Exchange templates: www.microsoft.com/exchange/default.mspx

- A collection of Windows templates: http://www.windowsecurity.com/articles/Understanding-Windows-Security-Templates.html. The use of these templates will at least give you a baseline of security on the applications to which they are applied.

Securing an Individual Workstation

There are a number of steps that any prudent individual can take to make their individual computer secure. These steps should be taken for both home computers and workstations on a network. In the former case, securing the individual computer is the only security option available. In the latter case, securing the individual computers as well as the perimeter allows for a layered approach to security. While some network administrators simply secure the perimeter via a firewall and/or proxy server, it is generally believed that you should also secure each and every machine in your organization. This is particularly vital in protecting against virus attacks and some of the distributed denial of service attacks that you learned about in Chapter 4, "Denial of Service Attacks."

FYI: Hardening a System

The process of securing a computer system against hackers, malware, and other intruders is sometimes referred to as *hardening* a system. You may see the terms *server hardening* or *router hardening* commonly used.

The first step with an individual computer is to ensure that all patches are appropriately applied. Microsoft's website has utilities that will scan your machine for needed patches for both Windows and Microsoft Office. It is critical that you do this on a regular basis—once per quarter as a minimum. You should also check your other software vendors to see whether they have some similar mechanism to update patches for their products. It is amazing how many virus outbreaks have been widespread despite patches being available to secure the flaws they exploited. Too many people simply do not ensure that patches are applied regularly. For a home computer, this is the most critical step in your security strategy and will protect you from a number of attacks designed to exploit security flaws. For a networked workstation, this is still a vital piece of the overall security strategy and cannot be ignored.

The second step in securing an individual computer is restricting the ability to install programs or alter the machine configuration. In a network environment, this would mean that most users do not have permissions to install software or change any system settings. Only network administrators and designated support staff should have that ability. In a home environment, this would mean that only a responsible party or parties (such as the parents) have access rights to install software.

One of the reasons for this particular precaution is to prevent users from accidentally installing a Trojan horse or other malware on their machine. If a person is prevented from installing any software, then there is no chance of inadvertently installing improper software such as a Trojan horse, adware, or other malware. Blocking users from altering the machine's configuration also prevents them from changing system security settings. Novice users may hear of some way to change some setting and will do so, not realizing the security risks they are exposing their system to.

A perfect example in which a novice might adversely alter security settings involves the Windows Messenger service. This is not used for chat rooms or instant messaging, as many novices incorrectly assume. It is instead used for network administrators to send a broadcast message to all people on a network. Unfortunately, some adware programs also use that service to circumvent pop-up blockers and inundate you with ads. Thus, a security-conscious person might disable that service. You would not want an inexperienced person to turn it back on by thinking it is needed for instant messaging.

It is absolutely critical in any network environment that limits be placed on what the average user can do to a machine's configuration. Without such limits, even well-meaning employees could eventually compromise security. This particular step is often met with some resistance from the organization. If you are in charge of a system's security, it is your job to educate the decision makers as to why this step is so critical.

The next step has been discussed previously in this book. Each and every computer must have antivirus and antispyware software. You must also set it to routinely automatically update its virus definitions. Updated, running antivirus software is an integral part of any security solution. The two-pronged approach of antispyware and antivirus software should be a major component in your individual computer security strategy. Some analysts feel that antispyware is a nice extra, but not a critical component. Others contend that spyware is a rapidly growing problem and will probably eventually equal or surpass the dangers of virus attacks.

Of course, if your operating system has a built-in firewall, it is a good idea to configure it and have it turned on. Windows 7 and Linux both come with built-in firewall features. Turn them on and configure them properly. The only significant problem you may encounter in implementing this step is that most networks require a certain amount of traffic between key servers (such as the DNS server) and individual computers. When you configure your firewall, make certain you are allowing appropriate traffic through. If you are at home, you can simply block all incoming traffic. If you are on a network, you must identify what traffic you need to allow.

Passwords and physical security, as discussed earlier in this chapter, are a critical part of computer security. You must ensure that all users utilize passwords that are at least eight characters long and consist of a combination of letters, numbers, and characters. In general, make sure that your password policy is complete and that all employees follow it. This will ensure that your physical security system is sound.

Following these guidelines will not make your computer totally impervious to danger, but these guidelines will make your workstation as secure as it reasonably can be. Remember that, even in a network environment, it is critical to also secure each individual computer as well as the perimeter.

Securing a Server

The core of any network lies in its servers. This includes database servers, web servers, DNS servers, file and print servers, and so on. These computers provide the resources for the rest of the network. Generally, your most critical data will be stored on these machines. This means that these computers are an especially attractive target for intruders and securing them is of paramount importance.

Essentially, to secure a server, you should apply the steps you would to any workstation and then add additional steps. There will not be a user on that machine routinely typing documents or using spreadsheets, so extra-tight restrictions are unlikely to cause the same difficulties for end users that they might on a workstation.

To begin with, you must follow the same steps you would for a workstation. Each and every server should have its software routinely patched. It should also have virus-scanning software and perhaps antispyware as well. It is critical that access to these machines, both via logging on and physical access, be limited to only those people with a clear need. There are, however, additional steps you should take with a server that you might not take with a standard workstation.

Most operating systems for servers (e.g., Windows 2008 Server, Linux) have the ability to log a variety of activities. These activities would include failed logon attempts, software installation, and other activities. You should make sure that logging is turned on and that all actions that might pose any security risk are logged. You then must make certain that those logs are checked on a periodic basis.

Remember that the data on a server is more valuable than the actual machine. For this reason, data must be backed up on a regular basis. A daily backup is usually preferred but, in some cases, a weekly backup might be adequate. The backup tapes should be kept in a secure offsite location (such as a bank safety deposit box) or in a fireproof safe. It is critical that you limit access to those backup tapes just as you would limit access to the servers themselves.

With any computer, you should shut down any service you do not need. However, with a server, you may wish to take the extra step of uninstalling any software or operating system components you do not need, meaning that anything not required for the server to function should be removed. But think carefully about this before proceeding. Clearly, games and office suites are not needed for a server. However, a browser might be necessary to update patches.

There is another step that should be taken with servers that is not necessary with workstations. Most server operating systems have built-in accounts. For example, Windows has built-in administrator, guest, and power user accounts. Any hacker who wants to try and guess passwords will begin by trying to guess the passwords that go with these standard users. In fact, there are utilities on the Web that will do this automatically for the would-be intruder. First, you should create your own accounts with names that do not reflect their level of permission. For example, disable the administrator account and create an account called basic_user. Set up basic_user as the administrator account, with appropriate permissions. (Of course, only give that username and password to those people you want to have administrator privileges.) If you do this, a hacker would not immediately guess that this account is the one that they want to crack. Remember, hackers ultimately want administrative privileges on a target system; concealing which accounts have those privileges is a vital step in preventing the hacker from breaching your security.

FYI: Handling Old Backup Media

Unfortunately, many network administrators simply throw old backup media in the trash. Persons with malicious intent who retrieve this discarded media could restore it to their own machine. This could give them access to your older data without breaking in to your system or could give them very valuable clues as to your current security practices, depending on what is found on that media. Old media (e.g., tapes, CDs, hard disks) should be thoroughly destroyed. For a CD, this means physically breaking it. For a tape, this means partially or completely melting it. Hard disks should be magnetized with a powerful magnet.

There are a variety of Registry settings in any version of Windows that can be altered to increase your security. If you use a scanning tool, such as Cerberus, it returns a report stating the weaknesses in your Registry settings. What items in the Registry settings might cause a security problem? A few items that are commonly examined include the following:

- **Logon:** If your Registry is set so that the logon screen shows the last user's name, you have done half of the hacker's work for her. Since she now has a username, she only needs to guess the password.

- **Default Shares:** Certain drives/folders are shared by default. Leaving them shared like this presents a security hazard.

These are just a few of the potential problems in the Windows Registry. A tool such as Cerberus will not only tell you what the problems are, but will make recommendations for corrections. To edit your Registry, go to Start, select Run, and then key **regedit**. This will start the Registry editor.

Securing a Network

Obviously, the first step in securing a network is to secure all computers that take part in that network, including all workstations and servers. However, this is just one part of network security. By now it should be clear that using a firewall and proxy server are also critical elements in network security. Chapter 12, "Cyber Terrorism and Information Warfare," will provide more details on these devices. For now, it is important to realize that you need to have them. Most experts also recommend using an IDS. There are a number of such systems available—some are even free. These systems can detect things, such as port scanning, which might indicate that a person is preparing to attempt a breach of your security perimeter.

If your network is at all large, then you might consider partitioning it into smaller segments with a firewall-enabled router between segments. Of course, "large" is a vague term and you will have to decide if your network is large enough to require partitioning. In this way, if one segment is compromised, the entire network will not be compromised. In this system, you might consider putting your most important servers (database, file) on a secure segment.

Since web servers must be exposed to the outside world and are the most common point of attack, it then makes sense to separate them from the rest of the network. Many network administrators will put a second firewall between the web server and the rest of the network. This means that if a hacker exploits a flaw in your web server and gains access to it, then he will not have access to your entire network. This brings up the issue of what should be on your web server. The answer is: only what you need to post web pages. No data, documents, or other information should be stored on that server, and certainly no extraneous software. The operating system and web server software are all that are required. You may add a few other items (such as an IDS) if your situation requires it. Any other software running on that server is a potential security risk.

Another concept you should consider is the DMZ. A DMZ is a *demilitarized zone*. It essentially involves setting up two firewalls, an outer and an inner firewall. Resources that must be accessible to the outside world are between the two firewalls. The outer firewall is more permissive, and the inner firewall is highly restrictive. There are even routers that include this functionality in a single box. By plugging into certain ports, you are adding a device either behind the inner firewall, or in the DMZ. This is shown in Figure 11.3.

FIGURE 11.3   DMZ.

You must also have policies that guide users in how to use the system, as we discussed earlier in this chapter. The most robust security in the world will not be of much use if a careless user inadvertently compromises your security. Keep in mind that you must have policies in place that guide users in what is considered appropriate use of the system and what is not.

Just as you take steps to harden your servers (e.g., patching the operating system, shutting down unneeded services), you should also harden your router. The specifics of what needs to be done will be contingent on your particular router manufacturer and model, but a few general rules should be followed:

- **Use good passwords:** All routers are configurable. They can be programmed. Therefore, you must obey the same password policies on a router that you would use on any server including minimum password length and complexity, age of password, and password history. If your router allows you to encrypt the password (as Cisco and other vendors do), then do it.

- **Use logging:** Most routers allow for logging. You should turn this on and monitor it just as you would monitor server logs.

- **Security rules:** Some basic router security rules should also be followed:

  - Do not answer to Address Resolution Protocol (ARP) requests for hosts that are not on the user local area network (LAN).

  - If no applications on your network use a given port, that port should be also shut down on the router.

  - Packets not originating from inside your LAN should not be forwarded.

These rules are simply a beginning. You will need to consult your vendor's documentation for additional recommendations. You must absolutely pay as much attention to securing your router as you do to securing your servers. The following links might be helpful:

- **Router security:** www.mavetju.org/networking/security.php

- **Cisco router hardening:** www.sans.org/rr/whitepapers/firewalls/794.php

Scanning Your Network

The only way to be sure your network is secure is to actually check for vulnerabilities and flaws. In this section, we will look at some commonly used vulnerability scanners. These tools can be an invaluable asset for any network administrator.

MBSA

Microsoft Baseline Security Analyzer is a free tool from Microsoft (just do a web search on the name to get the latest version). It is also very simple to use. Critics point out that it is not as robust as other tools, and that is an accurate assessment. However, it is easy to use, free, and ideal for a Windows administrator who may not be well versed in security.

MBSA (version 2.2 as of this writing) will check one or more Windows machines to see if they have the latest patches, have good password policies, and generally if they have basic security in place.

Once you run the program, you first choose whether you want to scan a single computer or multiple computers, as shown in Figure 11.4.

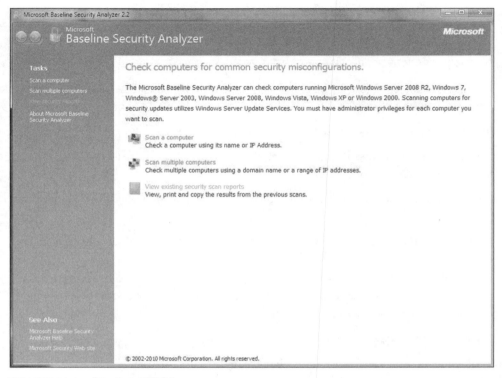

FIGURE 11.4   Starting MBSA.

For demonstration purposes, we will scan a single computer. When you choose that option, you will see a screen that allows you to designate the computer to scan (it defaults to the computer you are on) and what scans to perform. This is shown in Figure 11.5.

FIGURE 11.5   Scanning a single computer.

Then you simply start the scan. For a single computer, it won't take long, but for multiple computers it could take quite some time. When it is done, you will receive a report that details everything checked, if it was okay or not, and it has links for deeper explanations if you need them. This is shown in Figure 11.6.

While I agree with critics that there are more robust scanning tools, I personally feel this particular tool is an excellent choice for someone who is a security novice. It is easy to use and will give you actionable information quickly.

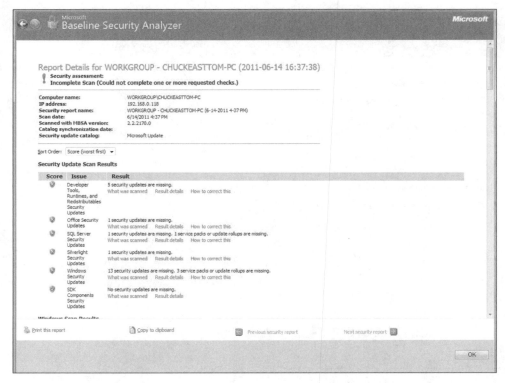

FIGURE 11.6   MBSA report.

NESSUS

Nessus (www.Nessus.org) is the premiere network vulnerability scanner. There is a free version for personal use and a commercial version. This is perhaps the most widely used vulnerability scanner available today. It is not nearly as simple to use as MBSA but has many more capabilities. We will explore the basic functionality. If you have an interest in learning more about Nessus, then it is recommended that you consult the documentation available at their website.

Once you install Nessus, you will have two icons on your desktop. One is the Nessus server the other is the client. We will launch the server first, shown in Figure 11.7. The first thing you have to do is register it. The process is quick, easy, and free.

FIGURE 11.7   Starting the Nessus server.

Once you register, it will take a few moments to download the latest plug-ins. When that is done, you will see the main Nessus server screen, shown in Figure 11.8.

FIGURE 11.8   Starting the Nessus server.

You can leave the default settings for now. But you need to click on the Manage Users button and add a user. For demonstration purposes, it does not matter what name and password you give them. When you have done that, you will close out of the server and launch the client, shown in Figure 11.9.

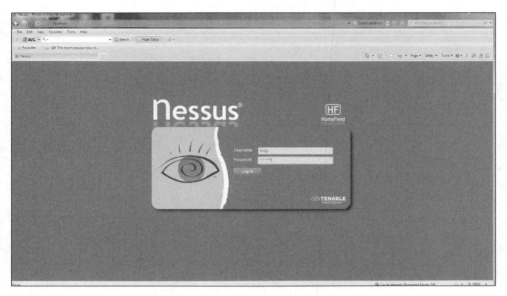

FIGURE 11.9   Nessus client login screen.

The Nessus client is actually a web interface. Once you log in, you will see a page with a toolbar at the top like the one shown in Figure 11.10.

FIGURE 11.10   Nessus client main screen.

It is important that you do things in a specific order. You first have to create a policy, then you can create a scan, and when the scan is done you will have a report. So we will start by creating a simple policy. When you click on Policy, you will see a screen like the one shown in Figure 11.11.

FIGURE 11.11   Policies.

As you can see, there are some default policies already there. But we will make our own simple policy just so you can see how it is done. If you click on the Add button, you will see a screen like the one shown in Figure 11.12.

FIGURE 11.12   Add a new policy.

Give your new policy some meaningful name. For demonstration purposes, something like *test policy* might be appropriate. We will leave default settings on this screen, but take the time to review all the various items on this screen.

We are going to skip credentials for now. That is only necessary if, as part of the scan, you need Nessus to be able to log on to various systems. We are going to go to the plug-ins screen, shown in Figure 11.13.

FIGURE 11.13   Selecting plug-ins.

The plug-ins are the real strength of Nessus. There are literally thousands of plug-ins for almost every conceivable type of vulnerability. When creating your own policies, they should be for specific types of scans. What you are scanning will determine the plug-in you select.

We are going to leave the default selection, but you should take time to review the options available to you. Nessus provides a truly impressive array of vulnerabilities it can scan for. For now, click the Next button, which will take you to Preferences, then click Submit. You have just created a policy. Now click on the Scan option on the toolbar at the top. You will see a screen like the one depicted in Figure 11.14.

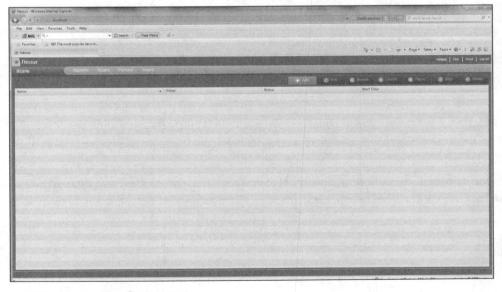

FIGURE 11.14   The Scan screen.

Now click the Add button and you will see a screen like the one shown in Figure 11.15.

FIGURE 11.15   Add a new scan.

Give your scan a meaningful name, then select the policy to use for this scan, enter the IP addresses to scan in the targets text field (you can either enter a computer name or an IP address) and start your scan. When it is done, you will be notified and you can go to the Reports screen, shown in Figure 11.16.

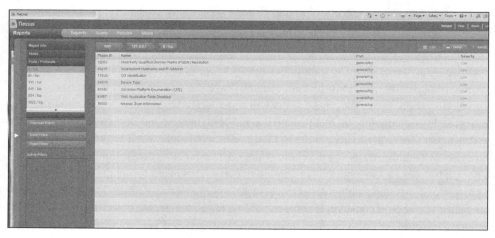

FIGURE 11.16   Reports.

The best thing about the Nessus reports is that you can click on any item and drill down for details. You can also export the report to several formats. Now in this section we have just given you a basic introduction to Nessus. It is strongly recommended that you take the time to become more familiar with Nessus.

Getting Professional Help

You may decide that you need outside help to set up and test your system's security. This option is one that most security professionals would highly recommend if at all possible, particularly if you are new to security. It can be extremely helpful to get a professional consultant to assist you in setting up your initial security strategy and policies and perhaps do a periodic audit of your security. As mentioned in Chapter 1, "Introduction to Computer Security," there are a number of people who claim to be hackers who are not. Frankly, there are also a number of self-proclaimed security experts who simply do not have the requisite skills. The question here is: How do you determine whether an individual is qualified? Following are some guidelines to consider in making this decision.

Experience is the most important factor when looking for a security professional. You want someone with a minimum of five years of IT experience, with two years related to security. Often, this will be a network administrator or programmer who has moved into security. Note that this is a minimum level of experience. More experience is always better. It is certainly possible that someone with less experience might have the requisite skill, but it is unlikely. Everyone needs a place to start, but you do not want your systems to be the place where someone is learning.

The quality of the person's experience is as important as the length of experience. Ask details about the person's experience. For example, exactly what role did she play in computer security? Did she simply set up policies, or did she actually do hands-on security work? What was the result? Was her system free from virus infections and hacker breaches or not? Can you contact her references? In short, simply because a person states that she was responsible for information security on her resume is not enough. You need to find out exactly what she did and what the results were.

Another important aspect of a security professional is education. Remember that computer security is a very broad subject. One needs an understanding of networks, protocols, programming, and more. It is entirely possible for a person with no formal education to have these skills, but it is less likely than if they had a formal education. Generally, these skills will most likely be found in a person with experience and a degree in a computer- or math-related field. That may sound somewhat intellectually snobbish, but it is a fact. There are many people in IT who are self-taught, such as people with history degrees that are network administrators or psychology majors that are now programmers. However, the more areas a person focuses in, the harder it is to obtain mastery. This is not to say that a person cannot be a security professional without a computer science, math, or engineering degree. The point is simply that this is one factor you should consider. If someone has an unrelated degree but meets or exceeds all other qualifications, you might still consider them. Some colleges are beginning to offer security-specific curriculum, and a few even offer security degrees. Clearly, specific training in computer security would be the most preferable security background.

Certifications have become very controversial in the IT profession. Some people swear by them. You can easily find many job advertisements that demand certain certifications, such as the CNE (Certified Novel Engineer) or MCITP (Microsoft Certified Information Technology Professional). Cisco certifications are also common (Cisco Certified Network Associate through Cisco Certified Internetworking Engineer). On the other hand, you would have no problem finding some IT professionals who denigrate certifications and consider them utterly worthless. A more reasonable position is somewhat between the two extremes. A certification can be a good indicator of a candidate's knowledge of a specific product. For example, if you want someone to secure your Microsoft network, looking at people who are Microsoft certified is not a bad idea. You should balance that, however, by keeping in mind that it is entirely possible for someone with a good memory to use the various study guides available on the Internet and pass a test they don't actually understand. That is where experience comes in. A certification coupled with appropriate experience is a good indicator of skill.

In addition to the certifications for network administrators, there are a number of security-related certifications. Some have more credibility than others. The Security+ exam from CompTIA and the CIW Security Analyst are both conceptual exams. This means that they test a candidate's knowledge of security concepts and not their ability to actually implement any security solution. This means that, by themselves, they may not indicate the skill level you need. But if, for example, you are securing a network using Novell, a candidate who is a CNE and has CIW Security Analyst or Security+ might be a good person to consider.

The most respected security certification is the CISSP (Certified Information Systems Security Professional). This test is a grueling six-hour exam and can only be taken if you first verify four years of security-related experience (if you also have a degree) or five years of experience (if you do not have a degree). CISSP holders are also required to submit a recommendation from another CISSP or an officer of their company and to take continuing education credits to maintain the certification. This is probably the most respected security-related certification.

The Certified Ethical Hacker certification is relatively new, and is sponsored by the EC-Council (www.eccouncil.org/). It is an interesting test in that it actually tests basic hacking skills. It has also been the subject of some controversy. One must keep in mind that it tests basic hacking skills, not a mastery of hacking. But if you keep that in mind, it is an excellent certification for any penetration tester or security administrator to have.

GIAC (www.giac.org/) has a number of security-related certifications. These all have a very solid reputation in the security industry. They are, however, more expensive than other tests, and for that reason there are fewer security professionals that have them.

All certifications get some critics. The fact is that some people do attend boot camps and cram just enough information in to pass a certification. However the same can be said of any qualification. It is certainly the case that there are medical doctors who are incompetent, but I am certain that if you are sick or injured you seek out a medical doctor. The reason is that you are more likely to get qualified help than simply selecting some random person. The same is true of certifications. I think you should keep in mind that certifications reflect a minimum skill level, not mastery. I would recommend any security professional have a minimum of CISSP, CEH, and one "elective" (Security+, Microsoft certification, Cisco Certification, etc.). You may wish to consult the following two articles for at least one view of the relative merits of various certifications:

- www.pearsonitcertification.com/articles/article.aspx?p=1652336
- www.pearsonitcertification.com/articles/article.aspx?p=1663684

With all of that being said, you should never hire a person based solely on certifications. Those certifications should simply be one element that you consider.

Finally, you should consider personal background. A security consultant or full-time employee will, by definition, have access to confidential information. Any legitimate security professional will not mind giving you

- References

- Permission to check their credit history

- Permission to check their criminal background

Anyone who seems reluctant to provide any of these items should be avoided. Therefore, an ideal security consultant might be a person with five or more years of experience, a degree in a computer-related discipline, a certification in your organization's operating systems as well as one of the major security certifications, and a completely clean background, with references. As a rule, you simply cannot be too careful in hiring a security consultant.

Unless you have a highly trained security expert on staff, you should consider bringing in a security consultant to assess your system at least once. In our current legal environment, liability for security breaches is still being hotly debated. Companies are being sued for failing to practice due diligence in computer security. It is simply a wise move, both from a computer industry perspective as well as from a legal perspective, to do everything reasonable to ensure the security of your systems.

Summary

This chapter has outlined some basic items to look for in any security assessment. You should periodically assess your network/system for security vulnerabilities. A general recommendation would be a quarterly assessment for noncritical/low-security sites and perhaps as frequently as a weekly assessment for high-security sites. In any case, what are outlined in this chapter are the basics of assessing the security of a network, and they should give you a start toward securing your own network.

Safe computing is a matter of securing your computer, your network, and your servers and using common sense on the Web. It is important to rigorously apply security practices and standards to all computers, whether they are home computers or part of an organizational network.

Test Your Skills

MULTIPLE CHOICE QUESTIONS

1. What are the six P's of security?

    A. Patch, ports, personnel, privacy, protect, policies

    B. Ports, patch, protect, probe, policies, physical

    C. Physical, privacy, patch, ports, probe, protect

    D. Ports, patch, probe, physical, privacy, policies

2. What is the most basic rule of computer security?

    A. Keep systems patched.

    B. Always use an IDS.

    C. Install a firewall.

    D. Always use antispyware.

3. How might you ensure that system patches are kept up to date?

    A. Use an automated patching system.

    B. Patch anytime you receive a vendor notification of a new patch.

    C. Patch whenever a new threat is announced.

    D. Use periodic scheduled patching.

4. What is the rule about ports?

    A. Block all incoming ports.

    B. Block ICMP packets.

    C. Block all unused ports.

    D. Block all non-standard ports.

5. Which of the following is a good reason to check dependencies before shutting down a service?

   A. To determine whether you will need to shut down other services as well

   B. To determine whether shutting down this service will affect other services

   C. To find out what this service does

   D. To find out whether this service is critical to system operations

6. If your machine is not used as a server and is not on a local network, what packet-filtering strategy should you use?

   A. Block all ports except 80.

   B. Do not block any ports.

   C. Block all ports.

   D. Do not block well-known ports.

7. Which of the following is the least essential device for protecting your network?

   A. Firewall

   B. Virus scanners on all machines

   C. IDS system

   D. Proxy server

8. What is the rule of thumb on data access?

   A. Data must be available to the widest range of people possible.

   B. Only administrators and supervisors should access sensitive data.

   C. Only those with a need for the specific data should have access.

   D. All employees should have access to any data used in their department.

9. What is password age?

   A. How long a user has had a password

   B. The length of the password history

   C. A reference to the sophistication (maturity) of the password

   D. A reference to a password's length

10. What is the minimum frequency for system probing and audits?

    A. Once per month

    B. Once per year

    C. Every other year

    D. Every other month

11. An audit should check what areas?

  A. System patching, review polices, check personnel records of all managers, and probe for flaws

  B. Only probe for flaws

  C. System patches, probe for flaws, check logs, and review policies

  D. Check all machines for illicit software, complete system virus scan, and review of firewall polices

12. Which of the following is true of the room in which the server is located?

  A. It should be in the most fire-resistant room in the building.

  B. It should have a strong lock with a strong door.

  C. It should be accessible only to those who have a need for access.

  D. All of the above.

13. What would be most important to block end users from doing on their own machine?

  A. Running programs other than those installed by the IT staff

  B. Surfing the Web and using chat rooms

  C. Changing their screensaver and using chat rooms

  D. Installing software or changing system settings

14. What is the preferred method for storing backups?

  A. Near the server for quick restore if needed

  B. Offsite in a secure location

  C. In the IT manager's office for security

  D. At the home of one of the IT staff

15. Which of the following is a step you would definitely take with any server, but might not be required for a workstation?

  A. Uninstall all unneeded programs/software.

  B. Shut down unneeded services.

  C. Turn off the screensaver.

  D. Block all Internet access.

16. Which of the following is a step you might take for large networks, but not for smaller networks?

  A. Use an IDS.

  B. Segment the network with firewalls between the segments.

  C. Use antivirus software on all machines on the network.

  D. Do criminal background checks for network administrators.

17. Which of the following is a common way to establish security between a web server and a network?

    A. Block all traffic between the web server and the network.

    B. Place virus scanning between the network and the web server.

    C. Put a firewall between the web server and the network.

    D. Do not connect your network to the web server.

18. What is the rule on downloading from the Internet?

    A. Do not ever download anything.

    B. Only download if the download is free of charge.

    C. Only download from well-known, reputable sites.

    D. Never download executables. Only download graphics.

19. Which of the following certifications is the most prestigious?

    A. CISSP

    B. PE

    C. MCSA

    D. Security+

20. Which of the following set of credentials would be best for a security consultant?

    A. Ten years of IT experience, one year in security, CIW Security analyst, MBA

    B. Eight years of IT experience, three years in security, CISSP, B.S. in computer science

    C. Eleven years of IT experience, three years in security, MCSE and CISSP, MS in information systems

    D. Ten years of experience as a hacker and cracker, MCSE/CIW/ and Security +, Ph.D. in computer science

EXERCISES

EXERCISE 11.1: Patching Systems

1. Using a lab system, find and apply all operating system patches.

2. Check with all vendors of software installed on that machine and apply patches for those applications as well (if available).

3. Note the time taken to fully patch a machine. Consider how long it would take to patch a 100-machine network.

4. Write an essay that answers the following questions: Are there ways you could speed the process of patching a 100-machine network? How might you approach such a task?

EXERCISE 11.2: **Learning about Policies**

1. Using the resources given or other resources, find at least one sample security policy document.

2. Analyze that document.

3. Write a brief essay giving your opinion of that policy. Did it miss items? Did it include items you had not thought of?

EXERCISE 11.3: **Learning about Disaster Recovery**

1. Using the resources given, or other resources, find at least one sample disaster recovery plan.

2. Analyze that document.

3. Write a brief essay giving your opinion of that disaster recovery plan. Also note any changes you would recommend to that policy.

EXERCISE 11.4: **Learning about Audits**

1. Using the resources given or other resources, find at least one sample security audit plan.

2. Analyze that document.

3. Write a brief essay giving your opinion of that plan. Do you feel the audit plan is adequate? What changes might you recommend?

FYI: Helpful Resources

For Exercises 11.2, 11.3, and 11.4, you may find the following resources helpful:

- www.cert.org/
- www.sans.org/
- http://csrc.nist.gov/fasp/
- www.information-security-policies-and-standards.com/

EXERCISE 11.5: **Securing Your Computer**

Using either your home computer or a lab computer, follow the guidelines given in this chapter to secure that computer. Those steps should include the following:

1. Scan for all patches and install them.

2. Shut down all unneeded services.

3. Install antivirus software. (A demo version can be used for this exercise.)

4. Install antispyware software. (A demo version can be used for this exercise.)

5. Set appropriate password permissions.

EXERCISE 11.6: Secure Passwords

1. Using the Web or other resources, find out why longer passwords are harder to break.

2. Also find out what other things you should do to make a password harder to crack.

3. Write a brief essay describing what makes a perfect password.

EXERCISE 11.7: Securing a Server

Note: This exercise is for those students with access to a lab server.

Using the guidelines discussed in this chapter, secure a lab server. The steps taken should include the following:

1. Scan for all patches and install them.

2. Shut down all unneeded services.

3. Remove unneeded software.

4. Install antivirus software. (A demo version can be used for this exercise.)

5. Install antispyware software. (A demo version can be used for this exercise.)

6. Set appropriate password permissions.

7. Enable logging of any security violations. (Consult your operating system documentation for instructions.)

EXERCISE 11.8: Backups

Using the Web and other resources as a guide, develop a backup plan for a web server. The plan should cover how frequently to back up and where to store the backup media.

EXERCISE 11.9: User Accounts

Note: This exercise is best done with a lab computer, not a machine actually in use.

1. Locate user accounts. (In Windows 2000 or Windows XP, this is done by going to Start > Control Panel > Administrative Tools > Computer Management and looking for Groups and Users.)

2. Disable all default accounts (Guest, Administrator).

PROJECTS

PROJECT 11.1: Writing and Executing an Audit Plan

With the knowledge you have gained while studying six chapters of this text and in examining security policies in the preceding exercises, it is now time to devise your own audit plan. This plan should detail all the steps in an audit.

Note: The second part of this project is contingent upon getting permission from some organization to allow you to audit their security. It is also ideal for a group project.

Taking the audit plan you wrote, audit a network. This audit can be conducted for any sort of organization, but you should make your first audit one with a small network (fewer than 100 users).

PROJECT 11.2: Forming a Disaster Recovery Plan

Using the knowledge you have gained thus far, create an IT disaster recovery plan for an organization. You may use a fictitious organization, but a real organization would be better.

PROJECT 11.3: Writing a Security Policy Document

Note: This project is designed as a group project.

It is now time to bring all you have learned thus far together. Write a complete set of security policies for an organization. Again, you may use a fictitious company, but real organizations are better. This set of policies must cover user access, password policies, frequency of audits (both internal and external), minimum security requirements, guidelines for web surfing, and so on.

PROJECT 11.4: Secure Web Servers

Using the information in this chapter as well as other resources, come up with a strategy specifically for securing a web server. This strategy should include the security of the server itself as well as securing the network from the server.

PROJECT 11.5: Adding Your Own Guidelines

Note: This project is ideal for a group project.

This chapter has outlined some general procedures for security. Write an essay detailing your own additional guidelines. These can be guidelines for individual computers, servers, networks, or any combination thereof.

Case Study

Juan Garcia is the network administrator for a small company that also maintains its own web server. He has taken the following precautions:

- All computers are patched, have antivirus software, and have unneeded services shut down.

- The network has a firewall with proxy server and IDS.

- The organization has a policy requiring passwords of ten characters in length, and they must be changed every 90 days.

Has Juan done enough to secure the network? What other actions would you recommend he take?

## Chapter 12

Cyber Terrorism and Information Warfare

Chapter Objectives

After reading this chapter and completing the exercises, you will be able to do the following:

- Explain what cyber terrorism is and how it has been used in some actual cases
- Understand the basics of information warfare
- Have a working knowledge of some plausible cyber terrorism scenarios
- Have an appreciation for the dangers posed by cyber terrorism

Introduction

Throughout this book, various ways have been examined in which a person might use a computer to commit a crime. This book has also looked into specific methods to make a system more secure. One issue that has not been addressed is that of cyber terrorism. People in countries around the world have grown accustomed to the ever-present threat of a terrorist attack, which could come in the form of a bomb, a hijacking, releasing a biological agent, or other means. Most people have not given much thought to the possibility of cyber terrorism.

The first question might be this: What is cyber terrorism? According to the FBI, *cyber terrorism* is the premeditated, politically motivated attack against information, computer systems, computer programs, and data that results in violence against noncombatant targets by subnational groups or clandestine agents (Dick, 2002). Cyber terrorism is simply the use of computers and the Internet connectivity between them in order to launch a terrorist attack. In short, cyber terrorism is just like other forms of terrorism—it is only the milieu of the attack that has changed. Clearly the loss of life due to a cyber attack would be much less than that of a bombing. In fact, it is highly likely that there would be no loss of life at all. However, significant economic damage, disruptions in communications, disruptions in supply lines, and general degradation of the national infrastructure are all quite possible via the Internet.

The real question might be what is the difference between cyber espionage and cyber terrorism. First and foremost, the goal of espionage is simply to gather information. It is preferable to the spy if no one is even aware that anything occurred. This is true for both corporate and international espionage. Cyber terrorism, on the other hand, seeks to cause damage, and it needs to be as public as possible. The idea is to strike fear into people. While some might find the topics related, they are actually quite different.

It is a strong possibility that, in time, someone or some group will try to use computer methods to launch a military or terrorist attack against our nation. Some experts make the case that the MyDoom virus (discussed in Chapter 4, "Denial of Service Attacks") was an example of domestic economic terrorism. However, an attack such as that may be only the tip of the iceberg. Sometime in the near future, our nation may be the target of a serious cyber terrorism attack. This chapter will examine some possible cyber terrorism scenarios, with the purpose of giving you a realistic assessment of just how serious a threat this is. In the exercises at the end of the chapter, you will have the opportunity to examine current acts of cyber terrorism, as well as potential threats, and the actions you can take to help prevent them.

The first edition of this book discussed cyber terrorism, as well. That was in 2004. At that time, some may have thought that the coverage of that topic was almost fiction. That there was no real threat from cyber terrorism. That has proven to not be the case. One of the first indications that cyber terrorism is a real threat was that in November 2006 the Secretary of the Air Force announced the creation of the Air Force Cyber Command. This Command's primary function is to monitor and defend American interest in cyberspace. The AFCC draws upon the personnel resources of the 67th Network Warfare Wing as well as other resources. It seems that the United States Air Force takes the threat of cyber terrorism and cyber warfare seriously and has created an entire command to counter that threat.

Actual Cases of Cyber Terrorism

Because some readers may wonder whether this is just fear mongering, let's look at some actual cases of cyber terrorism before we delve into the various aspects of it. How likely is a genuine cyber terrorist attack? Well let's look at some real-world cases. Later in this chapter, we will examine some older, historical cases, to get a sense of perspective. However, in this section, we will only look at recent attacks.

In May 2007, government offices of Estonia were subjected to a mass denial of service attack. This attack was executed because some people opposed the government's removal of a Russian WWII memorial. While this is a relatively minor attack, it was politically motivated and thus qualifies as cyber terrorism.

The year 2009 brought a number of Internet-based attacks, specifically against U.S. government websites, such as the websites of the Pentagon and the White House (in the United States) and various government agencies in South Korea. These attacks coincided with increased tensions with North Korea. Clearly, these where examples of cyber terrorism, albeit relatively minor.

In December 2009, a far more disturbing story came out. Hackers broke into computer systems and stole secret defense plans of the United States and South Korea. Authorities speculated that North Korea was responsible. The information stolen included a summary of plans for military operations by South Korean and U.S. troops in case of war with North Korea, and the attacks traced back to a Chinese IP address. This case is clearly an example of cyber espionage and a very serious one at that.

China Eagle Union

No discussion of cyber terrorism would be complete without a discussion of the China Eagle Union. This group consists of several thousand Chinese hackers whose stated goal is to infiltrate western computer systems. There are a number of web resources regarding this group:

- www.thedarkvisitor.com/2007/10/china-eagle-union/

- https://news.hitb.org/node/6164

- http://archives.cnn.com/2001/WORLD/asiapcf/east/04/27/chinA.hackers/index.html

Members and leaders of the group insist that not only does the Chinese government have no involvement in their activities, but that they are breaking Chinese law and are in constant danger of arrest and imprisonment. Many analysts find this claim dubious. Whether the Chinese government is involved in these attacks or not, some experts consider a state of cyber warfare to currently exist between China and the United States.

Economic Attacks

There are a variety of ways that a cyber attack can cause economic damage. Lost files and lost records are one way. Chapter 9, "Computer Security Software," discussed cyber espionage and mentioned the inherent value of data. In addition to stealing that data, it could simply be destroyed, in which case the data is gone and the resources used to accumulate and analyze the data are wasted. To use an analogy, consider that a malicious person could choose to simply destroy your car rather than steal it. In either case, you are without the car and will have to spend additional resources acquiring transportation.

In addition to simply destroying economically valuable data (remember that there is very little data that does not have some intrinsic value), there are other ways to cause economic disruption. Some of those ways include stealing credit cards, transferring money from accounts, and fraud. But it is a fact that anytime IT staff is involved with cleaning up a virus rather than developing applications or administering networks and databases, there is economic loss. The mere fact that companies now need to purchase antivirus software and intrusion-detection software and hire computer security professionals means that computer crime has already caused economic damage to companies and governments around the world. However, the general damage caused by random virus outbreaks, lone hacking attacks, and online fraud is not the type of economic damage that is the focus of this chapter. This chapter is concerned with a concerted and deliberate attack against a particular target or targets for the exclusive purpose of causing direct damage.

A good way to get a firm grasp on the impact of this type of attack is to walk through a scenario. Group X (which could be an aggressive nation, terrorist group, activist group, or literally any group with the motivation to damage a particular nation) decides to make a concerted attack on our country. They find a small group of individuals (in this case, six) who are well versed in computer security, networking, and programming. These individuals, motivated either by ideology or monetary needs, are organized to create a coordinated attack. There are many possible scenarios under which they could execute such an attack and cause significant economic harm. The example outlined below is just one of those possible attack modalities. In this case, each individual has an assignment, and all assignments are designed to be activated on the same specific date:

- Team member one sets up several fake e-commerce sites. Each of these sites is only up for 72 hours and pretends to be a major stock brokerage site. During the brief time they are up, the site's real purpose is only to collect credit card numbers/bank account numbers and so forth. On the predetermined date, all of those credit card and bank numbers will be automatically, anonymously, and simultaneously posted to various bulletin boards/websites and newsgroups, making them available for any unscrupulous individual who wishes to use them.

- Team member two creates a virus. This virus is contained in a Trojan horse. Its function is to delete key system files on the predetermined date. In the meantime, it shows a series of business tips or motivational slogans, making it a popular download with people in business.

- Team member three creates another virus. It is designed to create distributed denial of service attacks on key economic sites, such as those for stock exchanges or brokerage houses. The virus spreads harmlessly and is set to begin its distributed denial of service attack on the predetermined date.

- Team members four and five begin the process of footprinting major banking systems, preparing to crack them on the predetermined date. Footprinting is the process of gathering information. Some from public sources, others by scanning the target system/network.

- Team member six prepares a series of false stock tips to flood the Internet on the predetermined date.

If each of these individuals is successful in his or her mission, on the predetermined date several major brokerages and perhaps government economic sites are taken down, viruses flood networks, and files are deleted from the machines of thousands of businesspeople, economists, stockbrokers. Thousands of credit cards and bank numbers are released on the Internet, guaranteeing that many will be misused. It is also highly likely that the cracking team members four and five will have some success—meaning that possibly one or more banking systems are compromised. It does not take an economist to realize that this would easily cost hundreds of millions of dollars, perhaps even billions of dollars. A concerted attack of this nature could easily cause more economic damage to our country than most traditional terrorists attacks (i.e., bombings) have ever done.

FIGURE 12.1   A team member of Group X?

You could extrapolate on this scenario and imagine not just one group of six cyber terrorists, but five groups of six—each group with a different mission and each mission designed to be committed approximately two weeks apart. In this scenario, the nation's economy would literally be under siege for two and one-half months.

This scenario is not particularly far-fetched when you consider that, in past decades, nuclear scientists were sought after by various nations and terrorist groups. More recently, experts in biological weapons have been sought by these same groups. It seems extremely likely that these groups will see the possibilities of this form of terrorism and seek out computer security/hacking experts. Given that there are literally thousands of people with the requisite skills, it seems likely that a motivated organization could find a few dozen people willing to commit these acts.

Military Operations Attacks

When computer security and national defense are mentioned together, the obvious thought that comes to mind is the possibility of some hacker breaking into ultra-secure systems at the Department of Defense, Central Intelligence Agency (CIA), or National Security Agency (NSA). However, such an intrusion into one of the most secure systems in the world is very unlikely—not impossible, but very unlikely. The most likely outcome of such an attack would be that the attacker is promptly captured. Such systems are hyper-secure, and intruding upon them is not as easy as some movies might suggest. However, there are a number of scenarios in which breaking into less-secure systems could jeopardize our national defense or put military plans at risk.

Consider less-sensitive military systems for a moment, for example, systems that are responsible for basic logistical operations (e.g., food, mail, fuel). If someone cracks one or more of these systems, he could perhaps obtain information that several C-141s (an aircraft often used for troop transports and parachute operations) are being routed to a base that is within flight distance of some city—a city that has been the focal point of political tensions. This same cracker (or team of crackers) also finds that a large amount of ammunition and food supplies, enough for perhaps 5,000 troops for two weeks, is simultaneously being routed to that base. Then, on yet another low-security system, the cracker (or team of crackers) notes that a given unit, such as two brigades of the 82nd Airborne Division, has had all military leaves canceled. It does not take a military genius to conclude that these two brigades are preparing to drop in on the target city and secure that target. Therefore, the fact that a deployment is going to occur, the size of the deployment, and the approximate time of that deployment have all been deduced without ever attempting to break into a high-security system.

Taking the previous scenario to the next level, assume the hacker gets deep into the low-security logistical systems. Then assume that he does nothing to change the routing of the members of the brigades or the transport planes—actions that might draw attention. However, he does alter the records for the shipment of supplies so that the supplies are delivered two days late and to the wrong base. So there would be two brigades potentially in harm's way, without a resupply of ammunition or food en route. Of course, the situation could be rectified, but the units in question may go for some time without resupply—enough time, perhaps, to prevent them from successfully completing their mission.

These are just two scenarios in which compromising low-security/low-priority systems can lead to very significant military problems. This further illustrates the serious need for high security on all systems. Given the interconnectivity of so many components of both business and military computer systems, there are no truly "low-priority" security systems.

General Attacks

The previously outlined scenarios involve specific targets with specific strategies. However, once a specific target is attacked, defenses can be readied for it. There are many security professionals who work constantly to thwart these specific attacks. What may be more threatening is a general and unfocused attack with no specific target. Consider the various virus attacks of late 2003 and early 2004. With the exception of MyDoom, which was clearly aimed at the Santa Cruz Organization, these attacks were not aimed at a specific target. However, the shear volume of virus attacks and network traffic did cause significant economic damage. IT personnel across the globe dropped their normal projects to clean infected systems and shore up the defenses of systems.

This leads to another possible scenario in which various cyber terrorists continuously release new and varied viruses, perform denial of system attacks, and work to make the Internet in general, and e-commerce in particular, virtually unusable for a period of time. Such a scenario would actually be more difficult to combat, as there would not be a specific target to defend or a clear ideological motive to use as a clue to the identity of the perpetrators.

Supervisory Control and Data Acquisitions

These are industrial systems used to operate and monitor large-scale equipment (for example, power generators, civil defense alarms, water treatment plants). These systems are very attractive targets for cyber terrorism. In 2009, *60 Minutes* did a report on the vulnerability of power systems. They showed that penetration testers working for the Department of Energy were able to take over a power generator and potentially overload it, causing permanent damage and taking it offline. The famous Stuxnet virus that infected Iranian nuclear facilities was exploiting a vulnerability in SCADA systems.

These systems are of particular concern because damage to them is not simply an economic attack. It is entirely possible for lives to be lost as a result of cyber attacks on SCADA systems.

Information Warfare

Information warfare certainly predates the advent of the modern computer and, in fact, may be as old as conventional warfare. In essence, information warfare is any attempt to manipulate information in pursuit of a military or political goal. When you attempt to use any process to gather information on an opponent or when you use propaganda to influence opinions in a conflict, these are both examples of information warfare. Chapter 7, "Industrial Espionage in Cyberspace," discussed the role of the computer in corporate espionage. The same techniques can be applied to a military conflict in which the computer can be used as a tool in espionage. Although information gathering will not be reexamined in this chapter, information gathering is only one part of information warfare. Propaganda is another aspect of information warfare. The flow of information impacts troop morale, citizens' outlooks on a conflict, the political support for a conflict, and the involvement of peripheral nations and international organizations.

Propaganda

Computers and the Internet are very effective tools that can be used in the dissemination of propaganda. Many people now use the Internet as a secondary news source, and some even use it as their primary news source. This means that a government, terrorist group, political party, or any activist group could use what appears to be an Internet news website as a front to put their own political spin on any conflict. Such a website does not need to be directly connected to the political organization whose views are being disseminated; in fact, it is better if it is not directly connected. The Irish Republican Army (IRA), for example, has always operated with two distinct and separate divisions: one that takes paramilitary/terrorist action and another that is purely political. This allows the political/information wing, called Sinn Fein, to operate independently of any military or terrorist activities. In fact, Sinn Fein now has their own website, shown in Figure 12.2, where they disseminate news with their own perspective (www.sinnfein.org). In this situation, however, it is fairly clear to whoever is reading the information that it is biased toward the perspective of the party sponsoring the site. A better scenario (for the party concerned) occurs when there is an Internet news source that is favorably disposed to a political group's position without having any actual connection at all. This makes it easier for the group to spread information without being accused of any obvious bias. The political group (be it a nation, rebel group, or terrorist organization) can then "leak" stories to this news agency.

FIGURE 12.2   The Sinn Fein website.

Information Control

Since World War II, control of information has been an important part of political and military conflicts. Below are just a few examples:

- Throughout the Cold War, Western democracies invested time and money for radio broadcasts into communist nations. This well-known campaign was referred to as Radio Free Europe. The goal was to create dissatisfaction among citizens of those nations, hopefully encouraging defection, dissent, and general discontent. Most historians and political analysts agree that this was a success.

- The Vietnam War was the first modern war in which there was strong and widespread domestic opposition. Many analysts believe that opposition was due to the graphic images being brought home via television.

- Today, the government and military of every nation are aware of how the phrases they use to describe activities can affect public perception. They do not say that innocent civilians were killed in a bombing raid. Rather, they state that there was "some collateral damage." Governments do not speak of being the aggressor or starting a conflict. They speak of "preemptive action." Dissenters in any nation are almost always painted as treasonous or cowards.

Public perception is a very important part of any conflict. Each nation wants their own citizens to be totally in support of what they do and to maintain a very high morale. High morale and strong support lead to volunteers for military service, public support for funding the conflict, and political success for the nation's leader. At the same time, you want the enemy to have low morale—to doubt not only their ability to be successful in the conflict but also their moral position relative to the conflict. You want them to doubt their leadership and to be as opposed to the conflict as possible. The Internet provides a very inexpensive vehicle for swaying public opinion.

Web pages are just one facet of disseminating information. Having people post to various discussion groups can also be effective. One full-time propaganda agent could easily manage 25 or more distinct online personalities, each spending time in different bulletin boards and discussion groups, espousing the views that his political entity wants to espouse. These can reinforce what certain Internet news outlets are posting or they could undermine those postings. They can also start rumors. Rumors can be very effective even when probably false. People often recall hearing something with only a vague recollection of where they heard it and whether it was supported by any data.

Such an agent could have one personality that purports to be a military member (it would take very little research to make this credible) and could post information "not seen in newscasts" that would cast the conflict in either a positive or negative light. She could then have other online personas that entered the discussion who would agree with and support the original position. This would give the initial rumor more credibility. Some people suspect this is already occurring in Usenet newsgroups and Yahoo! discussion boards. Obviously, Usenet and Yahoo! are just two examples. The Internet is replete with various blogs, community sites, boards, etc.

FYI: Cyber Information Warfare Now

Anyone familiar with Yahoo! news boards (this is just one example, there are certainly many more) has probably noticed an odd phenomenon. At certain times, there will be a flood of posts from anonymous users, all saying essentially the exact same things—even using the exact same grammar, punctuation, and phrasing—and all in support of some ideological perspective. These flurries often happen in times when influence of public opinion is important, such as when an election is nearing. Whether or not these postings are coordinated by any well-known or official organization is debatable. However, they are an example of information warfare. One person or group of people attempt to sway opinion by flooding one particular media (Internet groups) with various items advocating one view. If they are lucky, some individuals will copy the text and email it to friends who do not participate in the newsgroups, thus crossing over to another media and spreading opinions (in some cases entirely unfounded) far and wide.

> ### FYI: Disinformation—A Historical Perspective
>
> While disinformation campaigns are certainly easier to conduct since the advent of mass communication, particularly the Internet, such activities did exist prior to the Internet, or even television. For example, in the weeks leading up the famous D-Day invasion of World War II, the Allied forces used a number of disinformation techniques:
>
> - They created documents and communiqués listing fictitious military units that would invade from an entirely different location than the real invasion was planned.
>
> - They used Allied double agents to spread similar disinformation to the Germans.
>
> - A few small groups simulated a large scale invasion to distract the German army.

Disinformation

Another category of information warfare that is closely related to propaganda is disinformation. It is a given that a military opponent is attempting to gather information about troop movements, military strength, supplies, and so forth. A prudent move would be to set up systems that had incorrect information and were just secure enough to be credible, but not secure enough to be unbreakable. An example would be to send an encrypted coded message such that, when the message is decrypted, it seems to say one thing, but to those who can complete the code it has a different message. The actual message is "padded" with "noise." That noise is a weakly encrypted false message, whereas the real message is more strongly encrypted. In this way, if the message is decrypted, there exists a high likelihood that the fake message will be decrypted and not the real one. General Gray, USMC, put it best when he said, "Communications without intelligence is noise; intelligence without communications is irrelevant" (Information Warfare, 2004).

The goal of any military or intelligence agency is to make certain our communications are clear and that the enemy can only receive noise.

Actual Cases

It should be noted that there are voices in the computer security industry that think cyber terrorism or cyber war are simply not realistic scenarios. Marcus Ranum of *Information Security* magazine states as much in the April 2004 issue. He and others claim that there is no danger from cyber terrorism and that, in fact, "The whole notion of cyberwarfare is a scam" (*Information Security*, 2004). However, computer warfare and cyber terrorism have already been used on a small scale. It seems quite plausible that, in a matter of time, it will be seen on a much larger scale.

Even if you believe that the scenarios outlined in the earlier sections of this chapter are merely the product of an overactive imagination, you should consider that there have already been a few actual incidents of cyber terrorism, although much less severe than the theoretical scenarios. This section examines some of these cases so as to show you how such attacks have been carried out in the past.

The incidents listed below were reported in testimony before the Special Oversight Panel on Terrorism Committee on Armed Services U.S. House of Representatives (Cyberterrorism, 2000). Earlier in this chapter, we listed more recent attacks, but these older attacks are important to illustrate just how long this problem has been going on.

- In 1996, a computer hacker allegedly associated with the white supremacist movement temporarily disabled a Massachusetts ISP and damaged part of the ISP's record-keeping system. The ISP had attempted to stop the hacker from sending out worldwide racist messages under the ISP's name. The hacker signed off with the threat, "You have yet to see true electronic terrorism. This is a promise."

- In 1998, ethnic Tamil guerrillas swamped Sri Lankan embassies with 800 emails a day over a two-week period. The messages read, "We are the Internet Black Tigers and we're doing this to disrupt your communications." Intelligence authorities characterized it as the first known attack by terrorists against a country's computer systems.

- During the Kosovo conflict in 1999, NATO computers were blasted with email bombs and hit with denial of service attacks by *hacktivists* (the name applied to individuals who work for their causes using cyber terrorism) protesting the NATO bombings. In addition, businesses, public organizations, and academic institutes received highly politicized virus-laden emails from a range of Eastern European countries, according to reports. Web defacements were also common. After the Chinese embassy was accidentally bombed in Belgrade, Chinese hacktivists posted messages such as, "We won't stop attacking until the war stops!" on U.S. government websites.

The good news is that these particular attacks caused little damage and were clearly the product of amateurs. However, it may only be a matter of time before more-damaging attacks are perpetrated by far more skilled cyber terrorists. Yet it is clear that cyber terrorism, at least on a low–intensity scale, is already beginning. These warnings can be heeded and the issues taken seriously, or they can simply be ignored until disaster strikes.

In addition to those cases listed above, there have been other credible threats or actual incidents of cyber attacks in the past several years:

- In 2002, Counterpane Internet Security reported (as shown in Figure 12.3) a credible threat of a Chinese-backed, all-out cyber attack planned on the United States and Taiwan (2002). A private group of Chinese hackers, called the Chinese Eagle Union, planned to attack routers and web servers across the United States and Taiwan. The attack never materialized, but unconfirmed reports suggested that the CIA took the threat seriously.

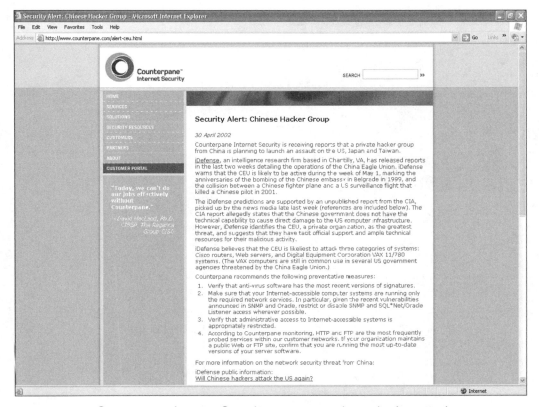

FIGURE 12.3   Counterpane Internet Security report on a planned cyber attack.

■ In June of 2000, Russian authorities arrested a man they accused of being a CIA-backed hacker. As shown in Figure 12.4, this man allegedly hacked into systems of the Russian Domestic Security Service (FSB) and gathered secrets that he then passed on to the CIA (BBC Report, 2000). This example illustrates the potential for a skilled hacker using his knowledge to conduct espionage operations. This espionage is likely occurring much more often than is reported in the media, and many such incidents may never come to light.

FYI: The Threat of Cyber Terrorism

Fortunately, to date, the examples given in this text are about the most dramatic that have been made public. Cyber terrorism is not a big problem today; it is the problem that is looming on our horizon.

Alternative media sources have been reporting that both the CIA and NSA have employed hackers for some time. This might be easily dismissed as false were it not for the fact that such hackers have actually been caught, as in the Russian story. One might even go so far as to say that, in our modern age, for intelligence gathering agencies not to employee cyber intelligence-gathering techniques would be a dereliction of their duty.

FIGURE 12.4   BBC report on an arrested hacker.

What is also frightening to consider are reports that our satellites, used for communication, weather, and military operations, could be vulnerable to hacking (Info World, 2002). Such vulnerabilities seem less likely simply because of the skill level required to execute such an attack. As previously mentioned, hacking/cracking is like any other human endeavor—by the law of averages, most people are mediocre. The level of skill required to compromise security on a satellite system is far greater than that required to compromise the security of a website. Of course, that does not mean that such an attack is impossible, but simply that it is less likely.

Future Trends

By carefully analyzing what is occurring presently in cyber crime and terrorism along with the recent history of that field, you can extrapolate and make reasonably accurate estimates for what trends will dominate in the near future. This section will endeavor to do that. There are certainly positive and negative trends that should be considered.

Positive Trends

It does seem that various governments are beginning to take notice of this problem and are taking some steps to ameliorate the dangers. For example, then Senator John Edwards (D-NC) proposed two bills in 2002 aimed at allocating $400 million for cybersecurity efforts. The first measure, called the Cyberterrorism Preparedness Act of 2002 (Tech Law, 2002), a portion of which is shown in Figure 12.5, allocated $350 million over five years for improving network security, first for federal systems and then for the private sector. It would also create a group assigned to gather and distribute information about the best security practices. The Cybersecurity Research and Education Act of 2002 (The Orator, 2002), a portion of which is shown in Figure 12.6, would provide $50 million over four years for fellowships that would be used to train IT specialists in cyber security. It also calls for the creation of a web-based university where administrators can get updated training. The Cybersecurity Research and Education act was passed and became Public Law 107-305. The Cyberterrorism Preparedness Act of 2002 was not passed. However, many of its goals where addressed by the Patiort Act.

FIGURE 12.5   The Cyberterrorism Preparedness Act of 2002.

FIGURE 12.6   The Cybersecurity Research and Education Act of 2002.

Title VIII of the U.S. Patriot Act specifically deals with cyber terrorism. The number of cyber attacks included in that definition of *cyber terrorism* is expansive, including attempts to damage or alter medical records and releasing a virus in a target system. Penalties are also clearly set out.

More recently, in 2010 the United States Department of Defense established the U.S. Cyber Command (USCYBERCOM). This unit is based in Ft. Meade, Maryland, and is a joint task force representing components of all four U.S. armed services.

Negative Trends

Unfortunately, as legislative bodies become aware of this problem and focus some resources on the issue, the threats continue to grow. In a paper commissioned by the Rand Corporation (Hoffman, 2003), it is noted that even groups such as Al Qaeda—who have not used cyber terrorism as one of their attack modalities as of this writing—have used Internet and computer technology resources to plan their various activities and coordinate training.

As early as 2000, the U.S. General Accounting Office warned of several possible cyber terrorism scenarios (*The Tech Law Journal*, 2000). As shown in Figure 12.7, their concerns involved far more lethal attackers than any of the scenarios that have been outlined in this chapter. They proposed possible attack scenarios in which the computer-controlled machinery in a chemical plant was altered in order to cause a release of toxic chemicals into the environment. This could be done in a variety of ways, including simply causing the machinery to drastically overproduce, overheat, or perhaps prematurely shut down equipment. The panel also contemplated scenarios in which water and power supplies were interrupted or compromised via computer systems. In essence, their focus was on the potential for massive casualties as a direct result of a cyber-based attack rather than the economic damage on which this chapter's scenarios focused.

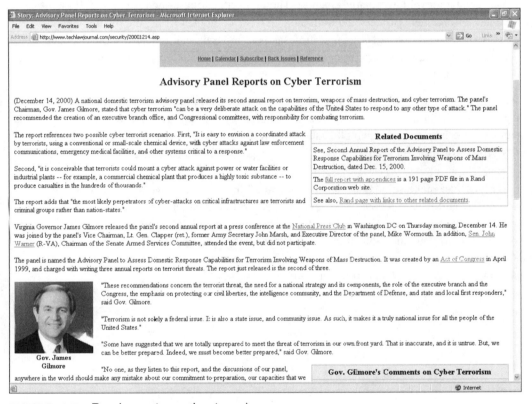

FIGURE 12.7   Rand report on cyber terrorism.

Defense against Cyber Terrorism

As the world becomes more dependent upon computer systems, the danger of cyber terrorism will grow. Clearly, there must be a much stronger emphasis on computer security. In addition to the basic security measures already recommended in this book, there are also some recommendations for preparing for and protecting systems against cyber terrorism:

- Many recommend a Manhattan Project-level government program designed to prepare for and defend against cyber warfare.

- Major academic institutions must begin dedicated research and academic programs that are devoted solely to computer security.

- Computer crime must be treated far more seriously, with stronger punishments and more active investigation of suspected crimes.

- It is unreasonable to ask every police department to have a computer-crime specialist on staff. However, state-level investigative agencies should be able to hire such personnel. Rather than take law enforcement officers and train them in basic computer crime, the recommendation exists to take highly skilled computer professionals and train them in law enforcement. To adequately combat cyber terrorism, one absolutely must first and foremost be a highly qualified computer expert.

- An emergency reporting system may need to be implemented so that security professionals from various industries have a single source where they can report attacks on their systems and can view the issues with which other security professionals are dealing. This could enable security professionals as a group to more quickly recognize when a coordinated attack is occurring.

In addition, you can make some additions to and variations on your existing security measures. For example, you should have a recovery process in place so that data can be quickly recovered should someone delete important files. You should also, as recommended in Chapter 9, assess what data is of most value and focus your attention on that data. But, as this chapter points out, you must also consider how data that would at first appear to be of less value may actually reveal more information about you personally or your company than is prudent.

Summary

It is clear that there are a variety of ways in which cyber terrorist attacks could be used against any industrialized nation. Many experts, including various government panels, senators, and terrorism experts, believe that this is a very real threat. This means that it is more important than ever to be extremely vigilant in securing your computer systems. You must also look beyond the obvious uses of data and see how someone with an intent to harm or cause economic hardship could use seemingly unimportant information. In the exercises at the end of this chapter, you will have a chance to explore various cyber terrorism and information warfare threats.

Test Your Skills

MULTIPLE CHOICE QUESTIONS

1. What is the most likely damage from an act of cyber terrorism?

   A. Loss of life

   B. Military strategy compromised

   C. Economic loss

   D. Disrupted communications

2. Which of the following is not an example of financial loss due to cyber terrorism?

   A. Lost data

   B. Transferring money from accounts

   C. Damage to facilities including computers

   D. Computer fraud

3. Which of the following military/government systems would most likely be the target of a successful computer hack?

   A. The most sensitive systems of the CIA

   B. Nuclear systems at NORAD

   C. Low-security logistical system

   D. Military satellite control systems

4. Which of the following might be an example of domestic cyber terrorism?

   A. Sasser virus

   B. Mimail virus

   C. Sobig virus

   D. MyDoom virus

5. What differentiates cyber terrorism from other computer crimes?

    A. It is organized.

    B. It is politically or ideologically motivated.

    C. It is conducted by experts.

    D. It is often more successful.

6. Which of the following is a political group that has already used the Internet for political intimidation?

    A. Internet Black Tigers

    B. Al Qaeda

    C. Mafia

    D. IRA

7. What is information warfare?

    A. Only spreading disinformation

    B. Spreading disinformation or gathering information

    C. Only gathering information

    D. Spreading disinformation or secure communications

8. Which of the following would most likely be considered examples of information warfare?

    A. Radio Free Europe during the Cold War

    B. Radio political talk show

    C. Normal news reports

    D. Military press releases

9. Which of the following is a likely use of Internet newsgroups in information warfare?

    A. To spread propaganda

    B. To monitor dissident groups

    C. To send encoded messages

    D. To recruit supporters

10. Sending a false message with weak encryption, intending it to be intercepted and deciphered, is an example of what?

    A. Poor communications

    B. Need for better encryption

    C. Disinformation

    D. Propaganda

11. Which of the following best describes the communication goal of any intelligence agency?

    A. To send clear communications to allies and noise to all other parties

    B. To send clear communications to allies and noise only to the enemy

    C. To send disinformation to the enemy

    D. To send clear communications to allied forces

12. Which of the following conflicts had a cyber warfare component?

    A. 1989 invasion of Panama

    B. 1990 Kosovo crisis

    C. 1990 Somalia crisis

    D. Vietnam War

13. Which of the following agencies has allegedly had one of its cyber spies actually caught?

    A. NSA

    B. KGB

    C. FBI

    D. CIA

14. According to the October 2002 *InfoWorld* magazine article, which of the following systems may be vulnerable to attack?

    A. NORAD nuclear weapons control

    B. Low-level logistical systems

    C. Satellites

    D. CIA computers

15. Which of the following is a cyber attack that would likely cause imminent loss of life?

    A. Disruption of banking system

    B. Disruption of water

    C. Disruption of security systems

    D. Disruption of chemical plant control systems

EXERCISES

EXERCISE 12.1: **Finding Information Warfare**

1. Pick a current political topic.

2. Track that topic on multiple bulletin boards, Yahoo! newsgroups, or blogs.

3. Look for signs that might indicate an organized effort to sway opinion or information warfare. This might include posts allegedly made by separate individuals that have highly similar points, grammar, and syntax.

4. Write a brief essay discussing what you found and why you think it constitutes information warfare.

EXERCISE 12.2: **Cyber Terrorism Threat Assessment**

1. Pick some activist group (e.g., political, ideological) that you find intriguing.

2. Using only the Web, gather as much information about that organization as you can.

3. Write a brief dossier on that group, including what you think is the likelihood that such a group would engage in information warfare or cyber terrorism and why.

EXERCISE 12.3: **Finding Information Policies**

1. Using the Web or other resources, locate several examples of organizational policies regarding information dissemination.

2. Find points common to all such policies.

3. Write a brief essay explaining why these policies might be related to either propagating or preventing information warfare.

EXERCISE 12.4: **How Companies Defend against Cyber Terrorism**

1. Interview the IT staff of a company to find out whether they take information warfare or cyber terrorism into direct account when they are securing their systems.

2. Find out what steps they take to protect their company's systems from these threats.

3. Write a brief essay explaining what you have found out.

EXERCISE 12.5: **Pulling It All Together**

Pulling together what you have learned from previous chapters, what information can you apply to the protection of a system against cyber terrorism or information warfare? Write a brief outline of the steps you would take to secure a system against these threats.

PROJECTS

PROJECT 12.1: **Computer Security and Cyber Terrorism**

Consider the various security measures you have examined thus far in this book. Given the threat of cyber terrorism, write an essay discussing how those methods might relate to cyber terrorism. Also discuss whether or not the threat of computer-based terrorism warrants a higher security standard than you might have otherwise used, and explain why or why not.

PROJECT 12.2: **The Law and Cyber Terrorism**

Note: This is meant as a group project.

Using the Web or other resources, find and examine laws that you feel relate to cyber terrorism. Then write an essay describing legislation you believe needs to be written regarding cyber terrorism. Essentially, your group should act as if it were technical advisors to a congressional committee drafting new legislation.

PROJECT 12.3: **Cyber Terrorism Scenario**

Considering any of the theoretical cyber terrorism scenarios presented in this chapter, write a security and response plan that you feel addresses that scenario and protects against that specific threat.

Case Study

Jane Doe is the network administrator responsible for security for a small defense contractor. Her company does handle some low-level classified material. She has implemented a strong security approach that includes the following:

- A firewall has all unneeded ports closed.

- Virus scanners are placed on all machines.

- Routers between network segments are secured.

- All machines have the operating systems patched monthly.

- Passwords are long, complex, and change every 90 days.

What other recommendations would you make to Jane Doe? Explain the reasons for each of your recommendations.

Chapter | 13

Cyber Detective

Chapter Objectives

After reading this chapter and completing the exercises, you will be able to do the following:

- Find contact information on the Web
- Locate court records on the Web
- Locate criminal records on the Web
- Use Usenet newsgroups to gather information

Introduction

In the preceding chapters we have examined many facets of computer security. Three of those issues lead us to the content of this chapter. The first is identity theft, the second is hacking, and the third is investigating potential employees for sensitive positions.

In order for a criminal to perpetrate identity theft they have to take a small amount of information they find on their target and use that to garner even more information. Perhaps a discarded credit card receipt or utility bill becomes the starting point from which the perpetrator finds enough information to assume the victim's identity. This chapter will show you some techniques that use the Internet to find additional information about a person. You need to be aware of how this is done, in order to be better prepared to defend against it and so that you are aware of what information about you personally is available.

Hackers, at least skilled hackers, will want information about a target person, organization, and system in order to assist in compromising security. Whether the perpetrator is attempting to use social engineering or simply trying to guess a password, having information about the target will facilitate the task. Once you realize how easy it is to gain personal information about someone, you will realize why security experts are so adamant that you must not use passwords that are in any way associated with you, your profession, your hobbies, or anything that might be traced back to you.

Finally, when you are hiring employees that might have access to sensitive data, simply calling the references they provide is not an adequate method of checking into their background. And hiring a private investigator may be impractical. The information in this chapter might be of use to you in conducting some level of investigation on your own.

This may surprise some readers, but network administrators are of particular significance to be investigated before hiring. Most companies perform the same cursory check of network administrators as they do of any other person. That usually consists of verifying degrees/certifications and calling references. With some companies it might include a credit check and a local criminal check. However, a network administrator should be more thoroughly investigated. The reason is quite simple, regardless of how tight your security is, it cannot keep out the person who sets it up and maintains it. If you are considering hiring a network administrator for your company, knowing that he or she has been affiliated with hacking groups might be of interest to you. Or simply knowing that they have had lapses in judgment might indicate a stronger possibility that they will have similar lapses in the future. This may seem a bit paranoid, but by this point in this book you should have developed a little healthy paranoia.

The Internet can be a valuable investigation tool. It can be used to find out about potential employees, babysitters, etc. Much of the information on the Internet is also free. Many states have court records online, and there are many other resources you can use to find information. In this chapter, we will examine some of the various resources you can use on the Internet to locate critical information.

Before beginning this discussion, a few points need to be made clear, the first being that this information is a two-edged sword. Yes, you can use it to find out if a potential business partner has previously been sued or declared bankruptcy or if your child's little league coach has a criminal record. However, as we briefly mentioned, a less-scrupulous person can also use these techniques to gather detailed information about you, either for the purpose of identity theft or perhaps stalking. Some people have suggested to me that perhaps I should not put this information (and some other items that appear in various chapters) in this book. However, my opinion is that the hackers, crackers, and perpetrators of identity theft already know about these resources. My hope is to level the playing field. I would also warn all readers that invading other people's privacy is fraught with ethical, moral, and in many cases, legal ramifications. It would be advisable to obtain written permission before running a background check on any person—or, better yet, play it safe and only perform searches on your own name. It must also be stressed that I am neither an attorney nor a law enforcement officer. I am simply providing you with techniques and resources. If you have questions about legality, you should refer those questions to an attorney.

General Searches

Sometimes you simply want to find an address, phone number, or email address for a person. Or perhaps that is the starting point for a more thorough investigation. There are a number of absolutely free services on the Web that will allow you to perform this sort of search. Some are better than others, and obviously the more common the name you are searching for the harder it will be to find the right one. If you do a search for John Smith in California, you might have a tough time dealing with all the results you get. No matter what search mechanism you utilize (LinkedIn, Facebook, etc.) the problem is the same.

A fairly easy to use service is the Yahoo! People Search. When you go to www.yahoo.com you see a number of options on the page. One option is the People Search shown in Figure 13.1. Or you can simply go directly to people.yahoo.com.

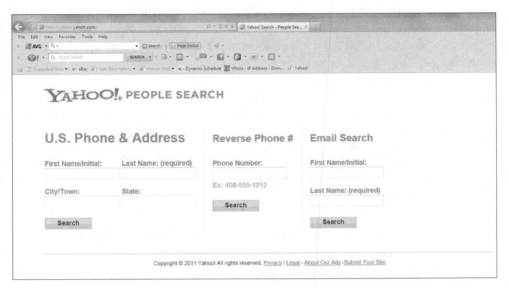

FIGURE 13.1   Yahoo! People Search.

When you select this option you will see a screen similar to the one shown in Figure 13.2. In this screen, you enter a first and last name, as well as a city or state. You can then search for either a phone number/address or an email.

First Name	Last Name (req'd)	City/Town	State	
Chuck	Easttom			Go
Chuck Easttom	WILLOW CREEK TRL MCKINNEY, TX 75071			
Chuck Easttom	WILLOW CREEK TRL MCKINNEY, TX 75071			

FIGURE 13.2   Search options.

To illustrate how this works, I did a search on my own name, in Texas (where I live). As Figure 13.3 shows, now it just so happens that I recently moved. The data shown is the old address, not the new one. That illustrates that these searches are not perfect. It also shows an inaccurate phone number. However, the address was accurate up until very recently. You may also note that in some cases (as with mine) the search with options is the same as the search without. The issue is that I have a less common last name. If you are searching for someone with a common name, then the options can be very useful in refining your search.

First Name	Last Name (req'd)	City/Town	State	
Chuck	Easttom			Go

Chuck Easttom   WILLOW CREEK TRL
MCKINNEY, TX 75071

Chuck Easttom   WILLOW CREEK TRL
MCKINNEY, TX 75071

FIGURE 13.3   People Search results.

Another useful site for addresses and phone numbers around the world is www.infobel.com. This site has the advantage of being international, allowing you to seek out phone numbers and addresses in a variety of countries. As you can see from Figure 13.4, the first step is to select a country to search in.

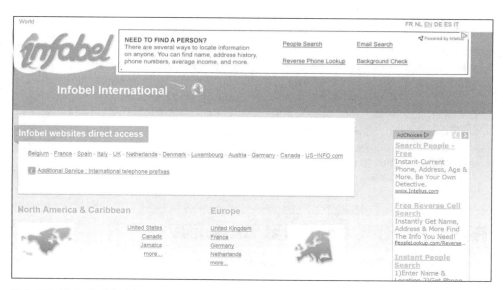

FIGURE 13.4   Infobel home page.

Once you have selected your country, you can then narrow your search further by providing as much information as you can on the person you are trying to locate. A first and last name, however, is a minimum.

These are just two of the many sites that allow you to investigate and discover a person's home address or telephone number. Several other good sites you should consider are listed here:

- www.yellowpages.com

- www.theultimates.com/white/

- www.FaceBook.com

- www.whowhere.com

- www.switchboard.com

- www.LinkedIn.com

It is important to remember that the more information you can provide, and the more you narrow down your search, the greater the likelihood of finding what you are looking for. All of these websites can assist you in finding phone numbers and addresses, both current and past. For a background check on an employee, this can be useful in verifying previous addresses.

FYI: Respecting Privacy

You might wonder why I would be willing to put my home address and phone number in a published book. To begin with, anyone reading this chapter could easily have done their own search and found my information. And, in order to illustrate the process, I needed a name to use. For the liability reasons mentioned earlier, I could not have used someone else's name. However, should readers wish to contact me, they are strongly encouraged to do so via my website (www.chuckeasttom.com) and email address (chuckeasttom@yahoo.com) rather than via phone. I try to answer all my email, but frequently avoid my phone. And I am certainly not encouraging anyone to make a surprise visit to my home!

Court Records and Criminal Checks

A number of states are now putting a variety of court records online. Everything from general court documents to specific records of criminal history and even lists of sex offenders. This sort of information can be critical before you hire an employee, use a babysitter, or send your child to little league. In the following sections, we discuss a variety of resources for this sort of information.

Sex Offender Registries

First, you should become familiar with the online sex offender registries. The FBI maintains a rather exhaustive list of individual state registries. You can access this information at www.fbi.gov/hq/cid/cac/Registry.htm. Every state that has an online registry is listed on this website, as shown in Figure 13.5. Obviously, some states have done a better job of making accurate information public than have others. For example, Texas has a rather comprehensive site. You can find it at http://records.txdps.state.tx.us/. This site allows you to either look up an individual person or to put in a ZIP code (or city name) and find out any registered sex offenders in that area. Figure 13.6 shows the search screen for the Texas site mentioned.

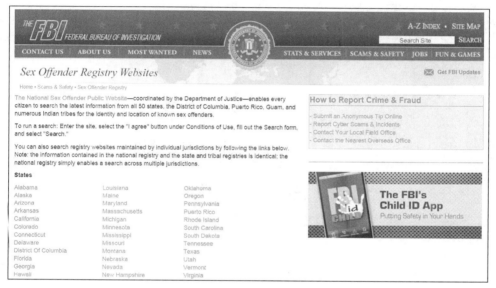

FIGURE 13.5   FBI state registry of sex offenders.

One of the most compelling things about the Texas sex offender registry is that it lists the offense the person was convicted of as well as a photo of the offender. This is important since the term *sex offender* covers a wide variety of crimes. Some of which may not, for example, impact whether you should hire this person. It is important to know what a person was convicted of before you decide they are unsuitable to be interacting with your children or working in your organization.

It should also be noted that there in an app for the iPhone/iPad called Offender Locator that will take your GPS location and list registered sex offenders nearby.

Some sex offenders have committed heinous crimes and many parents will want to use this information to find out about potential babysitters and coaches. This information may also be applicable to employment screenings. However, anytime any information is used for employment screening, it is advisable to check the laws in your area. You may not legally be able to base employment decisions on certain information. As with all legal questions, your best course of action is to consult a reputable attorney.

FIGURE 13.6   Texas sex offender search page.

Caution

Mistaken Identity

There have been cases of mistaken identity with sex offender lists. Any time you find negative information on a person you are investigating—whatever the source—you have an ethical responsibility to verify that information before you take any action on it.

Civil Court Records

There are a variety of crimes, as well as civil issues, a person might be involved in that would make them unsuitable for a particular job. If you are hiring a person to work in your human resources department and oversee equal opportunity issues, knowing if they had been involved in domestic violence, racially motivated graffiti, or other similar issues, might affect your employment decision. Or, if you are considering a business partnership, it would be prudent to discover if you prospective partner has ever been sued by other business partners, or has ever filed for bankruptcy. Unfortunately, in any of these cases, you cannot simply rely on the other parties' honesty. You need to check these things out for yourself.

Unfortunately, this area of legal issues has not been transferred to a web format as well as sex crimes. However, many states and federal courts do offer online records. One of the best organized and most complete on this issue is the state of Oklahoma. You can find their website at www.oscn.net/ applications/oscn/casesearch.asp, and their home search page is shown in Figure 13.7.

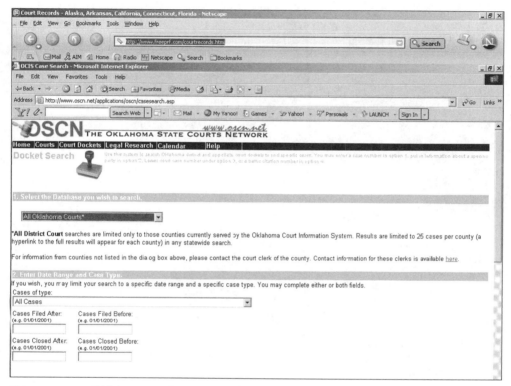

FIGURE 13.7   Oklahoma online court records.

This site allows you to search by last name, last and first name, case number, and more. You will get a complete record of any case you find, including current disposition and any filings. This includes both civil and criminal proceedings. Oddly enough, there are at least five different websites offering information on Oklahoma court cases for a fee—when all of that information is online and free. This illustrates a key point to keep in mind. There are a number of sites/companies that offer to do searches for you, for fees ranging from $9.95 to $79.95. It is true that they can probably do it faster than you. But it is also true that you can find the exact same information these people do, for free. And hopefully this chapter will equip you with the information you need to do that successfully.

Other Resources

There are many other websites that can be quite helpful for your searches. There are a few that deserve particular attention. The National Center for State Courts has a website at www.ncsconline.org/D_KIS/info_ court_web_sites.html that lists links to state courts all over the United States. It also lists several international courts in countries like Australia, Brazil, Canada, and the United Kingdom. This website, as shown in Figure 13.8, is an excellent starting point if you are seeking court records. There is a government access site that helps you find all federal courts. That website is www.uscourts.gov/court_locator.aspx.

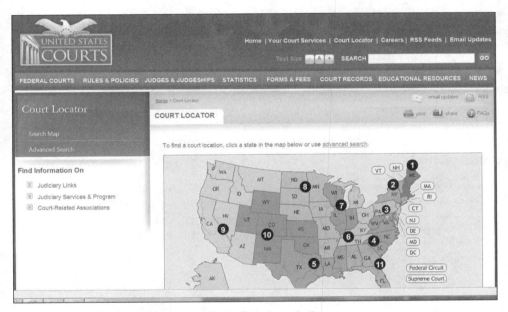

FIGURE 13.8   National Center for State Courts website.

The following list is designed to give you a starting point for online searches across the United States. These websites should help you start your search for court records:

- **Pacer:** www.pacer.psc.uscourts.gov/

- **Prison searches:** www.ancestorhunt.com/prison_search.htm

- **Federal prison records:** www.bop.gov/

- **Public records:** www.searchsystems.net/

- **United Kingdom public records:** www.pro.gov.uk/

- **The Bureau of Federal Prisons:** www.bop.gov/

As you begin searching the Internet, you will find other sites that appeal to you. This may be due to their ease of use, content, or other factors. When you do find such sites, bookmark them. In a short time, you will have an arsenal of online search engines. Also, your proficiency with using them will increase and you will learn which to use for which kind of information. This will allow you to become adept at quickly finding information that you need online.

Usenet

Many readers who are new to the Internet (in the past five years) may not be familiar with Usenet. Usenet is a global group of bulletin boards that exist on any subject you can imagine. There are specific software packages used to view these newsgroups, but for some time now they have been accessible via web portals. The search engine Google has an option on their main page called Groups. When you click on that option, you are taken to Google's portal to Usenet newsgroups, as shown in Figure 13.9.

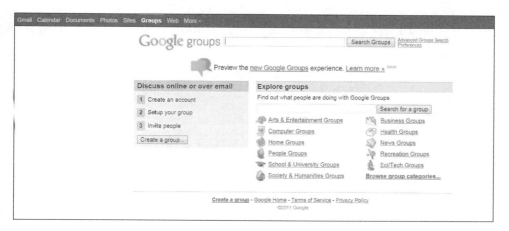

FIGURE 13.9   Google access to Usenet groups.

Caution

Usenet Information

Anyone can post anything on Usenet. There are no restrictions at all. So simply because you find a negative comment about a person on Usenet, it is not wise to automatically assume that comment is true. These postings can only be viewed as part of an investigation and only credible if other facets of the investigation also support the postings you find.

As you can see, newsgroups are divided into broad categories. For example newsgroups devoted to science topics would be found under the heading sci. This includes groups like sci.anthropology, sci.logic, sci.math.stat, and more. The heading alt is a catchall for anything and everything. This category includes things ranging from alt.hacking to alt.adoption.

You may be thinking that, while all this is fascinating, it does not have anything to do with tracking down information. But actually it does. If, for example, you were hiring a network administrator, you could see if she had posted in various network administration groups, and if those postings revealed key information about her network. This tool may be the single most important investigative tool you have, if you are willing to take the time and ferret out the information you need.

Summary

We have seen in this chapter that the Internet can be a valuable resource for any sort of investigation. It is often one of the tools that hackers and identity thieves use to gain information about their target. However, it can also be a valuable tool for you in researching a prospective employee or business partner. It can also be invaluable for you to routinely find out what information is on the Internet about you. Seeing strange data that is not accurate can be an indication that you have already been the victim of identity theft.

Test Your Skills

MULTIPLE CHOICE QUESTIONS

1. How might an identity thief use the Internet to exploit his or her victim?

   A. He or she might find even more information about the target and use this information to conduct their crime.

   B. He or she could find out how much the target has in their savings account.

   C. The identity thief usually does not use the Internet to accomplish his or her task.

   D. Identity thieves use the Internet to intercept your email and thus get access to your personal life.

2. Which of the following is not an ideal place to seek out phone numbers and addresses?

   A. Yahoo! People Find

   B. People Search

   C. The international phone registry

   D. Infobell

3. Why do you not want too much personal data about you on the Internet?

   A. It might reveal embarrassing facts about you.

   B. It might be used by an identity thief to impersonate you.

   C. It might be used by a potential employer to find out more about you

   D. There is no reason to worry about personal information on the Internet.

4. How could a hacker use information about you found through Internet searches?

   A. It could be used to guess passwords if your passwords are linked to personal information such as your birth date, address, or phone number.

   B. It could be used to guess passwords if your passwords are linked to your interests or hobbies.

   C. It could be used in social engineering to ascertain more information about you or your computer system.

   D. All of the above.

5. If you are hiring a new employee, which of the following should you do?

    A. Verify degrees and certifications

    B. Call references

    C. Perform an Internet search to verify contact information and to check for a criminal record

    D. All of the above

6. Which of the following would be *least* important to know about a potential business partner?

    A. Past bankruptcies

    B. A 15-year-old marijuana possession arrest

    C. A lawsuit from a former business partner

    D. A recent DUI

7. What information would provide the most accurate results for locating a person?

    A. First name and state

    B. First name, last name, and state

    C. Last name and state

    D. First name and last name

8. Of the websites listed in this chapter, which would be the most useful in obtaining the address and phone number of someone who does not live in the United States?

    A. The FBI website

    B. Yahoo!

    C. Infobell

    D. Google

9. Where would you go to find various state sex offender registries?

    A. The FBI website

    B. The national sex offender online database

    C. The interstate online sex offender database

    D. The special victims unit website

10. What is most important to learn about a person listed in a sex offender registry?

    A. The extent of his punishment

    B. How old she was when she committed her crime

    C. How long he has been out of prison

    D. The nature of her specific crime

11. Which web search approach is best when checking criminal backgrounds?

   A. Check primarily the person's state of residence

   B. Check primarily federal records

   C. Check the current and previous state of residence

   D. Check as many places as might have information

12. What advantages are there to commercial web search services?

   A. They can get information you cannot.

   B. They can get the information faster than you can.

   C. They can do a more thorough job than you can.

   D. They are legally entitled to do searches, you are not.

13. Which would you use to begin a search for information on a United States court case?

   A. The National Center for State Courts Website

   B. Infobel

   C. Yahoo! People Search

   D. Google Groups

14. Which of the following is the most accurate description of Usenet?

   A. A nationwide bulletin board

   B. A repository of computer security information

   C. A large-scale chat room

   D. A global collection of bulletin boards

15. Which of the following is the most helpful data you might get from Usenet on a person you are investigating?

   A. Postings by the individual you are investigating

   B. Security tips to help you investigate

   C. Criminal records posted

   D. Negative comments made by others about your target

EXERCISES

For all exercises and projects in this chapter, you will concentrate your investigation on some person. It is best if you investigate yourself (which makes it easier to evaluate the accuracy of what you find) or if someone in the class or the instructor volunteers to be the target of the investigation. There are ethical issues with simply investigating random people without their knowledge or permission. It is also important to avoid embarrassing someone in the classroom. So the volunteer targets of the investigation should be certain they will not be embarrassed by whatever is found. Substitute the name of the person you are investigating for John Doe or Jane Doe in the projects and exercises.

EXERCISE 13.1: **Finding Phone Numbers**

1. Beginning with Yahoo! People Search, seek out phone numbers and addresses for John Doe.

2. Use at least two other sources to look up John's phone number.

Did you get too little information or too much information? Were you able to determine the correct, current number?

EXERCISE 13.2: **Criminal Records Checks**

1. Using sources listed in this chapter or other websites, look for criminal background information about John Doe. Start with the state John currently resides in, then check other states, particularly those that might have shown up with John's name in Exercise 1.

2. Expand your search to check for federal crimes as well.

EXERCISE 13.3: **Checking Court Cases**

1. Search court records for any court cases for Jane Doe's business.

2. Check state licensing agency websites, if applicable, for any history or complaints on John's business.

EXERCISE 13.4: **Finding Business Information on Usenet**

1. Access Usenet.

2. Search bulletin boards and other groups that Jane Doe may have posted to in connection with her business.

Were you able to find out more about Jane's business through her postings to a Usenet group?

EXERCISE 13.5: **Blocking Information**

This chapter illustrated the many ways you can access information about someone and pointed out the potential hazards of having too much personal information available on the Internet. So, what can you do to prevent unscrupulous individuals from finding out too much about you? Check the primary websites listed in this chapter (i.e., Yahoo! and Google) to see if they provide any means to block your information from being distributed. Are there any other means of blocking access to your personal information?

PROJECTS

PROJECT 13.1: **Investigating a Person**

Using all of the web resources in this chapter, and any others you come across, do a complete investigation of Jane Doe. Try to determine her address, phone number, occupation, age, and any criminal history. You might even check Usenet postings and find out clues as to Jane's hobbies and personal interests as well. Create a brief report on Jane based on your findings.

PROJECT 13.2: **Investigating a Company**

Using all of the web resources in this chapter, and any others you come across, do a complete investigation of John Doe's business. How long has he been in business? Are there any complaints about the business with any regulatory agency? Any complaints on Usenet boards? Any business relationships? Any past court proceedings? Write a report discussing your analysis of this business based on your findings.

PROJECT 13.3: **The Ethics of Investigation**

Write an essay discussing the ethics of online investigations. Do you feel these investigations are an invasion of privacy? Why or why not? If you do feel they are an invasion of privacy, what do you think can be done about it? Are there problems with getting inaccurate information?

Case Study

Henry Rice, the owner and CEO of a small company, has been conducting a search for a new human resource administrator. After many rounds of interviews, he has narrowed his search down to two individuals that he feels are the best candidates. Each has very similar qualifications so Henry's decision may very well be based on the information he finds when he checks their references and performs a background check.

Henry has received written permission from each to conduct a background check. Where should Henry begin his search? What sites or sorts of information would be most critical for him to check? What type of information could weigh heavily for a person working in human resources? Write a brief essay outlining the steps Henry should take in conducting his research.

## Chapter 14

Introduction to Forensics

Chapter Objectives

After reading this chapter and completing the exercises, you will be able to do the following:

- Understand basic forensics principles
- Make a forensic copy of a drive
- Use basic forensics tools

Introduction

In the preceding 13 chapters, you have been introduced to a variety of security topics: from concepts like the CIA triangle, to attacks such as session hijacking, to counter measures like IDS and honey pots. In this chapter, we are going to cover the basics of computer forensics. This is a very important topic for anyone involved in computer security or network administration. It is frequently the case that the first responder to a computer crime is the network administrator, not a law enforcement officer. And if you fail to handle the evidence properly, you may render it unusable in a court and ruin any chances of convicting the perpetrator.

However, remember that the steps outlined in this chapter are general guidelines. You should definitely consult whatever forensics standards are used in your jurisdiction. If you are not a law enforcement officer, you will still want to familiarize yourself with the procedures used by local law enforcement and to follow the same steps. If for some reason you cannot acquire the procedures used by your local law enforcement agency, then you can find federal guidelines. Here are some sources:

- **United States Secret Service:** www.secretservice.gov/ectf.shtml
- **Federal Bureau of Investigation:** www.cert.org/tech_tips/FBI_investigates_crime.html
- **FBI Computer Forensics:** www.fbi.gov/news/stories/2009/august/rcfls_081809

It is also important to keep in mind that a few jurisdictions have passed laws requiring that in order to extract the evidence the investigator must be either a law enforcement officer or a licensed private investigator. This is a controversial law, given that normally private investigator training and licensing does not include computer forensics training. You should check with specifics in your state. However, many of those states will allow you to forensically examine a computer if you have the permission of the owner. So this would not prohibit you from forensically examining computers in your company.

General Guidelines

There are some general guidelines you should always follow in any forensic examination. You want to have as little impact on the evidence as possible. This means you want to examine it, and not to alter it. You want to have a clear document trail for everything that is done. And of course you want to secure your evidence.

Don't Touch the Suspect Drive

The first, and perhaps most important, is to touch the system as little as possible. You do not want to make changes to the system in the process of examining it. Let's look at one possible way to make a forensically valid copy of a drive. Some of this depends on Linux commands, which you may or may not be familiar with. If you are not, I have had students with no Linux experience use these same commands and be able to accomplish the task of making a forensic copy of a drive.

First you will need a bootable copy of Linux. Some books recommend Knoppix, but I have found Back-Track to be more consistently reliable. You will actually need two copies. One on the suspect machine and one on the target machine. Whichever version of Linux you use, the steps will be the same:

First you have to completely wipe the target drive.

```
dd if=/dev/zero of=/dev/hdb1 bs=2048
```

Now we need to set up that target forensics server to receive the copy of the suspected drive we wish to examine. The Netcat command helps with that. The specific syntax is as follows:

```
nc -l -p 8888 > evidence.dd
```

We are telling the machine to listen on port 8888 and put whatever it receives into evidence.dd.

Now on the suspect machine we have to start sending the drive's information to the forensics server:

```
dd if=/dev/hda1 ¦ nc 192.168.0.2 8888 -w 3
```

Of course, this assumes that the suspect drive is hda1. If not, then replace that part of the command with the partition you are using. This also assumes the server has an IP address of 192.168.0.2. If not, replace with whatever your forensics server IP address is.

You will also want to create a hash of the suspect drive. Later you can hash the drive you have been working with and compare that to the hash of the original drive and confirm that nothing has been altered. You can make a hash using Linux shell commands:

```
md5sum /dev/hda1 ¦ nc 192.168.0.2 8888 -w 3
```

When you are done, you have a copy of the drive. It is often a good idea to make two copies: One you will work with, and another will simply be stored. But in no case do you do your forensic analysis on the suspect drive.

Document Trail

Beyond not touching the actual drive, the next issue is documentation. If you have never worked in any investigative capacity, the level of documentation may seem onerous to you. But the rule is simple: *Document everything.*

When you first discover a computer crime, you must document exactly what events occurred. Who was present and what were they doing? What devices were attached to the computer, what connections did it have over the network/Internet? What hardware was being used and what operating system?

Then when you begin your actual forensic investigation you must document every step. Start with documenting the process you use to make a forensic copy. Then document every tool you use, every test you perform. You must be able to show in your documentation everything that was done.

Secure the Evidence

First and foremost, the computer must be taken offline to prevent further tampering. Now there are some limited circumstances where a machine would be left online to trace down an active, ongoing attack. But the general rule is take it offline immediately.

The next step is to limit access to the machine. No one who does not absolutely need access to the evidence should have it. Hard drives should be locked in a safe or secure cabinet. Analysis should be done in a room with limited access.

You must also be able to document every person who had access to the evidence, how they interacted with it, and where the evidence was stored. There must be no period of time that you cannot account for the evidence. This is called *chain of custody*.

FBI Forensics Guidelines

Beyond the general guidelines we have just discussed, the FBI gives some specific guidelines. In most cases, they will overlap with what we have discussed, but it is still useful to cover the FBI recommendations.

If an incident occurs, the FBI recommends that the first responder preserve the state of the computer at the time of the incident by making a backup copy of any logs, damaged or altered files, and of course any files left by the intruder. This last part is critical. Hackers frequently use various tools and may leave traces of their presence. Furthermore the FBI warns that if the incident is in progress, activate any auditing or recording software you might have available. Collect as much data about the incident as you can. In other words, this might be a case where you do not take the machine offline, but rather analyze the attack in progress.

Another important step is to document the specific losses suffered due to the attack. Losses typically include the following:

- Labor cost spent in response and recovery. (Multiply the number of participating staff by their hourly rates.)

- If equipment was damaged, the cost of that equipment.

  If data was lost or stolen, what was the value of that data? How much did it cost to obtain that data and how much will it cost to reconstruct it?

- Any lost revenue, including losses due to downtime, having to give customers credit due to inconvenience, or any other way in which revenue was lost.

Documenting the exact damages due to the attack is just as important as documenting the attack itself.

The FBI computer forensic guidelines stress the importance of securing any evidence. The FBI also stresses that you should not limit your concept of *computer evidence* to PCs and laptops. Computer evidence can include the following:

- Logs (system, router, chat room, IDS, firewall, etc.)
- Portable storage devices (USB drives, external drives, etc.)
- Emails
- Devices capable of storing data such as iPod, iPad, tablets
- Cell phones

The FBI guidelines also stress making a forensic copy of the suspect drive/partition to work with and creating a hash of that drive.

Finding Evidence on the PC

Once you have secured the evidence and made a forensic copy, it is time to start looking for evidence. That evidence can come in many forms.

Finding Evidence in the Browser

The browser can be a source of both direct evidence and circumstantial or supporting evidence. Obviously in cases of child pornography, the browser might contain direct evidence of the specific crime. You may also find direct evidence in the case of cyber stalking. However, if you suspect someone of creating a virus that infected a network, you would probably only find indirect evidence such as the person having searched virus creation/programming-related topics.

Even if the person erases his history, it is still possible to retrieve it. Windows stores a lot of information in a file called index.dat (information such as web addresses, search queries, and recently opened files). There are a number of tools you can download from the Internet that will allow you to retrieve and review the index.dat file. Here are a few:

- www.eusing.com/Window_Washer/Index_dat.htm

- www.acesoft.net/index.dat%20viewer/index.dat_viewer.htm

- http://download.cnet.com/Index-dat-Analyzer/3000-2144_4-10564321.html

Finding Evidence in System Logs

Regardless of what operating system you are using, the operating system has logs. Those logs can be critical in any forensic investigation and you should retrieve them.

Windows Logs

Let's start with Windows XP/Vista/7. With all of these versions of Windows, you find the logs by clicking on the Start button in the lower-left corner of the desktop and then clicking the Control Panel. You then will click on Administrative Tools and the Event Viewer. Here are the logs you would check for. (Note that not all appear in every version of Windows.)

NOTE: With all of these you have to turn the logging on; otherwise, there will be nothing in these logs.

- **Security log:** This is probably the most important log from a forensics point of view. It has both successful and unsuccessful login events.

- **Application log:** This log contains various events logged by applications or programs. Many applications will record their errors here in the application log.

- **System log:** The System log contains events logged by Windows system components. This includes events like driver failures. This particular log is not as interesting from a forensics perspective as the other logs are.

- **ForwardedEvents log:** The ForwardedEvents log is used to store events collected from remote computers. This will only have data in it, if event forwarding has been configured.

- **Applications and Services logs:** This log is used to store events from a single application or component rather than events that might have systemwide impact.

Windows servers will have similar logs. However with Windows systems you have an additional possible concern. It is possible that the attacker cleared the logs before leaving the system. There are tools that will allow one to wipe out a log. It is also possible to simply turn off logging before an attack and turn it back on when you are done. One such tool is auditpol.exe. Using `auditpol \\ipaddress /disable` turns off logging. Then when the criminal exits they can use `auditpol \\ipaddress /enable` to turn it back on. There are also tools, like WinZapper, that allow one to selectively remove certain items from event logs in Windows

Linux Logs

Obviously Linux also has logs you can check. Depending on your Linux distribution and what services you have running on it (like MySQL), some of these logs may not be present on a particular machine:

- **/var/log/faillog:** This log file contains failed user logins. This can be very important when tracking attempts to crack into the system.

- **/var/log/kern.log:** This log file is used for messages from the operating system's kernel. This is not likely to be pertinent to most computer crime investigations.

- **/var/log/lpr.log:** This is the printer log and can give you a record of any items that have been printed from this machine. That can be useful in corporate espionage cases.

- **/var/log/mail.*:** This is the mail server log and can be very useful in any computer crime investigation. Emails can be a component in any computer crime, and even in some noncomputer crimes such as fraud.

- **/var/log/mysql.*:** This log records activities related to the MySQL database server and will usually be of less interest to a computer crime investigation.

- **/var/log/apache2/*:** If this machine is running the Apache web server, then this log will show related activity. This can be very useful in tracking attempts to hack into the web server.

- **/var/log/lighttpd/*:** If this machine is running the Lighttpd web server, then this log will show related activity. This can be very useful in tracking attempts to hack into the web server.

- **/var/log/apport.log:** This records application crashes. Sometimes these can reveal attempts to compromise the system or the presence of a virus or spyware.

- **/var/log/user.log:** These contain user activity logs and can be very important to a criminal investigation.

Getting Back Deleted Files

It is a fact that criminals frequently attempt to destroy evidence. And this is also true with computer crimes. The criminals may delete files. However there are a variety of tools you can use to recover such files, particularly in Windows. Disk Digger is a free tool that can be used to recover Windows files. This is a very easy to use tool. There are more robust tools, but the fact that this is free and easy to use makes it perfect for students learning forensics. Let's walk through its basic operation.

On the first screen, shown in Figure 14.1, you simply select the drive/partition you wish to recover files from.

FIGURE 14.1   Add a new scan.

On the next screen, you select the level of scan you want to do. This is shown in Figure 14.2. Obviously the deeper the scan, the longer it can take.

Then you will get a list of the files that where recovered. You can see this in Figure 14.3.

You can see the file and the file header. You can also choose to recover the file if you wish. Obviously, it is possible that Disk Digger will only recover a file fragment. But that can be enough for forensics.

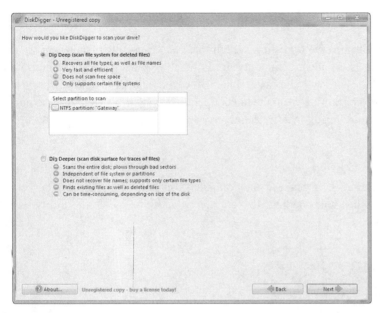

FIGURE 14.2   Select depth of scan.

FIGURE 14.3   Recovered files.

Operating System Utilities

There are a number of utilities built in to the operating system that can be useful in gathering some forensic data. Given that Windows is the most commonly used operating system, we will focus on those utilities that work from the Windows command line. However, one of the key issues in conducting forensics work is to be very familiar with the target operating system. You should also note that many of these commands are most useful on a live running system to catch attacks in progress.

Net Sessions

This command lists any active sessions connected to the computer you run it on. This can be very important if you think an attack is live and ongoing. If there are no active sessions, the utility will report that, as shown in Figure 14.4.

FIGURE 14.4   Net Sessions.

Openfiles

This is another command useful for finding live attacks ongoing. This command will list any shared files that are currently open. You can see this utility in Figure 14.5.

FIGURE 14.5   Openfiles.

Fc

Fc is a command you can use with a forensic copy of a machine. It compares two files and shows the differences. If you think a configuration file has been altered you can compare it to a known good backup. You can see this utility in Figure 14.6.

FIGURE 14.6   Fc.

Netstat

This command is also used to detect ongoing attacks. It lists all current network connections, not just inbound, but outbound as well. You can see this utility in Figure 14.7.

FIGURE 14.7   Netstat.

The Windows Registry

The Windows Registry is an incredible repository of potential valuable forensics information. It is the heart of the Windows machine. There are a number of interesting pieces of data you can find here. It is beyond the scope of this chapter to make you an expert in the Windows Registry, but it is hoped that you will continue on and learn more. One important thing you can find, from a forensics perspective, is any USB devices that have been connected to the machine.

The Registry key HKEY_LOCAL_MACHINE\System\ControlSet\Enum\UBSTOR lists USB devices that have been connected to the machine. It is often the case that a criminal will move evidence to an external device and take it with them. This could indicate to you that there are devices you need to find and examine.

Summary

In this chapter, you have seen the basics of computer forensics. The most important things you have learned are to first make a forensics copy to work with, and second, to document everything. You simply cannot over document. You have also learned how to retrieve browser information, recover deleted files, and you have learned some commands that may be useful forensically. Finally, you learned the forensics value of the Windows Registry.

Test Your Skills

MULTIPLE CHOICE QUESTIONS

1. In a computer forensics investigation, what describes the route that evidence takes from the time you find it until the case is closed or goes to court?

   A. Rules of evidence

   B. Law of probability

   C. Chain of custody

   D. Policy of separation

2. Where does Linux store email server logs?

   A. /var/log/mail.*

   B. /etc/log/mail.*

   C. /mail/log/mail.*

   D. /server/log/mail.*

3. Why should you note all cable connections for a computer you want to seize as evidence?

   A. To know what outside connections existed

   B. In case other devices were connected

   C. To know what peripheral devices exist

   D. To know what hardware existed

4. What is in the Index.dat file?

   A. Internet Explorer information

   B. General Internet history, file browsing history, etc. for a Windows machine

   C. All web history for Firefox

   D. General Internet history, file browsing history, etc. for a Linux machine

5. What is the name of the Standard Linux command that is also available as a Windows application that can be used to create bitstream images and make a forensic copy?

    A. `mcopy`

    B. `image`

    C. MD5

    D. `dd`

6. When cataloging digital evidence, the primary goal is to do what?

    A. Make bitstream images of all hard drives

    B. Preserve evidence integrity

    C. Not remove the evidence from the scene

    D. Not allow the computer to be turned off

7. The command `Openfiles` shows what?

    A. Any files that are opened

    B. Any shared files that are opened

    C. Any system files that are opened

    D. Any files open with ADS

8. "Interesting data" is what?

    A. Data relevant to your investigation

    B. Pornography

    C. Documents, spreadsheets, and databases

    D. Schematics or other economic based information

9. Which of the following are important to the investigator regarding logging?

    A. The logging methods

    B. Log retention

    C. Location of stored logs

    D. All of the above

EXERCISES

EXERCISE 14.1: **DiskDigger**

Download DiskDigger and search your computer for deleted files. Attempt to recover one file of your choice.

EXERCISE 14.2: **Making a Forensic Copy**

This exercise requires two computers. You must also download either Backtrack or Knoppix (both are free). Then attempt to make a forensic copy of computer A by sending its data to computer B.

Appendix | **A**

Glossary

This section contains terms from both hackers and security professionals. To truly understand computer security, you must be familiar with both worlds. General networking terms are also included in this glossary.

admin: Short for system administrator.

adware: Software that is used to display advertisements.

audit: A check of a system's security. This check usually includes a review of documents, procedures, and system configurations.

authentication: The process of proving that someone is who he or she claims to be.

back door: A hole in the security system deliberately left by the creator of the system.

bagbiter: Something that fails to work (such as a program or a computer) or works in a remarkably clumsy manner.

bid shielding: Hiding an item from other bidders by putting a fake, but very high bid on it to discourage other bidders.

bid siphoning: Attempting to lure bidders from a legitimate site to a site that may be used for malicious purposes such as phishing.

black hat hacker: Someone who uses hacking skills for malicious and illegal purposes.

BlowFish: A well-known symmetric key encryption algorithm that uses a variable-length key and was invented by Bruce Schneier.

braindump: The act of telling someone everything one knows.

breach: To successfully break into a system, to breach the security.

brute force: To try to crack a password by simply trying every possible combination.

bug: A flaw in a system.

Caesar cipher: One of the oldest encryption algorithms. It uses a basic mono-alphabetic cipher.

CHAP: Challenge Handshake Authentication Protocol, a commonly used authentication protocol.

CIA triangle: A common security acronym: confidentiality-integrity-accessibility.

cipher: Synonym for cryptographic algorithm.

cipher text: Encrypted text.

code: The source code for a program; or the act of programming, as in "to code an algorithm."

codegrinder: An unflattering reference to one who works in an uncreative corporate programming environment.

cookie: A small bit of data, often in plain text, that is stored by web browsers.

cracker: One who breaks into a system in order to do something malicious, illegal, or harmful. Synonymous with black hat hacker.

cracking: Breaking into a system or code.

crash: A sudden and unintended failure, as in "My computer crashed."

cryptography: The study of encryption and decryption.

cyber fraud: Using the Internet to defraud someone.

cyber stalking: Using the Internet to harass someone.

demigod: A hacker with years of experience, who has a national or international reputation.

DDoS: Distributed Denial of Service attacks are denial of service attacks launched from multiple source locations.

denial of service (DoS): An attack that prevents legitimate users from accessing a resource. This is usually done by overloading the target system with more workload than it can handle.

DES: Data Encryption Standard, a block cipher that was developed in the 1970s. It uses a 56-bit key on 64-bit blocks. It is no longer considered secure enough.

Encrypting File System: Also known as EFS, this is Microsoft's file system that allows users to encrypt individual files. It was first introduced in Windows 2000.

elliptic curve: A class of algorithms that provide asymmetric encryption.

encryption: The act of encrypting a message. Encryption usually involves altering a message so that it cannot be read without the key and the decryption algorithm.

espionage: Illicitly gathering information, usually from a government or corporate source.

ethical hacker: One who hacks into systems to accomplish some goal that he feels is ethically valid.

firewall: A device or software that provides a barrier between your machine or network and the rest of the world.

gray hat hacker: A hacker who usually obeys the law but in some instances will cross the line into black hat hacking.

hacker: One who tries to learn about a system by examining it in detail by reverse-engineering.

hash: An algorithm that takes variable length input and produced fixed-length output and is not reversible.

honey pot: A system or server designed to be very appealing to hackers, when in fact it is a trap to catch them.

hub: A device for connecting computers.

IKE: A method for managing the exchange of encryption keys.

information warfare: Attempts to influence political or military outcomes via information manipulation.

intrusion-detection system (IDS): A system for detecting attempted intrusions.

IP: Internet Protocol, one of the primary protocols used in networking.

IPsec: Internet Protocol Security, a method used to secure VPNs.

IP spoofing: Making packets seem to come from a different IP address than they really originated from.

key logger: Software that logs key strokes on a computer.

MAC address: The physical address of a network card. It is a 6-byte hexadecimal number. The first 3 bytes define the vendor.

malware: Any software that has a malicious purpose, such as a virus or Trojan horse.

MS-CHAP: A Microsoft Extension to CHAP.

multi-alphabet substitutions: Encryption methods that use more than one substitution alphabet.

NIC: Network interface card.

packet filter firewall: A firewall that scans incoming packets and either allows them to pass or rejects them. It only examines the header, not the data, and does not consider the context of the data communication.

penetration testing: Assessing the security of a system by attempting to break into the system. Penetration testing is the activity of most sneakers.

phreaker: Someone who hacks into phone systems.

port scan: Sequentially pinging ports to see which ones are active.

PPP: Point-to-Point Protocol, a somewhat older connection protocol.

PPTP: Point-to-Point Tunneling Protocol, an extension to PPP for VPNs.

proxy server: A device that hides your internal IP addresses and presents a single IP address to the outside world.

Router: A device that connects two networks.

RSA: A public key encryption method developed in 1977 by three mathematicians: Ron Rivest, Adi Shamir, and Leonard Adleman. The name *RSA* is derived from the first letter of each mathematician's last name.

RST cookie: A simple method for alleviating the danger of certain types of DoS attacks.

script kiddy: A slang term for an unskilled person who purports to be a skilled hacker.

smurf: A specific type of distributed denial of service attack.

sneaker: Someone who is attempting to compromise a system in order to assess its vulnerability.

sniffer: A program that captures data as it travels across a network. Also called a packet sniffer.

snort: A widely used, open source, intrusion-detection system.

social engineering: The use of persuasion on human users in order to gain information required to access a system.

SPAP: Shiva Password Authentication Protocol. SPAP is a proprietary version of PAP. This protocol basically adds encryption to PAP.

spoofing: Pretending to be something else, as when a packet might spoof another return IP address (as in the smurf attack) or when a website is spoofing a well known e-commerce site.

spyware: Software that monitors computer use.

stack tweaking: A complex method for protecting a system against DoS attacks. This method involves reconfiguring the operating system to handle connections differently.

stateful packet inspection: A type of firewall that not only examines packets but knows the context within which the packet was sent.

symmetric key system: An encryption method where the same key is used to encrypt and decrypt the message.

SYN cookie: A method for ameliorating the dangers of SYN floods.

SYN flood: Sending a stream of SYN packets (requests for connection) then never responding, thus leaving the connection half open.

tribal flood network: A tool used to execute DDoS attacks.

Trin00: A tool used to execute DDoS attacks.

Trojan horse: Software that appears to have a valid and benign purpose but really has another, nefarious purpose.

Virus: Software that is self-replicating and spreads like a biological virus.

War-dialing: Dialing phones waiting for a computer to pick up. War-dialing is usually done via some automated system.

War-driving: Driving and scanning for wireless networks that can be compromised.

white hat hacker: A hacker who does not break the law, often synonymous with ethical hacker.

worm: A virus that can spread without human intervention.

Appendix | B

Resources

Note: Links are valid as of October 2011.

General Computer Crime and Cyber Terrorism

Cyber crime: www.cybercrime.gov/

Computer security: www.cert.org

Department of Justice Computer Crime: www.usdoj.gov/criminal/cybercrime/compcrime.html

Symantec's antivirus site: www.symantec.com/avcenter/

Computer Associates Virus Information Center: www3.ca.com/virusinfo/

Department of Defense cyber crime: www.dcfl.gov/dc3/home.htm

General Knowledge

EC Council: www.eccouncil.org

Hellbound Hackers: www.hellboundhackers.org/

Hacker history: www.tranquileye.com/hackerculture/home.html

Hacker history: www.sptimes.com/Hackers/history.hacking.html

Cyber Stalking

www.crimelibrary.com/criminology/cyberstalking/

www.cyber-stalking.net/

Identity Theft

www.consumer.gov/idtheft/

www.idtheftcenter.org/index.shtml

www.usdoj.gov/criminal/fraud/idtheft.html

Port Scanners and Sniffers

NMap: www.nmap.org

Port scanners: www.hackfix.org/software/port.html

Port scanners and other tools: www.all-internet-security.com/security_scanners.html

More port scanners: www.mycert.org.my/resource/scanner.htm

More scanners and sniffers: is-it-true.org/pt/ptips13.shtml

www.prosolve.com/software/winscan.php

Password Crackers

Ophcrack: http://ophcrack.org/

Password crackers: www.password-crackers.com/

More password crackers: www.pcmag.com/article2/0,4149,696,00.asp

Countermeasures

Preventing port scanning: www.nwfusion.com/links/Encyclopedia/P/792.html

Various security and hacking tools: www.insecure.org

Snort, an open source IDS system: www.snort.org/

The SANS Institute IDS FAQ: www.sans.org/resources/idfaq/

The Association of Computing Machinery IDS page: www.acm.org/crossroads/xrds24/intrus.html

Spyware

www.youarethespy.com/spy-software.htm

www.keystrokekeyloggers.com/spy_anywhere.asp

www.keyloggers.com/

www.bestspyware.com/

www.spectorsoft.com/

www.spywareguide.com/

www.spywareinfo.com/

www.softactivity.com/

Counter Spyware

www.webroot.com/wb/products/spysweeper/index.php

www.spywarenuker.com/overture.php

www.webroot.com

www.enigmasoftwaregroup.com/jump8.shtml

Cyber Investigation Tools

WhoIs tool: www.whois.sc/

Sam Spade for Windows: www.samspade.org/ssw/

Various search tools: www.virtualgumshoe.com/

Viewing previous versions of websites: www.Archive.org

General Tools

www.maxwells-alley.com/tech/toolkit.html

www.all-internet-security.com/security_scanners.html

Scanning tool: www.rawlogic.com/netbrute/

www.totalshareware.com

Virus Research

CNET Virus Center: www.cnet.com/2735-2023_1-693.html

F-Secure: www.fsecure.com

Symantec virus encyclopedia: http://www.symantec.com/security_response/

Computer Associates Virus Information Center: www3.ca.com/securityadvisor/virusinfo/default.aspx

Index

B

C

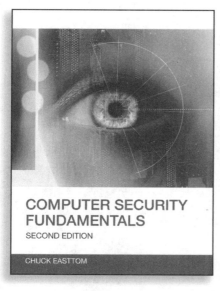

COMPUTER SECURITY FUNDAMENTALS
SECOND EDITION

CHUCK EASTTOM

FREE Online Edition

Your purchase of **Computer Security Fundamentals** includes access to a free online edition for 45 days through the Safari Books Online subscription service. Nearly every Pearson IT Certification book is available online through Safari Books Online, along with more than 5,000 other technical books and videos from publishers such as Addison-Wesley Professional, Cisco Press, Exam Cram, IBM Press, O'Reilly, Prentice Hall, Que, and Sams.

SAFARI BOOKS ONLINE allows you to search for a specific answer, cut and paste code, download chapters, and stay current with emerging technologies.

Activate your FREE Online Edition at www.informit.com/safarifree

> **STEP 1:** Enter the coupon code: BKBVFWH.

> **STEP 2:** New Safari users, complete the brief registration form. Safari subscribers, just log in.

If you have difficulty registering on Safari or accessing the online edition, please e-mail customer-service@safaribooksonline.com